Face in the Mirror

Face in the Mirror

Wayne Andre
with David W. Balsiger

BRIDGE PUBLISHING, INC.
South Plainfield, NJ

Unless otherwise indicated, all Scripture has been quoted from the *New American Standard* version of the Bible.

Face In The Mirror
ISBN 0-88270-678-0
Library of Congress
    Catalog Card #93-072057
Copyright©1993 by Overcomers/ FMC Enterprises Ltd. Partnership

Published by:
Bridge Publishing Inc.
2500 Hamilton Blvd.
South Plainfield, NJ 07080

This book is gratefully and affectionately dedicated to
Raymond F. Culpepper
and the congregation of
the Metropolitan Church of God.

Contents

Acknowledgments

The life and sermons of Pastor Raymond Culpepper have guided me in understanding the meaning of wholeness, the grace of caring, and the fullness of life found in being "conformed to the image of Christ." He has been a friend, adviser, consultant, and motivator.

The people at Metro accepted me with a spirit of love when I was unlovable and walked with me step-by-step on the pathway of healing. They unselfishly assisted me in building my dream, free from bondage and mediocrity, and to realize that I could be a creative leader and guide others in believing that God *is* love.

Wayne Andre

The authors wish to thank those who helped to make this book a reality and the many friends who offered prayer and support, including:

T & T Enterprises, Neil P. Damron, Kathryn Damron, Newman M. Evans and Associates, J. Lindy Davis Jr., John O. Tabor, Jack and Becky Harris, Peggy R. Culpepper, Alan Walters, Milner and Associates, Savage Enterprises, Sheri L. Washburn, Daryl O. Davis, Paul H. Blackwell Jr., Joyce B. McKay, Kevin H. and Anissa Kelley, Lisa K. White, Charles Buzbee, Melinda G. Higginbotham, Jo Ann H. Stennis, Evelyn Coleman, Patricia Wallace, Tom and Judy Morrow, Jim and Carlene Snow, Dr. and Mrs. D. Keven Bowdle, E.T. Smith, Wayne Gentry and Billy McDonald.

Prologue

Hope for the Sexually Broken

The day I hit bottom is still clear in my mind.

Thomas and I were invited to a jazz concert by one of the women who worked in the salon we owned. Although partying was the last thing I wanted to do, I agreed to go.

That night, Laura and her daughter took us to an old barroom in the basement of a dingy building. We selected a table and ordered drinks. The musicians sailed into their first song.

I quickly downed my first glass and started on another. Idle talk droned around me. I tried to participate, but kept losing the thread of the conversation. Nothing made sense, not the music nor the talk. The longer I sat there, the more I realized my life was shattering into sharp, hurting pieces. Finally in desperation, I excused myself and bolted for the men's room.

I hit the restroom door with a bang and stumbled to a dirty, scratched sink. Water trickled out of the rusted faucet and gurgled wearily down the pipe throat.

I stared into the streaked mirror. A sunken-eyed, gaunt-faced, bearded creature glared back.

Is that me? I froze before the image of myself—the drug addict, the old faggot, the queer, the sissy. I am everything people have called me for years.

I could barely endure the sight of my aging face. In it, I saw the reflection of everything I had done wrong, acts not worthy of human behavior.

My mind raced like a horror video on fast forward. I remember the day I left Patricia and my kids and the time I told my mother I was gay. The agony in their faces haunted me.

Memories of greed flashed through my mind—living in high style, avoiding alimony and child support, "borrowing" money from the business tax account, letting checks bounce, neglecting to pay employee benefit premiums, pushing our hair salon ever closer to bankruptcy.

I saw the effects of my addiction to cocaine and alcohol and remembered the needle tracks across my arms. Scenes from my nearly twenty years of homosexuality exploded through my mind like camera flashes. The endless hours in gay bars. The succession of partners. The sordid acts. The bitter fights. The draining of another person to feed my own insatiable desires and needs. The desperate search for the missing pieces of my broken self. Years of hazy days and nights swam together in waves.

Suddenly, Thomas's face wavered before me. He's going to leave me one day soon, I groaned. I'm too old to start over with someone new. And who would want an old, used, forty-three-year-old man like me?

I raised my arm, the one with the heavy cast, until I could see it in the mirror. My career's gone, too. How can I be a hairdresser without two hands? My head dropped.

I rubbed the spot where I'd tried to shoot an overdose of cocaine in my useless hand a few days ago. Another failure, I winced.

A thick, black wave of despair poured over me like suffocating hot tar. I was drowning in my own horror and pain.

Throwing my hands in the air, I moaned, "Lord God. Help me. Save me. Do something. I can't live like this anymore!"

The only answer was the echo of my own words bouncing off the gray tile walls.

I desperately wanted a new beginning, but my future seemed hopeless. How could someone who had made a complete mess of his life start over? The anguish I had experienced had plunged me into an abyss too deep to scramble out of. Wasn't I born a homosexual? Wasn't I powerless to change my behavior?

Too aghast for tears, I stumbled back to my friends more determined than ever to end it all.

But God did answer my helpless cry the very next day. He extended His healing hands of mercy and grace to a man who had wasted himself in an ever-draining homosexual lifestyle. He gave me His forgiveness, acceptance and unconditional love. He filled me with joy. He began to change me from the inside out, creating a wholeness I could never imagine possible.

Today, I have something that satisfies completely—a relationship with Jesus Christ. And I have Christian friends and a loving wife who accept me in spite of my sin and weakness-

es. They have borne with me through my dark times and re-joiced with me over my victories.

Perhaps you, too, are struggling with the questions that had plagued me for so long. I'm sure you've heard all kinds of opinions about homosexuality. Some claim it is normal, an acceptable alternative life-style. Others hate gays and do all they can to humiliate them. Which attitude is right? How does God view the homosexual? What should our attitude be toward them?

Only God has the answer to our inner turmoil and needs. He has taught me many things since that night in the bar. I have learned how deeply sexual brokenness can run in a person's life. My eyes have been opened to the devastation and pain that a gay life-style inflicts on everyone involved.

Through my experiences, I'd like to show you where homosexuality leads. I'd like to give you practical principles that will help you understand your emotions and how to deal with your inner pain. And I want to give you simple tools to help you encourage others who are trying to come out of the gay life-style.

I assure you that you can find freedom from homosexual feelings and behaviors. You can feel whole again. And through God's power, you can help someone who is overcome by compulsive and addictive behaviors live a fulfilled and happy life.

Now, let me share my story with you....

1

The Secret of the Stone

"Andre, party of two...," a pleasant voice called.

The stylishly dressed couple stepped forward. "Good evening, Mr. Andre. Your table is ready. Right this way."

Wayne Andre let an artful smile creep across his lean "Cajun" face as he and Hinano Vincent followed the chic hostess into the dining room to their table. His plan was ingenious.

He pulled the chair out for Hinano and waited patiently for her to sit down. Dexter's on the Lake with its beautiful candlelight, white tablecloths, elegant dinnerware, and fresh flowers could not have been a more romantic setting for what he had in mind. He had sent ahead a huge rare lily—the only one of its kind in all Birmingham—for their table and had reserved a place next to the window overlooking the lake.

"What a beautiful lily!" She gazed at the white flower with its mysterious splashes of pink, then glanced around the room at the floral arrangements on the other tables. Hinano's warm Hawaiian eyes danced. Her auburn hair swayed gently on her shoulders with each movement. Wayne couldn't take his eyes off her as he stepped lightly to the chair across from her and sat down. In her white dress, with its scooped neckline edged in delicate lace, she looked more beautiful than the lily.

Chattering happily, Hinano picked up her menu and Wayne followed suit. Never in his life had he felt such tenderness in his heart for a woman. Usually he and Hinano were with friends when they went out to dinner. The fact that they were alone made him feel uneasy. Would being alone together in such a romantic setting arouse her suspicions? He hoped their casual conversation would distract her.

"Let's start with an appetizer—and maybe some passion tea," he grinned, motioning for the waiter. After placing their order, Wayne took a deep breath, leaned forward, and spoke in a roguish tone. "Someone told me a story that you're just not going to believe, and I want you to tell me what you think about it."

Hinano listened intently as Wayne began. "This guy walked up to a friend of mine—well, let's call him Jim. He gave Jim an engagement ring that he had bought for someone years ago. The guy said the Holy Spirit had told him to give the ring to Jim for the girl Jim wanted to marry."

"Oh, you've got to be kidding," Hinano gasped.

"No."

"Who is this guy?"

A grin tugged at the corners of Wayne's mouth. "You know him, but I'm not going to tell you 'cause he doesn't want anyone to know who it is." He continued the story as the waiter set down their drinks and a plate of sauteed mushrooms.

"This guy had bought the ring for a girl he was going to marry. But they had broken up, and he had kept the ring in his dresser drawer all this time."

Wayne savored the South Seas flavor of the tea as he told how his friend Jim refused to take the ring. "But the guy grabbed Jim's hand and forced it open. He said he had to obey the Holy Spirit and insisted that Jim take it. The guy pressed Jim's hand shut, then walked away."

Wayne helped himself to a mushroom then dabbed at his mouth and mustache with a napkin. "Jim opened his hand and stared at the ring. 'Oh, God, what am I supposed to do?' he thought. 'This thing looks so puny!' He had purchased a costly ring for his girl friend but was unable to make the payments and had taken it back. He was heartbroken and thought that because he couldn't afford the expensive ring, God didn't want him to marry the girl."

Hinano shook her head sympathetically. "Just how expensive was it?"

"Almost $8,000," Wayne confided.

"She must have been very special."

"Yeah, she was." Wayne toyed with his napkin as he related how his friend had gone to a back room in their place of business where he could pray. "Jim said that God showed him the reason he had bought the expensive ring was because he wanted to look big when he gave it to his girl, not because he loved her."

The polite voice of the waiter interrupted the conversation. "Are you ready to order, or do you need a few more minutes?"

"No, we're ready." Wayne nodded to Hinano.

She pointed to the fish entrees. "I'll have the red snapper."

"Guess I'll have the same," Wayne chimed in.

The waiter wrote down their order and turned back to Hinano. "Soup or salad, ma'am?"

They finished selecting their food, and Wayne continued as the waiter picked up the menus and left.

"Jim said God spoke so clearly to him that he just started crying. He told his pastor about what happened and asked him if he thought it was a miracle. The pastor said, 'I would say that the Holy Spirit gave you this ring.' When Jim finally realized that God had given him the ring, it meant more to him than anything he could have bought."

"Wow, Wayne, that's too much! Then what happened?" Hinano's eyes beamed.

"Jim took the ring to a jewelry store and had the diamonds remounted on a new wedding band." Wayne paused to form his words just right. "He doesn't quite know how to handle the situation. He called and wanted to know if I thought he should give the girl this particular ring, ask her to marry him, and if I thought she would say yes."

Wayne let his words sink in. "What do you think? Should he give her that ring? Should he marry her?"

"I'll tell you what I think!" Hinano blurted. She leaned forward as though to speak confidentially. Her

4

brown eyes beamed. "If that would happen to me, I would know beyond a shadow of a doubt—that was the person I was supposed to marry. Of course he should give her the ring! That story has God written all over it."

"Do you want to know who Jim is?" Wayne smiled proudly.

"Yes, of course!"

Wayne reached into the pocket of his Sunday-best gray suit coat and pulled out a little brown velvet bag. He took his time loosening the drawstring. "That friend is me, and you're the girl. Will you marry me?" He held out the ring to Hinano. She seemed frozen, her chin cradled between open hands, her mouth open.

Wayne felt suddenly aware of a tightness in his shirt collar. Had the air stopped? A million eyes, it seemed, were watching them. "Hinano, take the ring," he whispered.

Finally she stammered, "Wayne—I—I—don't know about this."

Wayne glanced furtively at the surrounding tables. "All right, look. Just take the ring, think about it, and if the Lord leads you not to take it—well, we can call it off and you can give me the ring back. No pressure."

Someone at the next table sang out, "Marry him." Others took up the chorus, "Marry him. Marry him."

Hesitantly, Hinano reached for the ring and slipped it on her finger.

"I really love you, Hinano, and I hope your answer will be yes. I'm willing to wait." Wayne paused while the waiter set their dinners on the table. Fear tugged hard at Wayne's confident air, and he felt his stomach tighten.

Hinano cut into her fish with her fork and shook her head. "I can't believe this," she laughed. "I can't believe the way you did that. You're slick. I fell for it—hook, line and sinker."

Wayne grinned. The tension was broken. He explained how Tony Vincent, an employee at his beauty salon, had called him aside one morning and given him the ring. "I offered him money," Wayne explained, "but he wouldn't take it."

Suddenly Wayne's voice quivered. "I just fell apart when the Holy Spirit told me, *The ring you have in your hand now is more valuable than anything you can ever buy, because I gave it to you.*'"

As Wayne recounted more details of how Tony gave him the ring, Hinano laughed, "Did Tony really do that? God told him to give you the ring?" Her voice broke as she dabbed at her eyes. "And Tony said that? I can't believe this!"

Hinano admired the ring on her finger, twisting her hand to view the diamonds from different angles. A large stone flanked by clusters of triangular diamond chips gave the setting the appearance of a little flower burst. "It's absolutely gorgeous!"

Still, she did not say "yes" to Wayne's proposal. As Hinano prattled on about the ring, the waiter interrupted. "Would you like anything else, sir? More tea? Dessert perhaps?"

"No, thanks," Hinano smiled.

Wayne laid cash on the small tray holding their bill, and Hinano plucked the lily from its vase as they rose to leave. They walked silently out of the restaurant toward her car. He owned a black pickup truck with dark tinted windows, but on special occasions like this they always went in her Nissan.

Beside the car, he stepped close to Hinano and studied her eyes. All he could think to say was, "Well?"

Hinano looked away from his gaze. "Well...I don't know. I'll have to think about it...." Her voice trailed into nothing.

Wayne had not expected that. Not wanting to press the matter further, he gently opened the car door for her. "I'll bring you home," he suggested, trying hard to hide his disappointment. "If you decide you really want to marry me, then tell me tomorrow."

Wayne swallowed hard as he walked around to the driver's side and got in. Hinano looked at him and laughed heartily. "I can't believe all this. I'm overwhelmed!" She stared at her ring again. "I just can't believe it!"

Wayne felt perplexed. The whole evening had been wonderful. He had rehearsed his story until it was down pat. The artful manner in which he had led Hinano to give the right answer, her excitement over the ring, and just the way she laughed and appeared to enjoy herself left him with no doubts that she would say, "Yes." But why was she hesitating?

The drive to her apartment seemed endless. Hinano's mother, brother and two sisters were there when they arrived. She showed them the ring, and they all became excited. After some of the congratulations died down, Wayne approached Hinano's mother. "Victoria, will you let her marry me?"

She laughed. "Yes! Of course I will!"

One by one, each of her family—Peter, Kathryn and Mary—gave their hearty approvals, but Hinano remained silent. No one seemed to notice that the bride-to-be had not yet given her consent.

Wayne went along with the events like everything was okay. Finally, it came time for him to leave. He and Hinano embraced, and she whispered, "I'll think about it and let you know."

At home, he quickly unlocked the front door and sat down on his living room sofa to think. He remembered another evening when the two of them had talked about their future. He told her he wanted to pay off all his bills before thinking seriously about marriage. She had looked lovingly at him and said, "You don't have to do that. I'd marry you right now if you asked because you'll probably never have your life straight."

What had changed? Had he been too slick in his proposal? Or was it because of his past? He wished the uneasiness inside would go away.

2

"Swamp Man" in Waiting

Early the next morning, Wayne determined to do what he always did when faced with a difficult situation. He would go to work at his hair salon early, lock himself in a back room and pray; then when the shop opened, he would keep himself busy until Hinano could figure out an answer. But this time she would not be able to help him. She was the "difficult situation."

Feeling utterly alone, he started his truck and headed toward the salon. He had been so sure last night that Hinano would say "yes" to his proposal. The fact that she wanted to think about it stirred fears that she might reject him.

After leaving the homosexual life-style, he had looked for a woman who would understand him. Hinano was that woman. He was sure of that. Over the last few months he had been telling her a lot about himself, things that most women would probably run from. But she had been compassionate and accepting as though his past didn't matter. Now he wondered whether she was having second thoughts about his past.

Wayne pulled up behind a car stopped at an intersection. His mind traced many of the conversations he and Hinano had had in recent months. She seemed like a sensitive person, and he had offended her on several occasions. Sometimes when the two of them got into heavy discussions, she would retreat. It was difficult to talk with each other face to face on certain issues, so they would spend hours on the telephone, he lying in his bed and she in hers. The distance between them that the phone permitted had helped them express themselves more freely. The problem came when they would go out together. Sometimes they could not say fifteen words to each other.

During their conversations, Wayne had been open about his homosexual past, but he hadn't told her all the sordid details. She knew about his former lovers. In fact, she worked at the shop with Thomas, Wayne's long-time business partner and former lover. Thomas had gone practically everywhere with them during the early part of their courtship. What Hinano didn't know, and what lay heavily on Wayne's mind as he rolled into a parking space near the shop, was the depth of his sexual promiscuity and the guilt he felt about it.

Wayne closed the front door of the shop and locked it behind him before heading for the back room. Sure, God had forgiven him, but he found it difficult to forgive himself. His sexual life-style had been rough—degrading talk, sadomasochism, sodomy, group sex. He was afraid it would be hard to get back into normal heterosexual activity. "Lord, what's going to happen to me now?" he agonized. "Is Hinano afraid that I may go back into the gay life? Does she think I can't be the tender, loving person she needs?"

Wayne's prayer time was interrupted by the sound of employees coming to work. Thomas was the first to arrive, then Tony Vincent and several other hairdressers. Wayne bounded out of the back room and pretended to be cheerful. Before Hinano could arrive, he let everyone know what had happened the night before. "Then I gave her the ring, and you should have seen her face," he laughed.

"What did she say?" someone chimed in.

"She just couldn't get over the way I...."

"Did she say yes? That's what we want to know," another teased.

Wayne started to answer but stopped short at the sight of Hinano entering the front door. All eyes focused on her ring finger. Hinano wasn't wearing the ring! Wayne felt the tenseness in the room and tried to distract her from it with a cheerful greeting.

Saturday was the busiest day at the salon, and today was no exception. Try as he might, he found it difficult to keep his mind on his work. Even the steady chatter of Mrs. Chamberlain, one of his more fashionable clients who gloried in gossip about Birmingham's "in" society, seemed lost in his volley of thoughts. Occasionally he would interject a polite response.

Something she said about AIDS brought to mind two of his former lovers. He had contacted them recently to ask their forgiveness and had learned that both had tested positive for AIDS. Wayne had had himself tested twice in the last couple of years and was clean. He considered himself lucky, especially since neither he nor his lovers had taken precautions against the deadly virus. But he knew that sometimes it went undetected for months or years after infection. So as an extra precaution, he intended to be tested once again before he got married.

"...And do you know she went and did it anyway?" Mrs. Chamberlain chuckled. "I just don't know what got into the old girl. What do you think, Wayne? Should I say something to her about it?"

Her question jerked Wayne out of his reverie. "Ah, about what, ma'am?"

"Wayne! Aren't you listening to me?" Mrs. Chamberlain cocked her head upward. "You seem so quiet today. Anything wrong?"

"Ah, no, ma'am." Wayne glanced in Hinano's direction as he finished combing out his client's hair. He didn't want to think about what would happen to him and Hinano if the AIDS test results came back positive. Hinano hadn't seemed concerned. At least she hardly spoke of it. But could this be weighing on her mind, too?

Wayne unfastened the pastel cape around Mrs. Chamberlain's shoulders as she prattled on, primping in front of the mirror. "Beautiful, just beautiful," she sang, then hurriedly handed Wayne some bills and waltzed out the door. As usual, she had left him a generous tip. Motioning to his next customer, Wayne smiled and carried the cash to the register. "I'll be right with you, Mrs.

Tate. Have a seat." He quickly thumbed through the mail which had just been delivered and shook his head.

"Anything decent in the mail today, Wayne?" Thomas called.

Wayne tightened his lips until they virtually disappeared beneath his mustache. "Naw. Just bills." Then to himself he murmured, "Probably past due."

Although business was going well for a change, poor management, unwise spending and their former extravagant life-style had left Wayne and Thomas with serious financial problems. It seemed they could never get caught up. Wayne and Hinano had talked about this often, and it was a major concern between them.

Since her divorce, Hinano had established good credit in her own name. Wayne worried that his ruined credit rating would affect her sense of security. The fact that she had been willing to help him through his money problems had prompted him to go ahead with the marriage proposal. But now he was beginning to wonder. Had he moved too fast? She knew he was digging out from under a pile of debts and improving his credit situation. But maybe she wanted to wait until he had fully recovered.

Wayne greeted his next customer and prepared to give her a shampoo. "Same as usual today, Mrs. Tate?"

Other thoughts about finances raced through Wayne's mind as he gently guided her head onto the neck rest of the sink and wet her hair. He had no doubts he could look after himself financially. But getting married meant that what he considered adequate for himself would not be enough for two. Hinano would need more security. This meant he would have to settle down and take root, a scary thought because he had been like a gypsy most of his life.

Carefully massaging in a fragrant lather, Wayne was thankful that Mrs. Tate wasn't the talkative kind. A frequent customer, she carried an air of quiet confidence which he envied. Especially now. With gentle precision, he rinsed her hair and dried it with a towel, then tilted her upright.

Hardly one fear escaped his thoughts before another replaced it. Wayne even felt concerned about the difference in age between him and Hinano. Eight years older than she, he always seemed to go for the younger set. Somehow age had not been a problem between him and his male lovers. He hoped it didn't matter to Hinano either, though he knew some women had serious hang-ups about age.

Wayne began to trim Mrs. Tate's hair with skillful snips. Hinano's age weighed on his mind for another reason. She wanted children. After his first wife, Patricia, became pregnant with their third child, Wayne had had no intention of being a father again. He had a vasectomy to make sure.

Hinano had asked if he would be willing to reverse the vasectomy and give her a baby. At the time, he didn't know how to answer her. He was forty-five, already had three grown children, and dreaded the thought of how old he would be when his and Hinano's child would be ready for college. Even so, he had agreed to consider having another baby because that was the only way he thought she would consent to marry him.

Wayne shook his head. He knew how much Hinano loved children. He could tell by the glow on her face when she was around them. He had looked into his chances for a reversal and the costs of the operation. *Lord, what can you do?* he fretted. *It's been twenty years since my operation. The prognosis for reversal is less than ten percent. And the cost—more than $6,000!*

Wayne stretched to reach his hair dryer and began drying and styling Mrs. Tate's hair. He stole a glance at Hinano and wondered, *if she does get pregnant, how am I going to take care of both her and the baby?* Wayne had not been a good provider for his first wife and children. He had fallen far behind in child support during his homosexual years. Since he believed that God would honor his marriage to Hinano only if he made things right with his first family, he didn't want anything in this marriage to hinder him. Amazingly enough, Hinano had accepted the fact that he would be making restitution. But did she worry, too, that he might not be able to support her and another child adequately and give to his original family as well?

Wayne and Hinano had gotten to know each other pretty well over the past few months. Another good reason for her to turn him down could be the differences in their cultures and backgrounds. Wayne characterized her as a "concrete woman," the big-city type, because she was from Los Angeles and was used to a faster pace of living. He saw himself as a "swamp man," a typical southerner who lived a slower life, made jokes about women and expected them to like it. Most southern women were used to ribbings from their men and would not be bothered by their innuendos. At least they would ignore the comments. But Hinano was ready to fight over some of the things he said. Didn't she know that he meant no harm and just said them for laughs? He wondered how they would get along.

The difference in their spiritual lives was of concern to Wayne as well. Hinano was well-grounded in her Christian faith. Wayne was a new believer. The fact that she knew more about the Bible than him sometimes worried him. He was just beginning a new ministry to gays who wanted to be free of their life-style, and she was helping him. He could only imagine how hard it was for her to let him comment on a Bible verse when she could say so much more on the subject. Often she would say things about the lesson, but he knew that out of deference to him, she limited her comments. Wayne knew that as a man he would have to lead Hinano spiritually. Was he ready for it? How long could she hold back before he caught up with her?

Wayne couldn't let the thought of Hinano saying "no" linger in his mind. He had no doubt God had led him to propose to her and was bringing them together. Surely if she rejected him now, God would reveal this to her, and she would change her mind and say "yes" somewhere down the line.

Still, Wayne didn't know how he could handle Hinano's rejection if she were to turn him down. He was sure, however, that it would be the ultimate in devastation to his sense of masculinity. Hinano had been married to a guy who looked macho—stocky, dark-skinned with black hair and beard. On top of Wayne's other concerns, if Hinano said "no," he feared it would be because he didn't look, talk or walk like "real" men do. In fact, he still got accused of being a homosexual because of his effeminate characteristics. He knew, of course, that not being macho didn't make him less of a man. But his ego was still fragile in this area.

One thing he knew for sure, whatever Hinano decided, he would not return to his gay life-style; his commitment to Christ and living straight was too strong for that. If he wasn't "man enough" for Hinano, he would remain celibate the rest of his life.

While Wayne's overriding fear was that Hinano was going to say "no" to his proposal, the impact of his greatest fear suddenly hit him like a left hook to the jaw. *What if she said "yes"!*

The thought of having to perform in bed on the wedding night was another matter. The fact that he had not been to bed with a woman in nearly twenty years frightened him even more than the fear that Hinano might say "no"! Wayne had been used to the touch and smell of a man. How would the soft feel and perfumed scent of a woman affect him? All that had been foreign to his mind since he had left Patricia for Gary Ross. If he couldn't perform as a husband, how would Hinano feel? He sighed at the thought, loudly enough to startle Mrs. Tate.

"Is something wrong?"

"Oh, no, Mrs. Tate," he assured her. "I was just thinking about something. Everything's okay." He picked up the hair spray bottle and deftly sprayed her hair, patting it now and then. Finally he handed her a mirror. "There! How does that look?"

"It's beautiful!" She looked pleased. "Just the way I like it."

Wayne unfastened the cape from Mrs. Tate's shoulders and glanced at his watch. *Past 1:00, and I haven't had lunch,* he mused. He took Mrs. Tate's money, smiled his good-bye, and retreated into the back room to retrieve a sandwich from his lunch bag.

As the day wore on, Wayne buried himself in work and banter with his clients hoping to get some relief from the constant strain on his emotions. At closing time, Hinano was among the last to leave. She seemed cheerful, but Wayne detected a note of awkwardness in their parting "good-night."

Exhausted from standing on his feet all day and from the emotional turmoil, he left Thomas to lock up and headed for his truck. Surely, hopefully, Hinano would say "yes" tomorrow.

All day long, his doubts about Hinano had increased more and more. But his concern about the wedding night became monumental in his mind. If she said "yes" or "no," his worst fears would be realized. Even with God, he wasn't sure how he'd overcome the circumstances of either situation.

Why had he ever thought she would want to get involved with a man with so many problems? He had no answer to that question. His thoughts turned back to the events in his life that had brought him to this day....

3

A Louisiana Heritage

Probably neither Wayne nor any of his family gave much thought to their family roots. Had they done so, they might have discovered how their French heritage and the circumstances of their ancestors' coming to Louisiana had shaped their fortunes.

They could have known little of the seventeenth-century struggle between the French and the English for supremacy in North America. And what of Robert Cavelier who in 1682 descended the Mississippi River and claimed the entire valley in the name of Louis XIV of France? After the British finally obtained permanent possession of the continent at the Treaty of Utrecht in 1713, they bore with the Acadian French settlers for more than forty years. Finally the long-suffering Acadians were dispossessed of their lands—which became the province of Nova Scotia—and many were exiled to Louisiana.

To the Andre family, however, this would all have been purely academic speculation. Nor would the vast land deal in 1803 in which the United States purchased from France a huge tract of land[1] for fifteen million dollars have been of interest to them either—their own finances were too marginal.

Albert and Grace Andre had simply chosen to live in a French "Cajun" (corruption of "Acadian") community some thirty miles west of Baton Rouge. At first, they lived in the little country town of Valverde where the day-to-day struggle for existence was coping enough. There, in a small wooden frame house, two of their four children were born: George (1938) and Wayne (1943). The last two, Marjorie (1950) and John (1955), joined the family after they moved into the city.

Although Albert worked for Standard Oil Company, they could afford to rent only a poor house in town, and for one year an aunt and uncle added to the congestion. Eventually, however, the Andres purchased a house in the blue-collar district of Algonquin Street, only a mile from the oil refinery. This was the childhood home Wayne was to remember best—the asbestos siding, the bare wooden floors and the crowding because of having only two bedrooms. Nonetheless, he was enchanted with his mother's choice of vividly flowered kelly-green wallpaper for the living room. He grew up to have a keen and natural interest in arranging things— in putting objects in the exact place where they would look best. While excitement prevailed over this move to the new house, emotional upheaval was never far away. Almost immediately, Albert became embroiled with the neighbor over the dividing line between the two driveways.

Still, no one could accuse the lean, angular Albert Andre of not working hard to support his family. He hired out as a farmhand. In good times he might make a dollar a day, otherwise it would be seventy-five cents or less. But Albert really lived for the hunting seasons. Louisiana's rich woodlands and swamps abounded in mink, otter, raccoon and opossum as well as deer, wildcats and a great variety of bird life. These possibilities provided an open invitation to hunting and sportsmanship, skills of which Albert and other Cajuns were very proud. He spent snowy winter months from October to January trapping animals back in the forests and selling the meat and the fur.

"I tell you, boy," he liked to say, "you don't know anything about snow these days." His swarthy face would light up. "But I used to lay my traps in anything from six to thirteen inches of snow in the old days."

Not surprisingly, guns obsessed Albert. And Wayne hated them. Frequently Albert would bring them all out onto the kitchen table to be oiled and cleaned. His hunting dogs also were his priority and took up a lot of his time. Wayne grew to realize that all of this was attention which could have been shared with him and the other children.

Although consistently a rebellious child, older brother George was the preferred son to go on hunting trips with his father. Wayne was seldom invited. Did his father think he wasn't man enough? Then, when he heard the stories father told about George, Wayne didn't feel sorry about being left home.

"Your brother, boy, has learned to hunt, you know." Albert ran a long hand through his black hair, his stern eyes boring through his younger son. "There was this squirrel up in the tree, and I says, 'Shoot, George! Shoot!'"

"Did he hit him?" Wayne asked, simply because his father had noticed him, but he didn't really want to hear the answer.

"Not right off. He shot at him five or six times and kept missing him. But I took care of that." Albert leaned back and crossed his long legs. "Yes sir, I did. I cut a vine off that tree and I just wore him out right there." Once more, his father looked carefully down his sharp nose at Wayne to see if the boy was getting a message. "And George's never missed a squirrel since. A whipping does a boy a whole lot of good, I reckon."

Wayne's mother, Grace Bernard, traced at least four generations of her Acadian ancestors back to Canada, while his father's people had come from France. When Wayne took up hairdressing as a profession, he would remember the stories he'd heard of his forebears doing the same work generations back in France. Albert Andre's broken English and persistent Cajun speech had always kept the family's roots well in the foreground—sometimes to the embarrassment of Wayne.

Life for Wayne was harsh from the start. One day at his uncle's farm, Wayne watched George and his cousin playing in the tar, thoroughly polluting themselves and their surroundings. The two fathers, without any discussion, took ropes and beat the boys. Wayne was sure that his brother would die. Shortly afterward, however, an incident occurred which curbed Albert's loss of control when he disciplined his children.

Wayne grew up in the company of his mother. Usually he liked helping her with the housework—dishes, housecleaning, dusting, and so on. In fact, he seldom minded doing "girl's work." He'd even sit for hours watching her sew clothes or wind her dark hair into pin curls—unconsciously, perhaps, planning for the hairdressing salon he would one day have. He thought her brown eyes and open, wide face were rather pretty.

One morning, however, he had a confrontation with his mother in the bathroom. "Wayne, you need to clean the house," she announced. "The floor must be mopped and then the whole place has to be dusted, and—"

"But, mom, this was the day I was going to—" Wayne's heart sank as his voice trailed off. Then, in a sudden spurt of unusual energy, he rebelled. He started cursing his mother with a stream of profanity which would have done credit to a drunken sailor, to say nothing of the vocabulary of a six-year-old.

He hadn't noticed that the bathroom window was open, however, so he had no way of knowing his father was just outside. The retribution came immediately. Albert strode indoors, livid. "You little animal!" He jerked Wayne across his knees. "I'll wallop you, Robert Wayne, for every word you said to her." He beat the boy almost to pulp. "For every word—," his muscular arms kept pummeling him, "for every word, I say!" Gasping for breath, Wayne felt waves of darkness sweep over him. Only his mother's intervention halted the beating.

After the bathroom episode, it seemed that Albert tried to set limits on himself, knowing that his violence could kill. Thereafter, Wayne might be hit occasionally, ridiculed or ignored—but never again would he be the recipient of such a pounding.

But Albert Andre had another side too—an odd sense of humor. His practical jokes, however, were wholly for his pleasure. The children used to go berry-picking along the gravel road in front of their house. "You gotta look out for snakes," father would warn them. They all knew about the rattlesnakes and the deadly water moccasins.

Terrified even to reach for another blackberry inside the bush, they huddled together on the roadside staring at the inaccessible berries. Then came a hissing sound, a sudden movement among the branches, and something clutching at their legs. Screaming, the children froze to the spot while their father scrambled out onto the road from under the bushes, laughing loudly. At supper that night he gleefully regaled the rest of the family with the joke. The unspoken emphasis, of course, lay on Wayne's cowardice and hysteria. Even a little boy could feel that sting of scorn.

Sometimes his father's jokes hurt Wayne in another deeper, and even more vulnerable, place. One Christmas Eve he slept on the couch in the living room because the grandparents had come over to stay for the night and had taken his bed.

At bedtime his father ambled in, fresh from another hunting expedition. "Well, well, son. You know I was deer stalking last week." Albert sat down with elaborate casualness on the arm of Wayne's couch-bed. "And you know that old Rudolph the Red-nosed Reindeer? I think we shot him."

Four-year-old Wayne looked up into his father's thin, dark face, afraid to ask. "Do you think Santa can...?"

"No, no, boy. I don't believe Santa Claus is coming tonight." His father hoisted his sinewy frame up and headed for the door. "He couldn't do it without Rudolph, you know. And I'm pretty sure we got 'im!"

But Wayne had a far greater grief than just missing Santa—something that his father would never be able to understand. The boy loved deer because they were pretty. Grandfather Andre had once taken him to see "Bambi," and he could remember crying when Bambi's mother was killed by a hunter.

Wayne could never be the masculine son Albert required. He was often embarrassed on the many occasions when he knew his father was ashamed of him. He simply couldn't measure up to the kind of man who roped calves in Louisiana rodeos, hung out with sportsmen, and worshiped guns.

To this day Wayne can understand little of the meaning of the word "father." In his experience it was simply a word in the dictionary. Albert fulfilled the definition materially but not emotionally or spiritually. His father was away almost constantly and when he did come home, little joy attended his arrival. He'd bring money home, but Wayne can't remember many "fun times" involving father.

His mother, on the other hand, planted in each of her children a considerable degree of commitment and purpose. Two of her precepts that have stuck with Wayne for life are: "Where there's a will, there's a way" and "Whatever you start—finish it!" She welded a family unit in which her husband became, by reason of both absence and personality, an outsider looking in.

And there was a reason for Grace Andre's strength. As the eldest of five children, she had had the task of raising her brothers and sisters because her mother was sickly. Responsibility thus came too soon for a young girl, and Wayne's mother, in turn, became a self-sacrificing woman—but a mother who wanted to manage everything.

For her own sake, it was probably well that she developed a controlling personality. But the effect on Wayne would be less than beneficial. Unlike her own mother who was enslaved to her husband, Grace controlled most of the money in the house. Unable to read or write, Albert left the management of household affairs to his wife and always turned his paychecks over to her. Ultimately, when he went to work for Standard Oil, the company educated him to where he could read at the sixth-grade level. Although basically illiterate, he was a whiz at mathematics, and no one could beat him at figures. Like many other boys in his time and place who had been pulled out of school to work on the farm, Albert never finished Grade 3.

Grace was an odd combination of sternness and passivity. Like most youngsters, Wayne could figure out just about how far he could push his mother. She'd yell at her children five or six times before she would take action. With her husband constantly away from home, she worked hard, tending the garden and canning the produce in order to keep the children fed.

She always kept an open house and reached out to help people far beyond her family duties. Wayne felt proud that his mother was like a community nurse. Whenever a family had a crisis, they'd send for Grace Andre because she always knew what to do. Moreover, she would drop everything and go. More than likely she would hurry off with a scarf over her pin curls. When she arrived, she could get the situation under control immediately and everyone would feel better.

One night the man in the house across the street had a heart attack and died. She dragged four-year-old Wayne into the house with her. He watched in awe as she took a mirror and put it to the dead man's face to see if he was breathing. "My, you know a lot of stuff," he whispered. "What did the mirror tell you?"

Reared in the Catholic Church where works really mattered, Grace often seemed like the ambulance itself, always rushing off on yet another mission of mercy. The effect on her children was not good, however, because priorities in the home were warped. Her constant giving, in fact, became one of the traps of piety. Always more ready to help someone outside the family than in, she taught her children to give—even when they didn't have it. Thus everyone felt perpetually diminished. Wayne resented the many times when the family would plan something, only to be disappointed because mother had rushed off to rescue someone.

All the difficulties notwithstanding, Albert Andre could hardly be charged with malice toward his children—he simply had never been equipped with the basics for parenting. One of the few occasions when Wayne was invited to go with his father on an errand to the drug store proved to be a case in point. The two-door black 1949 Chevrolet had faulty door locks which sprang open if the back seat went forward. At a sudden stop at an intersection, Wayne's seat in the back lunged forward and hit the door handle. The door opened and the boy fell out. His father grabbed his hand as he tumbled through the door, but before the car came to a complete stop, the six-year-old was under it.

Never more frightened in his life, Wayne sobbed uncontrollably. Albert could have taken him in his arms and comforted him, but he didn't. Indeed, he probably couldn't. Instead, he told and retold the story to friends, featuring his own prowess in preventing Wayne from being killed. The boy finally concluded that it had somehow been his fault that the car door had opened.

So the rocky years passed in which none of the children could relate to their father. He had become a demanding provider and nothing more. Although Albert never seemed to be part of Wayne's life, the schedules of the entire family revolved around his whims. Coming in late at night, he'd sleep late in the morning, and everyone had to be quiet until he woke up. When he got up to work in the garden or tinker with mechanical projects, he always put the boys to work—cleaning car parts, weeding the yard, whatever. After lunch he'd take another nap, and everyone else had to rest for two hours also. He resented the children playing, even if he couldn't hear them while he was lying down. Constantly they lived under the dictum: "Shhhh, be quiet. Your daddy's sleeping."

Albert had no capacity for enjoying anything—except on his own terms. Even though he was a rugged hunter and trapper, he was still full of deep fears. He <u>had</u> to be among known people in familiar places in order to protect his family. Vacations especially could be a nightmare. Occasionally, the family would try a vacation—usually up with Grace's sister in Springhill, Louisiana, northwest on the Arkansas line. From there the two families would take two cars and head up into the Ozarks.

But the further Albert got from home, the more he'd get bent out of shape. When they bought food, he complained about the price. If anyone suggested a diversion, he suspected that it would be dangerous. His words hung over them like a dark pall, no matter what the circumstances: "Whatever you're doing, stop it!" "I'm giving you one minute to quit—and that's all." In the end, he'd yell, "Get packed up. We gotta go home." It might have been 3:00 in the morning, but that made no difference. Just when the family was on the point of having fun, one way or another, it happened. Always Albert just walked in and jerked it away from them.

Wayne always enjoyed summer storms and tense weather. In the heat and humidity, he liked to sit on the roof of the garage behind the house and hear the rain beat on the tin roof and walls. He prayed for hurricanes and tornadoes, for trauma had come to mean adventure for him. Storms matched the dysfunctions of his family and paralleled his fear of his father—who, when the going was loud and rough, would take himself off to the refinery and thus, happily, out of the house.

Wayne spent several of his early summers at the farm, which technically belonged to his Uncle Clark but was ruled by grandfather Andre. He would eventually come to understand that his father's disabilities as a parent went back to grandfather Andre. "I used to hide under the house so my father couldn't find me and beat me," Albert would tell his children. "We could get a whipping simply because we were 'due' one."

Although he remained a shadowy figure in Wayne's mind, grandfather had a basic set of rules for children to live by: "Do as I say, not as I do." "Keep walking behind me and don't ask any questions." "You are to be seen and not heard." And whenever grandfather took Wayne to the movies, he would chug along in his old Model-T Ford (with running boards on the side and a rumble seat in the back) with a stone face and never let Wayne talk to him.

At home Wayne worked through several fantasies— both his own and his mother's. Wayne liked to dress up in his mother's bright, floral-print dresses. Because he always wanted to fly, he especially liked capes and he would use them to play Superman. No rag was too insignificant to serve as a cape. Later on, he took on the roles of Tarzan (who was gratifyingly undressed) and jungle natives. Perhaps that's why his first memory was at age three when he was in a swing, hung between two trees. Landing from a high sweep, however, he fell and broke his collarbone!

One day, perhaps frustrated with George's waywardness, his mother told Wayne that she wished he had been a girl. "You're too pretty to be a boy, so that's why I like to put dresses on you." When she dressed him up, combed his white-blonde hair, and took him off to New

Orleans on the train, people doted on the "lovely little girl." And she never told anyone he wasn't. Somehow this sank deep into Wayne's consciousness.

School unloaded another set of problems on his defenseless little head. A devout Catholic, Grace insisted that her children attend parochial schools. Wayne had a baneful beginning in first grade. His mother left him in a large classroom with twenty strange children and the nuns. The sisters' stiff black-and-white habits left only their hands, faces and shoes showing, and he wondered if they had any bodies under all the clothes. Surely a nun couldn't be a real human being. He cried and wanted to go home with his mother.

Later, on a sweltering day when he'd become more courageous, he asked one of the nuns, "Don't you ever get hot in those robes?"

She looked down at him loftily. "I'm cooler than you would be if you didn't have any clothes on." This didn't make sense to Wayne and confirmed his suspicion that the nuns weren't real people. He also detected some masculine-looking nuns among his teachers. They walked differently. And two of them, for some reason, didn't like Wayne. Never a violent child, he was often accused of starting the playground fights, and the nuns' charges against him hurt.

Priests, on the other hand, fascinated him. They were strong authority figures. The fathers, of course, wore pants under the "dresses"—and that was confusing.

One day in Mass he found that the life-size cross with the almost-naked body of Jesus on it, blood pouring out of his side, had a peculiar, sexually stimulating effect on him. At that time the man's body interested him much more than the implications of Christ's dying for his sins.

Wayne's first awareness of sexual stimulation, however, had come from a boy only a little older than himself. Also at about this same time, a brief but secret interlude under the azalea bushes with the little girl next door inducted Wayne into what a sexual act might be like. They played "mamma and baby" to the point that Wayne knew that this was something that "felt good."

One day something happened which added immeasurably to the stresses within the Andre home. Wayne's memories of living in the country included grandfather and grandmother Bernard, whose property adjoined that of his family at the back. They came over every night to visit, and when his mother was away on a "rescue mission" they would come and stay the night with the children.

Wayne was only seven when his father suffered an almost-fatal accident in his work at the Standard Oil refinery, and home itself suddenly became a permanent rescue mission. Albert was vacuuming up the debris of metal fragments on the floor when the machine exploded. He caught the shrapnel, like steel bullets, in the abdomen. He remained on the critical list in intensive care for two months, and for the rest of his life he had precarious health. He consumed great quantities of medication and endured numerous surgeries for adhesions and blockages. Kidney stones and infections called for still more surgeries. He seemed to be in the hospital for some kind of chronic condition about twice a year, and he came to the edge of death at least thirty-five times.

In the end, he went on a dialysis machine, and when he died he had only one-fourth of a kidney left.

Although compensation cared for the family's financial needs, the household was thrown into turmoil that seemed never to end. When Albert came home from his surgeries, Grace would often be unable to cope and would simply leave the house. She taught little Wayne how to care for his father's post-surgical needs. Although this really was too much to ask of a seven-year-old, Wayne had some unusual compensations. After he'd changed the surgical dressing, his father would pat him on the head and say, "You did a good job." Only in the nursing care did Wayne get *any* affirmation from his father.

During his father's illness, his Bernard grandparents virtually replaced Wayne's own parents. But he had no model father here either. In fact, he grew to resent his grandfather Bernard for treating his grandmother like a slave. It didn't escape Wayne's notice that when she opened her wallet, she'd be lucky if she had even two dollars in it. Grandfather's wallet, in contrast, was always fat—bulging with bills.

"Why don't you ever give her any money, grandfather?" Wayne asked once.

"She don't need no money, boy." Grandfather dragged his chair up to the kitchen table where his long-suffering wife had placed a big bowl of warm water for his daily shampoo. "All she needs to do is to cook, clean and make sure I'm happy."

Wayne would watch his grandmother wash her husband's hair, dry it and carefully comb in into place. And

Wayne would sit there seething with fury and fighting down his desperate desire to punch his grandfather in the face—or better still drown him in the shampoo bowl.

Meanwhile, Wayne's stormy connection with brother George augmented his problems at school. When Wayne started first grade, George had his own friends and interests, and there was no "taking little brother under his wing." "You're too young, Wayne. Lemme alone," became a dismal counterpoint to the brothers' relationship all through the years.

In the end, Wayne failed the first grade and had to watch his friends go on to the next grade. He knew that everyone thought he was a dummy who couldn't do anything right. He believed it himself, and George's laughing at him only confirmed his belief.

Being accident-prone, Wayne broke his arm during that first year, only two years after he had broken his collarbone. Like the playground, home was no better. One cold winter morning while warming himself in front of the gas bathroom heater, he caught his flannel pajamas on fire. Running in terror down the hall, he tripped on the floor-furnace grate and fell. Out of his mind, he screamed for his mother. She ran from the kitchen crying, "Oh, my God! Oh, my God!" Bundling him in a blanket, she put out the flames.

At the hospital, the doctor talked to Grace Andre as if Wayne wasn't even there. In a quiet monotone he explained, "The burn here behind his right knee is so deep that we may have to amputate his leg!"

But even the saving of his leg had its dark side. During the long recuperation, someone taught Wayne how to crochet. Albert hadn't been too concerned at the time of the accident, though he did come to the hospital a few times. But when he did, Wayne self-consciously hid his crocheting under the bedclothes. He just couldn't stand any more ridicule from his father.

George was so much like their father in disposition that he kept Wayne in a perpetual state of trauma. He also had a penchant for practical jokes. One rainy night Wayne went to visit a friend. "When you see the lights go on in our house, come home right away," his mother instructed him.

On cue he saw the little frame house light up, and, scared as he was of the dark, he ran home. Just as he walked in the door, the lights went out. "Mamma! Mamma!" he called. No answer.

Then out of the darkness loomed a figure in a black hat, black slicker raincoat and dark glasses. In absolute hysteria, Wayne jumped out of the back door and dropped fifteen feet to the ground below. Bruised and winded, he looked up to see his brother George take off the glasses, lean over the rail and laugh at him.

Perhaps the birth of his baby sister helped Wayne more than anyone else. He screamed with joy to learn that the baby was a girl. Now he had someone below him, someone he could rule over as George ruled him.

By now Wayne had begun, in desperation, to hate not just both his grandfathers, but his father and brother too. Every man he saw he assumed to be a replica of all the males in his family. Although he could relate to most boys, as far as he could tell they'd all grow up to act like his father and his grandfathers. They'd dominate their wives and intimidate their children. So where did one go to find a friend?

By the time he entered his teens, Wayne had an ominous combination of frustrations in his life. His mother was his role model. His father was a "non-person" much of the time whose absence was not nearly as hard to bear as his being home. Wayne was rejected by his brother, ridiculed by many of his peers and hounded by some of his teachers. There simply wasn't much left out of which to build a self-image.

Today Wayne would be the first to say that his parents never did him any intentional harm and that they loved him in the best way they knew how. Nevertheless, a price would have to be paid for such a quantity of woe.

[1]The Louisiana Purchase consisted of 800,000 square miles, covering all of the south-central American states.

4

Rites of Passage

Wayne instinctively hunted for escape from the realities of his world. He became a steady movie-goer—especially enjoying westerns, cartoons and musicals. In fact, one of the few things the whole family could agree on was spending Saturday night with Roy Rogers, The Lone Ranger, Audie Murphy or John Wayne.

His visits to the farm *should* have been pleasurable for him, but seldom were. As he grew older, Wayne was expected to tend cattle and hogs and to work the corn and cotton. And somebody always corrected him for every move he made. "You don't pick corn. You *pick* cotton and *pull* corn, boy." Although Wayne didn't take to farm life, he enjoyed watching the animals. He preferred that to the perpetual arguing that went on in the house.

Often he took refuge among the black hired hands. His uncle would shout at them endlessly, though he never physically abused them.

Even at the farm, however, Wayne couldn't elude a shadow which had begun to haunt him. He was about eleven years old when, for a laugh, his cousins and George wrestled him to the ground and put him into a girl's bathing suit. Outside, a construction crew was resurfacing the road. The boys threw him out the door, screaming and crying, while the men on the street whistled at him and called him names. Everyone was bigger than Wayne, so fighting wasn't an option.

These years brought a succession of small trials which constantly reaffirmed Wayne's belief that he could never do anything right. At the farm his cousins would give him a Mason jar almost full of cream. "If you just stand there and shake it, it'll turn into butter." So eager to be accepted, Wayne would shake the jar until he thought his arms would fall off. But nothing ever happened.

"Now look here, dummy!" After about thirty minutes, the big kids would take the jar back—at just the right moment, give it a few shakes and the butter would form. "You just don't know how to do it, Wayne. You simply don't have the touch." So, they'd walk off laughing, leaving him feeling frustrated and foolish yet again.

Wayne reached his junior-high-school years and still hadn't resolved his inability to be a hunter in the image of his father. Despite misgivings, he was thrilled one day when Albert Andre invited him to accompany him on an adventure into the woods with some twenty members of a rather exclusive "deer club."

Once on location, Andre singled his son out, put him alone in a stand, and left him there. At first Wayne enjoyed the songbirds and the view, feeling like some kind of flower-child in the wilderness. Then suddenly the dogs erupted in a frenzy of barking and ran a beautiful deer directly toward his stand. Wayne took one look at the lovely, terrified animal, and a sharp pain shot through his own heart. *I can't do it!* He tried but couldn't even pick up his gun. *I just can't!* Thinking himself alone, he moaned and pulled his raincoat over his head, heartily wishing himself back on the streets of Baton Rouge.

But he hadn't realized that his father had seen the whole episode. When all the sophisticated hunters had gathered at the lodge at the end of the day, Wayne saw that the deer had been skinned and the meat divided. The blood had been kept in order to initiate a new hunter by smearing it on him. *Not on me!* Wayne thought, revolted at the idea.

Then he heard his father's strident voice. "Come on, everybody. Gather over here because I have a story to tell you. It's about this son of mine!"

"What do you mean?" Wayne couldn't imagine how he'd failed this time. "What did I do?"

"Just be quiet, boy. I'm the one to tell the story." Andre regaled them all with the tale of his lily-livered son. "And he was sitting in that deer stand and, lo and behold, that deer ran right up on him. Ya' know what he did?" Wayne felt every eye fixed on him. "He took the raincoat and put it over his head. And the deer trotted back into the woods."

The men roared and thought it was a great joke. "So just what kind of a deer were you expecting?" someone teased.

Then the conversation drifted among the other fathers, some of whom had also had difficulty "hardening up" their sons. Wayne, meanwhile, seethed with fury. He knew that he could have taken up his gun at that point and, without a qualm, shot his father in the head!

Home from the wretched weekend, Albert simply went to sleep and then was off to work the next morning as if nothing had happened. But his son would never forget.

Convinced that he could not be a man in his father's eyes, Wayne drew back into himself and vowed never to go into the woods with him again. Now the hate in his heart grew like a cancer, and he began to pray that his father would die.

Hunting still shadowed Wayne's life, however, because Albert loved his hunting dogs and would often hug and kiss them. The innocent dogs vexed Wayne because he had to bathe and feed them for his father. Forced to serve the very creatures who replaced him in his father's affections, Wayne felt the ironic twist of pain in his heart every time he had to care for the dogs.

Wayne couldn't forget that his dad would never say he loved him or could not even touch him in a loving way. Disciplining and whipping his desperately unhappy son was all the man knew. Throughout his childhood the knowledge that his father could "wipe him out" if he didn't do everything right was a thought never far from Wayne's mind.

As far back as anyone could remember, the Andre family had been "just getting by." Shortly after the hunting episode, however, a television finally came into the house. Looking at sitcoms now revealed to Wayne something he was missing. Why couldn't *his* father be like the one in "Ozzie and Harriet" and all the rest? "Fathers on TV talk to their children and they *care*," Wayne would plead. "Why can't daddy be like them?"

"But your father loves you," mother would say. "You know he loves you. He wouldn't be working so hard for us if he didn't love us." What could she say? What could anyone say? When Albert Andre heard the question, he would never answer his son.

But Albert's own father had never learned anything else to do with *his* children either, and so the sins of the fathers *did* come down upon the children. Wayne still prayed daily that his father would die. Later he would stand, a terrified rebel, by his father's death-bed as he clutched the bedclothes and whispered, "I love you, daddy." But the father just stared mutely at his son and then looked away. He could not, even at the final moment, say the words. Later, Wayne was to suffer the anguish of realizing that anger is murder. Had he really killed his father? Every day?

At age thirteen, Wayne realized a long-time dream. Under the ministry of Father McMillan, Wayne became an altar boy. He found the intense training as a respondee answering the priest's Latin prayers exciting. No one in the congregation could participate in that special way. He used to hope for a funeral during the school hours so that he could escape the woes of the classroom. At other times, the altar boys had to cut the grass and keep

41

the grounds of two churches—the Church of St. Catherine in Livonia, and another in Fordoche, Louisiana.

Because he was bent on pleasing the priests, his mother, and everybody else so that he would be accepted, Wayne actually derived some spiritual benefits from the altar-boy experience. He could feel, for once, that he was doing something right. Already, however, he was dissatisfied with the shortness of the sermonette. He believed that fund-raising received attention all out of proportion to the attention that was paid to God himself.

Surprisingly it was at church and not at school that Wayne, as a ninth-grader, first succeeded in physically defending himself—a positive step forward. He fought off six or seven boys who were trying to hold him down and smear his face with Polaroid chemicals. These opportunities for victory were relatively short-lived because at sixteen, the altar boys had to give way to younger applicants.

If church gave him any security or satisfaction, it was obliterated by what happened at his new school. Andre had decided to move his family permanently back to the country, and registration day merged him with a casual, ragged population of blue jeans and checkered shirts. To be sure, those children of simple country homes had limited graces. Wayne, on the other hand, had experienced the exalted expectation of the nuns and the dignities of a school uniform—starched shirt, tie, khaki pants and all the rest. Obeying his mother's desire to "do better," however, he wore his city clothes—only to be ridiculed as a "city slicker." Soon the names "sissy," "faggot," and "queer" almost became his legal label. But

Wayne wasn't sure what they meant—and probably none of the kids, even the name-callers, knew what a homosexual was either.

Marking this transition from private to public school made seventh grade probably one of the hardest years of Wayne's life. With the exception of one kind Jewish substitute teacher, the rest of the teachers ignored him. He was not called on to recite. He was always the last one chosen for games. He could only assume that he was the most born-loser ever to walk the earth—a chronic charity case.

The academic scene offered neither challenge nor security for him. Students who should have been in ninth or tenth grade still lagged in seventh grade. If after three years they still couldn't pass, they got promoted anyway. Furthermore, the school was filled with bullies. One of the boys chewed tobacco and spit it amazing distances. No one corrected him.

His refined sensibilities outraged, Wayne couldn't relate to anything around him. So he started staying inside at recess, hanging around the cafeteria and making friends with girls who were also repulsed by the bullies. Instinctively he seemed to know how to "do girl talk." As the tallest and skinniest kid in the classroom, Wayne slouched forward, trying to get himself down in size. He couldn't show an ounce of muscle anywhere, it seemed. So, by the end of that year, the environment had closed in on him. He failed the seventh grade!

As for the girls he knew, he thought of them only as friends, never in terms of dating. Actually he preferred to be home playing with his little sister. He loved to dress her in the beautiful dresses her mother made for her, to comb her hair (he always loved combing girls' hair) and then to sit down and look at her. A variation on this theme occurred when the girls wore hoops to school—hoops so wide that their skirts stopped traffic in the aisles. These feminine arrangements utterly fascinated Wayne.

On the other hand, keeping up with the boys (usually older than himself) reduced Wayne to utter despair. Urged on by a pair of predatory, world-wise twins who daily pared their teachers to tears, he attempted fondling the girls. Then came sexual abuse from the tough guys. To the shouts of "queer" and "faggot," they would drag him to a corner of the school yard and pull his pants off and abandon him. Other times they would call on him to watch while they stimulated themselves, and then inquire, "Do you like it, Waynie?" Horrified, Wayne didn't know where to turn for refuge. Had he complained to the teachers, it would have proved to be more than his life was worth.

Finally, when Wayne had nearly reached "point zero," the tide turned. A husky weight-lifter took pity on Wayne and befriended him—indeed, he became like a brother to Wayne. Intimidated by the hulk of Josh Green, the kids granted Wayne a little peace, and he basked in the wonder of having, at last, a bodyguard and a friend. Josh saved him from withdrawing completely from life. Only one thing sometimes hurt Wayne. He saw that Josh and his father had great conversations with each other and did things together. *That* was something

Wayne could never hope for, so he just watched, listened, and felt his heart break.

Now that he didn't always have to be on the run, Wayne tried hard to be heterosexual. First, he played football, since that was something the world believed males were supposed to do. Actually, he did quite well, but deep inside he never felt any zest for it. He'd rather have been a cheerleader than a football player. His athletic rival was George, of course. His older brother had played football back in the city. In fact, his desire to leave the Catholic school and attend public school had caused considerable family commotion. One wonders why, for all practical purposes, religious concerns became so prominent. No kind of church affiliation had yet made any discernible difference in the varied tribulations of the fractured Andre family. Always marginal in the sports world, however, Wayne spent hours in the gym, distracted by the muscular legs of the basketball players and longing to look and feel like those men—real men.

Wayne next tried dating girls. George, as usual, had everything sorted out to his satisfaction. Stocky, but dark and handsome, he *knew* about women. One day, Wayne discovered that the glove compartment of George's car was full of condoms, and he was able to figure out what his brother was doing.

Full of rhythm, Wayne was a good dancer. His mother allowed him to go double-dating with older boys to the dances at the community center. At sixteen, Wayne already knew his way into the bars, even though he didn't yet have a driver's license.

One of his first conquests here was Carol Landers, a blonde, "butch-looking girl," as he recalls. She loved horses and almost strangled Wayne when she hugged him. She then led him along to kissing and other games but, while he was somewhat excited, Wayne didn't feel much else. He still hadn't figured out what homosexuality was all about, but he suspected that whatever it was, it either got you killed or landed you in jail. So he tried hard to respond to women as all the other boys did.

Leigh Ann Vale was the first girl he really cared for—perhaps because she was almost as tall as he was. They enjoyed sitting together in study period and talking. After only a couple of dates, however, things fell apart because she became interested in a very masculine and well-built fellow.

Now the fear of being rejected on a date brought another cloud over Wayne's horizon. As his gaze roved fearfully over his rivals, he knew with agonizing certainty that every one of them looked better, talked better and walked better than he did. The only place where he had an edge was in dancing. It lifted his spirits a little when some of his competitors occasionally asked him to teach them the new dance steps.

Meanwhile, his other major satisfaction in those junior-high-school years was working with the Future Farmers of America. There he met Patricia O'Donnell, an eleventh-grader, six months older than he. Something of a tomboy, she interested Wayne immediately. They double-dated with a friend Ethan and his girl-friend, Jennifer. Drinking and dancing at the bars were the order of the day, and though they were all under-aged no one enforced the laws on minors.

The family's battle scars were now beginning to surface in a marked way. Only John, Albert Andre's youngest son, was spared the burning, bitter resentment which the other children bore toward their father. (He had been born after Andre was on total disability and didn't have the strength for harsh discipline anymore.)

Father-son relationships didn't actually die in the Andre family for the simple reason that they had never really been born. By this time, for anyone who had cared to look, Wayne's symptoms had hardened into a major trend—failure, low self-esteem, no family love, being bullied and being prone to accidents. In short, a total lack of sensitivity or consideration from any quarter. All the negatives outweighed any positive experiences to an alarming degree.

5

Surviving the Teens

In the wake of so many uncertainties and failures, Wayne was eighteen years old by the time he arrived at his final year of high school. Also, through his teen years, he still had to cope both with his father's hot temper and deteriorating health.

More and more frequently, Grace Andre spent days and nights with her husband at the hospital where Albert would be a patient for a month at a time. This left Wayne to help grandmother Bernard look after eleven-year-old Marjorie and five-year-old John. (To his relief, his older brother George had left home by this time.) He found himself stepping into the mother role easily, taking control of everything. He would turn Marjorie upside down and whip her for disobeying. John he would bring to his knees in the corner for his belting. That was the kind of discipline that had been practiced on him, and Wayne knew no other way to manage the house. When the red welts came up on John's and Marjorie's legs after the whippings, he could remember his own pain all too well.

But there were calmer interludes also—especially with Marjorie. Wayne would sometimes play dolls with her. Indeed, she herself was *his* doll. He liked to dress her up, style her dark brown hair and send her off to school. As the result of his care, she looked older than her years and much more sophisticated than her little friends.

At about this same time an incident occurred which did not come into focus until some time later. The Lion's Club sponsored a "beauty contest" in which men were to dress like women. Wayne joined in, totally "in drag" with wig, bosom and all. It was all in fun, and since the most *macho* men in town participated too, Wayne attracted no unfavorable attention. During the show, his own father looked him right in the face and didn't know who he was. This pleased Wayne, and his father was even proud of him when he took first prize.

Wayne's tormentors, however, still ridiculed him in the locker room and plagued him in the halls. Finally, some of them were expelled from school, and the ring leader himself was killed in a car accident. At last, in this rather odd, bittersweet way, several troublesome people walked out of his life, and he became free. Free to pursue his courtship of Patricia—which, according to society's prescription, was the next natural step for a man to take.

Now Wayne fell victim to the charms of Patricia O'Donnell. A pretty little ash-blonde, she was a cheerleader—and it was an advantageous thing for football players to go with cheerleaders. Besides, at the games, Wayne liked to hang around with the girls anyway. One day as they all sat in the second row of the bleachers, Patricia plopped herself on his lap. For fun, he suddenly straightened out his long legs. She slid off onto the ground and rolled almost into the ball court. Some kind of chemistry worked, and shortly thereafter he and Patricia became a recognized couple. His self-esteem improved as he began to feel like a real member of the male species.

Wayne was attracted not only to her trim looks but also to her feisty personality. He wanted a strong woman. Visits to her home had a ring of familiarity for him. It was a house full of girls, and tremendous family arguments would occur—pitched battles, in fact. But Patricia always came out on top—and Wayne liked that. Moreover, the mores of the countryside dictated that boys date girls from their own high school and the likelihood of their eventually marrying was high. Going with someone from a rival high school was something attempted only on a dare. Wayne had tried it only once before he settled on Patricia.

After Patricia graduated, she moved to Baton Rouge and lived in a boarding house for girls. She worked as a sales clerk in Chesterfield's Department Store. (Although Patricia was only six months older than Wayne, she graduated two years earlier than he.)

The Jaguar High School Annual of 1963, heavily autographed—particularly by Patricia—served as a checklist of their courtship. A variety of episodes monitored their relationship at the time and possibly forecasted things to come. Patricia got mad and sought her revenge by dating one of Wayne's classmates, Charles. Her temper flared again when he was very late picking her up for the South Seas Ball Night. Formal dancing to a live band, evening gowns and tuxedos made it a major event of the Mardi Gras season in the spring. But Wayne had been fixing someone's hair and hadn't watched the clock.

For Wayne, as for many other young people before and since, doing something with hair could be a major statement. In fact, for him it would become a career. The current fad in school was for the boys to grease their hair down with hair tonic until they looked like wet otters. Wayne was the first to go for the "Balboa Style" which called for lifting the sides up toward the middle and bringing all the hair forward to a curl on the forehead. Jimmy Clanton had popularized the fashion, and it pleased Wayne to find people thought he looked like the pop singer. At the same time, he went for the blonde hair which he'd always craved. He took hydrogen peroxide out of the medicine cabinet and started rinsing his hair with it.

Even though subtle, the change didn't escape his father. "What ya' doin' to your hair, boy? Bleachin' it?" he demanded.

"Why, no. Actually the sun is changing the color, I think," Wayne countered.

"Don't give me that junk," Albert yelled. "You better get that stuff outta your hair, or else I'm gonna do something!"

But Wayne knew he was old enough to run away from home if he had to. So he paid no attention and avoided his father. They lived under the same roof with as little communication as possible. He went on doing as he pleased with his hair and seeing Patricia as often as he could.

Their courtship tended to center on night spots. Above all, they loved to dance. Gifted with a light, bouncy step, Wayne was *fun* to dance with, so Patricia buried her occasional resentments. "Paula" was their favorite tune and, like everyone else, they did the Monkey and the Twist. And Wayne could inventively combine a half slow dance with a half jitterbug. Another attraction for them was the strip of nightclubs on the west bank of the Mississippi River. These clubs never closed, whereas Baton Rouge shut down at 2:00 a.m. For more meditative times, the lakes around home were a lovers' retreat for smooching on moonlit nights—Wayne and Patricia could be found among them.

Occasionally Wayne would stay overnight at Patricia's place in the city. Sometimes they even slept together. (One time they slept on a mat on the porch and found themselves in a nest of caterpillars in the morning.) Being a strongly sexual person, Wayne wanted to do what he supposed people usually went to bed to do. He wanted to join in what the boys at school always bragged about in the locker room. Patricia, however, would never allow intimacy beyond heavy petting.

Her reserve set her apart from most of the other girls. Nonetheless, at that time, boys hoped to finally marry virgins, regardless of what they themselves might do on the way to the altar. In practice this seldom worked, of course, even though the Church forbade premarital sex. As is the way of life, any concept of sin fades away when

53

the "flesh" takes over. Still, this "chastity clause" built into Wayne's and Patricia's courtship had a fascination of itself. Besides, Wayne was devoted and while going steady with Patricia, he never thought of touching anyone else.

Although he learned what it was to love Patricia, Wayne had not yet actually discovered what the gay life would be like. He was, in fact, repulsed when he discovered what homosexuals did. He knew what some of the school kids did in secret down at the levy, and he assumed, from their descriptions of how it "worked," that they were driven by the same weird urge as vampires when they went after blood. Somehow, he never related homosexuality to a life-style which could be like marriage, which could be founded on love and intimacy such as boys and girls could find together. His imagination, as yet, had not gone much beyond just looking at the male body and savoring it.

On one of his Saturday night trips to Baton Rouge to visit Patricia, he was almost "picked-up" in the bus station. He'd heard of homosexuals raping boys, so when he was in the restroom his mind was alert when an older man sidled up to him. At first Wayne froze when the man put his hand on his shoulder, and then he ran. The man kept up with him with surprising agility, but finally Wayne was able to shake him off. He ran the whole twenty blocks to Patricia's apartment. Then and there he decided not to ride the bus again—at least not late on a Saturday night.

Occasionally Albert Andre had permitted his son to take the family car on his courting journeys to the city, but most of the time he grumbled, sometimes long and loudly, because Wayne was putting on too many miles. And even that small privilege came to a loud and painful end. The showdown came on New Year's night in 1963, when father and son faced off. "All right, you can *take* your car and shove it!" Wayne shouted. "I'll walk."

Livid, Albert drew back to strike his son, but Wayne stood his ground and looked him right in the eye. He hardly ever spoke back to his father, but this time Wayne felt bold. Then slowly, Albert's fury waned, his fist wilted and came down and he stalked out of the room. Wayne trudged all the way to Patricia's place—a scary five miles in the dark.

Wayne's friend Ethan had more success in getting the use of *his* father's car. Even so the boys lied to their parents. "We're just going over to Joe's place out in the country," they'd say. In fact, they would make the high-speed, one-hour round-trip into Baton Rouge and be home by midnight. Another "friend in need" was Chad Stephens who had a big Impala. Whenever he went to Baton Rouge to see his girl friend, Wayne would try to go along. Thinking they were quite "somebody," the two couples would cruise around and then finish up with hamburgers and the trimmings at Romeo's Ice Cream Parlor.

Wayne's academic problems continued as he neared high school graduation, and he was not to achieve his next "rite of passage" without suffering. Although his grades had improved as he moved into senior-high-school, he fought an ongoing battle with English and French. In his last year he had a confrontation with the

English teacher, Stephen Walsh. It had to do with the rule about boys keeping their shirts tucked into their trousers. Wayne wore his outside because he was so thin that he wanted the flapping shirttail to cover his all-too-obvious bone structure. The shirt issue evolved into an ongoing problem in English, which he kept failing. Having also had trouble with the English teacher, Patricia stoutly encouraged Wayne to finish high school at any cost.

His academic failures along the way had dropped a mental block in his path. For several months he had his mind set on going to beauty college—something one could do, even an eighth-grade dropout. Still, he doggedly went on to finish what Patricia and everyone else expected him to do.

On the eve of graduation, with invitations already sent out, Wayne found that as a result of his controversy with his teacher, he now lacked half a credit in English. His graduation ring in hand and his gown in readiness, he went home in despair. This was one of the few times that his father ever went to bat for him—because the entire family was going to be embarrassed. Finally it was arranged that he could march up onto the gymnasium stage with his twenty-four classmates. When each name was called for receiving the diploma, his was passed over. His face burned, and he hoped that no one would notice. That summer, with no trouble, he took accounting to make up his credits.

Why Wayne failed French in school was a much more subtle difficulty. How could he bear the name of "Andre" and *still* not make even a "D" in French? His entire family spoke fluent French, and his parents had often used the language to block the children out of conversations. His grandmother Bernard had even tried to teach him, but he refused to learn. There were at least two reasons for his resistance. First and foremost, he felt a great distance from his family in almost every respect, and language became just one more protective wall around him. Second, using French in Louisiana at that time labeled one as being poor—a fact which Wayne hoped to disguise as much as possible.

What success he did have in his final year of high school seemed to be related to his somewhat brief experience center-stage in sports. Thin and light on his feet, he found himself the fastest runner in the school. The first time the coach timed him, he punched the clock, clapped him on the back and said "Wow!" That one word was music to Wayne's ears. Then came the day he won first place in high jumping and won a trophy for his school. The cheers of the fans rang in his ears like a whole anthem for weeks. True, the victory had no coverage other than in the local school paper, but Wayne's pleasure in his wins emphasized the great need he had in his life for approval. At last he'd done *something* that people could admire. Soon he was going to a variety of competitions—pole-vaulting, relay racing and jumping hurdles. He even earned a letter-jacket at track.

Whereas the track meets came to him as naturally as dancing, football posed more of a challenge. Even though Wayne disliked the meanness of many of the players, he needed to prove himself—both for the sake of his friend Josh Green who was a big lineman, for Patricia who had been a cheerleader and also for his ever-present need to be doing what *men* did. What he lacked in muscle and brawn, he had to make up for in nimble wits. When the coach set him to block a 200-pound bully, Wayne could only throw himself into his legs and let his opponent fall over him.

Playing third string that year, however, Wayne shared the public acclaim of being on a winning team. In fact, his notable contribution that season was a major touchdown. In one glorious moment he caught a pass and carried his tacklers more than forty yards to the goal line and scored. After months of bench-warming at the games, he was able for one golden instant to be a star. That euphoria lived with him for a long time.

Then school and life at home changed. The first ended, and the second fell into a new perspective. If one took another look at that old high school yearbook, he would find a query in Patricia's writing: "The plans we made for June 1964—will they come true?"

Knowing how much she wanted to be a June bride, Wayne had written beside her question a firm "yes."

6

Countdown to Marriage

Wayne's friendship with Patricia O'Donnell had been off and on for some time before the night when he asked her to go steady. He chose one of those unique occasions when his father allowed him to use the blue Plymouth. His older brother, George, had already destroyed two family cars, so Wayne's being allowed to get a driver's license and drive the Plymouth had been a major concession.

On that Saturday night he drove Patricia out into the oil fields on one of the gravel roads that laced the area. Lights off, he edged the car into a secluded spot. It was a perfect hideaway for parking, and they were soon deep into kissing. Suddenly, Wayne backed off. "I have something to ask you."

"What is it?" Surprised, Patricia also pulled away.

"Would you like to go steady with me?" In total darkness, Wayne held her face in his hands and went back to studying her body "in braille."

But she remained withdrawn and silent. Once again he asked her to go steady. She stiffened. "I'll have to think about it. I'm...I'm not quite sure I want to do that right now," she stammered. She had, after all, barely begun her life as an independent career girl.

Feeling such a strong physical attraction to her, Wayne simply couldn't take that for an answer. "You *have* to want to go with me, Patricia." He felt like a drowning man, grasping for what, he wasn't even sure. "I love you. Can't you see I want to be with you?"

He crushed her to him and planted a hard kiss on her lips. Having spent his energy in heavy kissing, he took her back to her apartment in the city and went home.

He waited all day Sunday for her to call him. Finally, in the early evening, the phone rang. "Yes," Patricia said, "I'll go steady with you."

The next day they exchanged their graduation rings. Wayne felt exhilarated—as if he'd scaled the highest mountain peak in the world. He had committed himself to a girl! Just like the other guys.

Coming as she did from a tempestuous household, Patricia's main goal had been to get away from her mother's house. Also, with the normal dreams of a country girl, she wanted to live in the city. In her final years of high school, she had worked as a waitress at Stacy's, afternoons and evenings. That, however, was not something she saw as a life work. Although she had once thought of becoming a secretary, she was now quite successful in her sales job at Chesterfield's in Baton Rouge.

Being a strong leader, she could take responsibility and do the right thing, and Wayne admired that trait in her.

Wayne realized he wasn't college material—his school career thus far had made that clear. What really interested him was hairdressing, and he'd already earned a certain degree of fame and notoriety as well.

He used to bring girls home and set up the kitchen as a salon. Cutting and styling hair in the kitchen upset his father, but Wayne had been more than glad to generate a little extra money while he was still in school. Not all of his efforts at this time were an unqualified success. One time, being carried away with the dangerous combination of zeal and ignorance, he played a prominent part in a high school prom. "Oriental gardens" had been chosen as the theme, and he did all the girls up as geishas. In order to create the Japanese effect, he vigorously teased their hair, French-laced it into a high coiffure, and "nailed" it in place with Nestle's spray. The moment of truth came after the dance when the girls found they couldn't disentangle the teasing out of the hair spray. The only way they could liberate themselves from the cement-hard headdress he'd created for them was to cut the knots out of their hair!

Nonetheless, Wayne's fame as a hairdresser had traveled far. His intentions were affirmed when the career recruiters came to his school for interviews. The owner of the National Beauty College in Baton Rouge invited him to enroll.

Wayne's opportunities for real money-earning jobs had heretofore been scarce. Apart from his sporadic earnings from his "kitchen hairdressing" work, the five-dollar-a-week allowance from his father had been his main income. This was not a generous amount because Albert wanted his children to work for whatever they got. Wayne got the message. He mowed lawns and would pick cotton and pull corn at harvest time. Occasionally when he helped his grandfather, he'd get another dollar or two.

Sometimes, when he wanted to take Patricia out, Wayne would ask his father for ten dollars. Whenever Albert acquiesced, he did so grudgingly. Still, he couldn't entirely deny Wayne because he wanted to encourage dating and, perhaps, thereby set his own mind at rest as to whether his son was "normal" or not.

Albert helped Wayne get his first job after he finished school—as a clerk in the Department of Education. He kept up the copy work and delivered and picked up mail at the capitol. This job gave him enough income to see him through beauty college.

Still, Albert had difficulty accepting the fact Wayne wanted to be a hairdresser. For him it was not a manly profession. In fact, in that part of the country, hairstyling invariably precluded homosexuality. Albert had to see the course as plain barbering rather than cosmetology. Even then he could never allow Wayne to cut his hair.

Going to cosmetology school in Baton Rouge finally gave Wayne the excuse he needed to leave home. For the first three or four months he lived with his aunt. Then, on the recommendation of Patricia's landlady, he found a tiny, one-room apartment behind the boarding house where Patricia lived. He had to share it with a sixty-five-year-old man, who (as time revealed) was the landlady's boyfriend. The cramped space, the odors, and the odd ways of the pathetic fellow vexed Wayne sorely. Therefore, Wayne stayed in the place only long enough to sleep, shower and then escape.

The light and cheerful precincts of the beauty college, on the other hand, came as a happy relief. Wayne and one other boy made up the entire male enrollment in the school. The girls, however, were an easygoing lot. They smoked, drank, did drugs and all the rest.

At the time, however, Wayne wasn't into any of those things. He was at school to work, to succeed and that was all. Unfortunately, his single-mindedness was not sufficient to curb Patricia's jealousy. When she'd come to the school to get her hair done, she'd eye all of the girls critically—assessing their curves, their mini-skirts and their talk. "I can't believe I allow you to come to this school with all these girls around," she'd tell Wayne. Sometimes she even sent spies to check up on him.

Such were Wayne's skills that after only two weeks in training, he was out on the floor cutting and styling hair. His talent generated so much income for the school that he was given a scholarship. Attending the night classes free, he still worked full-time at the Education Department.

Maria, the teacher's daughter-in-law, was Wayne's favorite guide. He thought she was the most beautiful woman he'd ever seen. Every day he watched her light touch with hair and admired her magic unreservedly. He learned more from Maria than from anyone else at the school.

But even now, while he succeeded in doing excellent work, he sometimes lapsed. A girl from the department store where Patricia worked wanted him to bleach her hair—white. Already heavily bleached, her hair was fragile and this made further treatment risky. This time Wayne confidently took too much on himself. The toners had to be carefully formulated, and this he did without help.

Suddenly, before his horrified eyes, the client's hair turned kelly green! The girl burst into tears, leaped out of the chair and slammed out of the room. "So that's what I get for coming to a *school!* I should have known better," she fumed.

Soon she returned with her boyfriend. He was not at all amused. The trauma almost overwhelmed Wayne, and he felt the end of the world had come.

But this time someone had sent for the teacher, who had not been on the premises at the time of the accident. Wayne sighed with relief as the supervisor took over. "We'll have to bleach it out again, Wayne," she said patiently, "and apply another color."

The final horror came when Wayne got the poor girl back to the shampoo bowl for the last time. At this point most of her hair fell out! Watching the long strands of hair accumulate in the sink and fill up the drain, he felt he should probably, at the very least, be shot at sunrise.

But the teacher was longsuffering. "You're going to have some special training on mixing colors, Wayne, before you get a chance to damage another client."

When she had recovered from the initial shock, the girl realized the sign at the door which announced all work was done by students and that everything was done at the "client's risk" was, in fact, infallible truth. Now she was awarded free conditioners, plus as good a hairstyle as could be salvaged out of the little hair she had left. She was a non-paying client until she recovered from the damages.

Wayne's native ability, however, was never called into question. Nine months and 1,500 hours of salon work later, he finished at the National Beauty College. Now, at only twenty-one, he had emerged as one of the best hair designers in the city.

Wayne and Patricia had been talking about getting married for some time. But several negatives entered the equation. Weekends they would go home to the country and have dinner with either his family or hers. It made no difference which house. There would be an argument, and they'd come away upset.

The conflicts often centered on race, with the debates ranging from separate restrooms for whites to blacks sitting in the back of the bus. Working for the Department of Education, Wayne had witnessed encounters in these areas at the capitol building which helped him understand and sympathize with the civil rights movement as it evolved. But both the Andres and O'Donnells were not to be dissuaded from their views.

One Sunday Wayne took Patricia to his parents' house on one of the "country weekends." Wayne let it slip that he'd recently been a judge at a beauty contest. He was telling his mother that the black girls had been beautiful and was elaborating on the texture and fine styling of their hair.

"You mean, boy, that you judged a *black* beauty contest?" his father thundered.

"Yes, I did."

"I can't believe it!" Albert shook his head incredulously. "What in the world were you doing in a place like that?"

"But, daddy," Wayne pleaded, "it was part of my business. I just went there and watched the models go by and graded the work that the stylist had done on them."

Albert remained unappeased. "To think you'd go into a total black place like *that* and sit your—-down there! And to carry the name of this family into that auditorium, too!"

"I'm sorry you feel that way." Wayne knew the smell of gunpowder, and he decided this time to "fire the first shot." "But it really didn't bother me in the least."

"Then I don't want you in my house anymore, you black —!" Albert exploded.

"You want to know something? I don't come here because I want to!" The two men leveled off, eyeball to eyeball, across the small kitchen table. "I come here because I still want to have a relationship with my mother and my sister and brother."

Albert threw his fork down on the table and shoved his chair back. Wayne stood up and slammed his fist on the table so that all the dishes jumped. "I really don't care what you think. I don't have to come back to this house ever—ever again in my life!"

His father turned back for one parting shot. "Hear this, boy. I am disowning you. You're not my son anymore." His black eye snapped. "No inheritance, no nothing! This—is—it!"

Poor grandfather rose from the table and beat a retreat, shaking his head and muttering, "I just can't believe this."

His mother wept, trying as usual to "fix" everything. "Please! Please! All of you! Control yourselves!"

Patricia just sat wide-eyed and silent because she knew how Wayne always gave in to his father. Wayne himself, when he'd cooled off, wondered where he got the guts to defy Albert Andre.

The O'Donnell household was really no better, and the racial heat never subsided there either. After church on Sunday, Patricia's rather passive father would retreat to the rocking chair in front of the television while mother cooked the dinner. Patricia's four sisters fought among themselves almost constantly—often about boyfriends. Discussion of blacks and other racial groups, however, really brought on the fireworks.

Surprisingly, Patricia was free of racial prejudice and she never minded imposing her views on her family. So, on every visit, the battle raged over the inequalities of blacks and whites. Some discoursed on the impossibility of their ever eating together. Some just knew blacks were dirty. Others claimed they weren't really human. Among all of his volatile women, father O'Donnell would never venture a word. Then, dinner over, someone would throw the switch, as it were, and everybody could relax and take a nap as if nothing had happened.

Wayne would stick his two cents' worth in, too. But when it got really hot, he'd just sit down and watch.

Unfortunately Patricia had inherited her family's tendency to be high-strung, and also their talent for arguing. She could go off into a tantrum without a moment's warning. In a restaurant, for instance, if she thought the waitress was not performing at top efficiency, she would make a scene. Wayne often cringed when she denounced some hapless waiter in a voice that could be heard out in the parking lot.

Away from their families, Wayne and Patricia managed, on the whole, to have a reasonably happy courtship. Always struggling against poverty, they would have welcomed a little money occasionally, but what they got when they went home were bags of groceries. Home-canned and frozen food were cultural necessities, and their parents wanted to be sure the children were eating well. Beyond that, the elders didn't give much thought as to how the young people might be paying their bills.

Going out to dinner occasionally, and afterward a movie or a dance, followed by a time of "making out" in one of their apartments—pretty well summed up their courtship. Or Patricia might rustle up one of her delectable chicken dinners for him. Then came the next natural step. Late one Sunday afternoon in September, 1963, Wayne proposed to her—after church and after the usual riotous dinner at the O'Donnell home. He set the stage as he had three years before when he'd asked Patricia to go steady with him. To his dismay, the pattern repeated itself.

This time he drove out into the country and parked on a shady little lane, and they talked about their future and about having the children they both wanted. In fact, they had always agreed on the pursuit of the American Dream—children, a nice home, lots of property and material assets. No farming—it would always be the city for them.

Now Wayne drew a deep breath, pulled Patricia toward him and kissed her. "Will you be my wife?"

To his surprise she seemed startled. After all, they had been together a great deal in the past three years. "I—don't know," she replied. "It's a big decision, and I need time to think about it."

Once again, as he had done the evening when he'd asked her to go steady, Wayne had to go home and wait for her answer. Now he had leisure to wonder why *he* was always the one to say, "I love you." Didn't she love him after all? He had time to figure out at least some of the possible reasons for Patricia's hesitancy.

He knew she'd been brought up in a home where sex was considered nasty. Patricia, he knew, had talked to her older married sister who had had one child but was frigid and determined to have nothing further to do with her husband. Wayne could imagine Patricia at home discussing his sexual advances with her very vocal mother and sisters. He feared they suspected him of homosexual tendencies. He wouldn't be man enough. *I should have been more romantic*, Wayne chided himself. But somehow he couldn't get the idea into focus very well because he had grown up with practically no love experience on which to draw in a time like this.

Then, too, they had had some doubts about their financial situation. Wayne, however, was prepared to argue that renting one apartment *should* be better than having to pay for two. Now he remembered that he hadn't had a ring to offer Patricia. This was, after all, his first time around! If he'd had the ring right there in his pocket, would he have been able to turn the tide in his favor?

Finally, three days later, Patricia gave her word. Yes, she really would marry him after all! Although Wayne might have taken warning from her reluctance, he didn't. Patricia's good looks appealed to his artistic soul—she was lovely, even without make-up. And now with her job in cosmetics at Chesterfield's, she looked like a model, always well-dressed, and he was proud of her. Moreover, her green eyes entranced him. Yes, if Patricia would have him, Wayne would marry her.

As might be expected, the news was not well received in the Andre home. "Boy, you really want to marry that woman?" his father demanded. "She's not a very calm person." Patricia's fiery personality had alienated both of Wayne's parents, and not even after they married would his parents accept her.

But Wayne wouldn't back down. He'd now achieved what the world expected of him—he was going to marry a girl. What else was he supposed to do anyway?

"Well, now, I'm warnin' ya right now. If you make your bed and put her in it, you're gonna sleep there!" Albert glowered at him. "And once you leave this house, that's it! You don't come whimpering back here, see?"

Patient and resigned, Wayne's mother sighed. "Well, if that's what you want to do, son, go ahead and do it."

While he appreciated her conciliatory tone, it did little to cheer him up. Wayne felt an emptiness in his life which he was still too young to measure. Part of the problem would forever go back to Albert Andre's total inability to give his love to his children. This circumstance ultimately drove all four of them apart and sent them off in different directions. For Wayne the dysfunction was to be homosexual. In fact, he would look back to this time of his life and realize he married for no better reason than to avoid going further in the direction in which his feelings seemed to be taking him.

But back in 1963, young and with sex drives strong, Wayne and Patricia believed they were getting what they both wanted. At first, they decided on a one-year engagement, but as plans went on, they moved the wedding date forward by six months. There seemed no convincing reason for waiting. Wayne had indeed entered upon his career, and both of them were twenty-one years old.

With problems apparently settled—for the moment—Wayne threw himself into planning the wedding. He and Patricia consulted the priest, attended a pre-marital seminar, and worked through all the instructions regarding children and education. Wayne even had to ask for the priest's permission for his Baptist cousin, Jessica, to come and play the organ in the church.

Finally, on February 1, 1964, it happened. It was a small wedding—just two bridesmaids and two small rings (purchased at Chesterfield's)—but a major point of transition to be sure. And the promise Wayne made that day was as sincere as he knew how to make it.

7

For Better or For Worse

The long-awaited day had come—the moment Wayne had dreamed about for years—his wedding day! He had pictured it in his mind over and over. Patricia would walk down the aisle and become his wife, and they would live happily ever after.

But a small cloud darkened Wayne's dreams. That morning he had awakened feeling feverish and queasy, as if he had an infection of some kind. As he prepared himself for the wedding at his parents' home, the hours passed slowly. The women had all gone to the church to get ready. Only he and his father were left.

Albert chose this opportunity to give Wayne one of his stern lectures. "Now that you're getting married," he scowled, "don't expect any more help from me. Once you're married, that's it." His eyebrows lowered ominously. "You made your bed, and now you'll have to sleep in it!"

Wayne bore the sermon in silence. Finally, the time came for him and his father to leave for the church. When he entered the vestibule, the smell of roses and carnations drifted heavily around his head. He shook off the hazy feeling and plunged into last-minute preparations.

An hour later, he stood waiting for his bride at the front of the church. A sinking feeling took hold of him. Now that he was standing still for the first time since breakfast, he realized just how ill he felt. His tuxedo seemed to get tighter and stiffer by the moment, and a wave of nausea made his face burn. *Not now*, he fretted, fighting back the sick feeling. *I can't let this infection ruin the most important day in my life!*

He tried to compose himself by looking around. The church was decorated beautifully. Flowers draped the ends of the pews and candles flickered on all sides. The organ's low tones swelled in full notes. Well-dressed people filled the seats. Even his father, properly grave on the front pew, looked good to Wayne.

It won't be long now, and I can take Patricia away and have her all to myself, Wayne thought excitedly. He mentally checked the contents of his packed suitcases as the bridesmaids promenaded down the aisle.

Suddenly the organ swelled into the full bridal march. Patricia floated down the aisle on her father's arm, her blonde hair shimmering under the veil. But as Wayne stepped out to meet her, an even stronger wave of nausea made his stomach wrench. He shakily reached for her hand and slipped it under his arm. She smiled sweetly at him.

A stab of fear pierced his heart. He remembered the priest solemnly insisting during the wedding rehearsal, "More grooms pass out on me than brides." He had looked directly at Wayne and said sternly, "I hope you're not going to do that." At that earlier moment, the suggestion had seemed ridiculous, but now Wayne was not so sure.

Wayne swallowed and breathed in deeply. The ill feeling subsided once again. Proudly, he helped Patricia and her gossamer train to the altar.

As they knelt side-by-side, the carpet in front of him began to swirl strangely. He let go of her arm to steady himself. As the Mass continued, the music, liturgy and fragrance began to spin in Wayne's head. Suddenly, the nausea returned with the force of a hammer blow.

The priest's words are coming true, he thought in horror. His heart raced faster. Gradually, he lost the sense of Patricia beside him as a thick blackness began to swallow him.

The events of the next few moments he learned later. A muted gasp went up from the congregation as Wayne fell over, pushing Patricia from her place. Her face whitened as she stared at his crumpled form on the floor. The priest, in the midst of an unstoppable ritual, didn't even glance at him.

George quickly stepped from the line of groomsmen and knelt beside his brother. "I think he's dead," Patricia whispered in a hysterical voice.

Josh Green, the best man, leaned over to help.

"Let's take him out," George muttered. The two men picked up Wayne's unconscious body and carried him down the aisle. His arms flopped as they hurried out the door.

The priest went on with the Mass without missing a word. After an embarrassed pause, Patricia resumed her kneeling stance, a solitary figure in white at the altar.

Outside, several people gathered around the prone form. "What happened?" someone asked.

"He fainted," Josh explained.

"I've got some smelling salts," an elderly aunt offered as she rummaged through her large, black purse. She slid a bottle under Wayne's nose. He began to turn his head.

Within minutes, Wayne was alert and sitting up. "I'm going back in," he insisted.

"Are you sure?" George asked.

Wayne nodded firmly.

"The priest's just beginning the offertory," Josh informed as he peeked through the heavy doors. "If you're going to go back in, do it now."

Shame-faced, Wayne walked up the aisle, followed by the groomsmen. He joined a grateful Patricia, and the Mass continued as before. Wayne's heart sank as he stole a glance at Patricia. *Dad's right*, he grimaced. *I can never do anything right.*

As Wayne expected, his father and brothers laughed heartily at Wayne's expense during the reception following the ceremony. The more they tipped their beer glasses, the louder their taunts became. Wayne brushed off their ridicule like he had had to do so many times before.

Feeling better after a few glasses of champagne, he danced with every woman who wanted the privilege of the groom's attention. According to custom, most of them slipped a bill into his tuxedo pocket to help with honeymoon expenses. As he whirled by Patricia, who was dancing with uncles, nephews, and others, he knew she would be receiving money, too. Wayne was glad for the old custom. He could hardly wait for the honeymoon to begin.

He and Patricia left as soon as they could gracefully excuse themselves. By the time they reached Gulf Port, Mississippi, a drizzle had begun to dot the windshield. Wayne pulled up to a motel and registered them as "Mr. and Mrs. Wayne Andre." He smiled with pleasure at the sight of the entry.

Wayne could see the tiredness in Patricia's eyes as he helped her into the room and deposited the suitcases near the bathroom. She had worked so hard to make this wedding beautiful.

"A whole week together!" he exclaimed. "Just you and me, and the beach."

Her eyes lit up. "I can hardly wait to hit the water."

But Wayne was eager to get undressed. The girl whose hair had turned green from the perm he gave her last month had confided how many times she and her new husband had made love during their honeymoon night. Seven times! Wayne had vowed to her that he could better that score. And he was determined to do just that.

By morning, he had fulfilled his vow. But somehow the wedding night hadn't turned out as wonderful as he expected. Patricia seemed withdrawn, and the drizzle had turned into a cold rain. They spent the next day wandering through shops and waiting for the weather to clear.

By the second day, Wayne felt sicker than ever. He managed to take Patricia to a restaurant that evening, but he could hardly stand the sight of food. Dull pains ran across the small of his back, making it uncomfortable to sit for long.

Once back in their room, Wayne admitted defeat. "Let's go home, Patricia. I feel terrible and the weatherman said the rain isn't going to let up for days."

She gently tucked him into bed, then lay beside him. "It is too cold to do much here, anyway," she said gallantly. "And you need to see a doctor."

The next morning, they packed their suitcases and set off for home. After a few hours of driving, Wayne realized he couldn't make it all the way back to Baton Rouge. He had to make several stops to rest and couldn't eat a thing. His head felt hot, and the dizziness had returned.

When they crossed the border into Louisiana, Patricia suggested, "Let's stop at my sister's place in La Plose."

Wayne nodded gratefully.

Upon their arrival, Patricia's sister took one look at Wayne and called the doctor. He came right over.

"Your temperature is 103," he observed, peering at his thermometer. He took out his stethoscope and began listening to Wayne's heart and lungs. Finally, he hung the stethoscope around his neck and looked squarely at Wayne. "I'd say you have a kidney infection. Are you on any kind of medication?"

Wayne nodded. "I wasn't feeling well before the wedding and went to see my doctor. He said I had an infection and prescribed an antibiotic."

"Well, I think you're having a mild reaction to your medication. I'm going to prescribe a different antibiotic. That should make you feel better in a couple of days."

It did take two days before Wayne felt well enough to travel the rest of the way to Baton Rouge. Patricia doted on him the entire time. As he began to feel more like himself, he thought, *This is like living happily ever after. Me and Patricia, just like I dreamed.*

But some of the fairy-tale magic started to wear off after he and Patricia got settled in their new home. They had rented an apartment at the top of a house on East Boulevard. It was a neat little place with hardwood floors, a kitchen, bathroom and combination living room-bedroom. Patricia had oohed and aahed over every nook and cranny as she arranged their belongings and sparse furniture. But soon she began complaining about a lack of privacy, and the apartment made Wayne feel cold.

Financial stresses and the realities of life also shattered their newlywed dreams. Patricia went back to work at Rosenfields, and Wayne continued with his beauty school and job at the Department of Education. But with only one car—an old orange Plymouth—they had to plan their schedules carefully. Having little money to spare, they worked hard to make ends meet.

One Saturday afternoon, Wayne took Patricia for a drive and stopped at a car dealership. "Sure would be nice to have a new car," he said nonchalantly.

"Oh, Wayne, we can't afford it!" she exclaimed.

"Let's just look." He opened his door and climbed out of the car. Patricia reluctantly followed.

After walking up and down the line of used cars, Wayne knew only one interested him, a beige 1963 Oldsmobile. It was long and streamlined and looked expensive. Sitting behind the wheel, Wayne felt important.

Patricia continued her vigorous protest. "We just *can't* afford it, Wayne." Getting out, Wayne glared at her and stalked off to the Plymouth.

Later that week, he drove by the car lot on his way home from school. The Oldsmobile still gleamed in its spot next to the showroom. On impulse, he pulled into the lot.

An hour later, he drove the long, beige dreamboat onto the street. Signed loan papers lay on the seat beside him. *Mine,* Wayne mused proudly. *And Patricia will look great behind the wheel.*

But when Patricia saw the car, she threw up her hands. "You didn't *buy* this, did you?" she demanded.

Wayne looked at her blankly.

Suddenly she spied the papers on the seat. "Another payment?" Wayne nodded.

"But how are we doing to dig up the money for another bill? And what if I get pregnant? How can we afford to start a family?" Her voice rose in anger with each question.

Wayne jumped out of the car and tried to explain. "We need a car we can be *proud* of," he began. "I hated to be seen in that old Plymouth." He rubbed a spot of dust from the hood.

"You're just a spendthrift," Patricia sputtered. The veins in her neck stood out. "You no-good bum. You have a beer pocket and a champagne taste."

Wayne's anger flashed. "I wanted it, so I bought it! Now we'll have to live with it!"

At this, Patricia turned, stomped up the stairs to their apartment and slammed the door behind her.

He slid behind the wheel of the Oldsmobile and turned the key. The motor sputtered, then purred. He backed out recklessly and sped down the street, the joy of his purchase ebbing away.

Hours later, he again pulled into the driveway. After parking, he slowly climbed the stairs, dreading another confrontation with Patricia. He found her sitting quietly on the couch. The light from the kitchen streamed across her feet, leaving her face shadowed.

"Still mad?" he ventured.

Silence.

He sat beside her and leaned back. "I love you."

She looked away, but he could feel her softening. "I know we can pay for the car," he argued gently. "I'll work hard, and soon I'll be in a salon making big money. You'll see."

She still didn't respond.

With a dramatic flourish, he fell to his knees in front of her. Grinning capriciously, he pleaded, "Please, please."

Her eyes met his and an unwilling smile tugged at her mouth.

"I'll be your slave forever!"

She laughed. "Sure! Sure! I'll believe *that* when I see it." She hugged him, and the tension shattered into harmless pieces.

Several days later, he thought about their fight. Sometimes, when he was honest with himself, he wondered about his dreams. Somehow, marriage wasn't exactly the Cinderella-and-Prince-Charming story he had imagined. Patricia didn't see things the same way he did. She wasn't as eager to have sex. In fact, some nights she seemed to avoid him. And he couldn't take her to nice restaurants or buy her gifts like he wanted to be able to do.

He decided that another apartment would solve their problems. A lady he knew had turned a garage behind her rooming house into an apartment. She would rent it to them for $50 per week. But how could they afford to pay the higher rent? About the same time, Patricia announced she was going to have a baby. Although delighted, Wayne was shocked. Their budget was already stretched. But with their first child on the way, the garage apartment seemed a necessity.

At first, Patricia was disappointed with the apartment. It was dirty, small and poorly insulated. But it had a private entrance, so she agreed to take it. After putting down the money for the first week's rent, Patricia became excited about the place. She began planning where to put the baby's things. She and Wayne scrubbed and cleaned, hung wallpaper and painted. By the time they finished, the place seemed like home. Putting aside what money they could, they saved enough to buy a window air conditioner which Wayne installed himself.

Some nights after work, he would relax in a chair and let the coolness flow around him. He liked to watch as Patricia turned the pages of a parenting magazine a few feet from him. She certainly looked good! He wanted to give her the best.

If I'm patient, he would think confidently, *things will turn out right. I'm close to finishing school, I'm going to be a father, and one day soon I'll open my own beauty salon. Then we'll be able to live in style!*

He had no doubts he could make all his dreams come true. He had put the dark clouds in his past behind him and made a new life for himself. It would just take a little time.

8

Deepening Conflict

Wayne bolted upright in bed as a scream ripped through the air. Patricia's side of the bed was empty.

He flew out of the bedroom to the closed bathroom door. "Patricia, are you all right?" he panted. Peeking in, he saw her ashen face.

"I don't know what happened," she sobbed. "I've been having cramps and now a bloody discharge. Hurry, call the doctor!"

Wayne ran for the phone. He dialed the doctor's home, explained who he was when the doctor answered and described what had happened.

"Bring her to the Lady of the Lake emergency room immediately," the doctor ordered.

Slamming down the receiver, Wayne wrapped Patricia in her bathrobe and carefully escorted her to the car. He gently settled her in the seat, then hurried to the driver's side.

The thought of losing his child only months into the pregnancy terrified him. Patricia sobbed uncontrollably beside him. Glancing at her white face, he tried in vain to calm her. *O God*, he prayed frantically, *is she going to die?*

In the emergency room, the nurses wheeled Patricia to an exam cubicle, leaving Wayne alone in the waiting area. He couldn't sit; he couldn't think. Instead, he rummaged through magazines without reading a word on a page.

After a few moments, Patricia's doctor stepped through the emergency room door into the waiting area. "What did you do with the discharge?" he asked Wayne quickly.

"It's still in the commode."

"Go home, dip it out, and bring it to me." The doctor handed him a container and disappeared into emergency again.

In a daze, Wayne did exactly as he was told. He could barely look at the watery mess in the bottle as he drove back to the hospital.

Wayne sat forlornly in the lobby until the doctor returned some time later and motioned to the examining room. "Mr. Andre, I'd like to talk to you."

Wayne followed him to Patricia's side. She lay on the table, ashen and red-eyed.

"She had a miscarriage," the doctor explained. "The fetus was in the discharge."

Wayne's heart sank.

"I know I'll never have another baby," Patricia cried hysterically.

"Mrs. Andre," the doctor soothed, "I know this seems like an immense tragedy. But many first pregnancies end in miscarriages. It doesn't mean you can't have more children. Most women go on to have as many babies as they want."

He turned to Wayne. "Sometimes the womb is not completely developed at the first pregnancy. But it matures after a miscarriage."

He patted Patricia's arm. "I'm going to check you into the hospital for a couple of days. When you go home, I want you to refrain from intercourse until you have completely healed. But everything's just fine."

And Patricia was just fine—physically. But the trauma of the miscarriage played on her mind. She insisted she never wanted to go through the pain of another pregnancy that would probably end in miscarriage anyway.

After that, Wayne began to feel more frustrated about their sex life. Patricia rarely wanted to enjoy him as he did her. Most of the time he had to wheedle or manipulate her into making love. Even then, it was apparent that she didn't enjoy it. Realizing she had come through a dreadful experience, Wayne tried to be patient. But his needs just weren't being met.

After many months, he despaired of ever getting Patricia to have sex as often as he wanted it, which was every night. Sometimes, a week or even two would pass before she was willing. Most nights, his pleading or manipulation would only lead to an argument. "You're just like a rabbit," she would shout. "You want it all the time and don't have any consideration for me!"

"You're just frigid," he'd fling back.

87

"And you're over-sexed!" She'd grab her pillow and march out to the couch, her white flannel nightgown flowing around her. Wayne would plump up his pillow and try to fall asleep, but a deep sense of loneliness and rejection would keep his mind churning.

Her lack of response intimidated Wayne. *I just can't function right*, he concluded. *Obviously, I'm not giving her what she needs.*

As the weeks and the coldness between them continued, he felt more and more inadequate. Finally, hoping to resolve their problem, he made an appointment for them both with a psychiatrist.

The afternoon of the appointment, he had to coax Patricia into the car. She insisted she didn't need to see "a shrink." But she did come.

Wayne pulled up in front of the gray brick office building and parked the car. Glancing at Patricia, he saw that stubborn set to her chin. "C'mon," he urged, "let's get this over with."

"I'm not coming! There's nothing wrong with me."

Wayne pleaded with her. "We've got an appointment, Patricia. The doctor's waiting for us."

But she wouldn't budge. Finally Wayne went in alone. But the doctor canceled the session. "I can't do anything until your wife comes in here," he said.

Wayne didn't speak all the way home. In his heart he knew things probably would never get better in their sex life.

Despite the disappointment of losing his baby and his marital problems, life looked good to Wayne. Shortly before graduating from cosmetology school, he was offered a business deal he couldn't refuse.

Stephano Nicholas, an Italian with strong Catholic beliefs who owned the barber shop in Livonia, wanted to open a beauty salon next door to his business. He approached Wayne and his high school buddy, Chad Stephens, to negotiate the terms of the arrangement. Stephano would buy all the equipment and put up the building. Wayne and Chad would rent the entire shop without having to invest a dime. The deal sounded good to Wayne, except for one thing. He had always dreamed of having an exclusive salon in a big city like Baton Rouge. He knew he had the talent to build a thriving, elite clientele. Livonia had only 700 people. It could never help him prosper the way he dreamed. Even so, Wayne concluded, it was a place to start.

At first business was slow. He and Chad would hang around doing nothing for days at a time. When women did come in, they demanded the same old types of styles. No one wanted to look fashionable and smart. But the income helped ease his budget problems.

One day, Patricia suspected she was pregnant again and made an appointment with her doctor. Needing something new in their relationship—something that would pull them together—Wayne hoped the results would come back positive.

On the third day after her tests, Patricia received the telephone call. "Hello." Suddenly her face lit up. "Really? You sure?" Hanging up the phone, she began jumping up and down. "The doctor said the rabbit died. I'm pregnant! I'm pregnant!"

Wayne ran up to give her a huge hug, then restrained himself. "Better be careful," he grinned. "I wouldn't want to hurt the mother-to-be." He grabbed her hands and kissed her repeatedly. "This time nothing's going to happen," he promised.

Time began to fly for Wayne. Now he had something exciting to work for. Every time an elderly lady insisted on a hairstyle she'd worn for decades, he reminded himself of his new responsibility. He was earning money for his new son or daughter.

Patricia quickly grew irritable. Sick most of the time, she did little around the house. Wayne bit his tongue over mentioning the clothes on the floor or the mess in the bathroom. Then, strangely, he began to feel nauseated in the mornings, too. "Sympathy pains," Patricia's doctor explained.

Although feeling a little embarrassed at the doctor's diagnosis, Wayne sensed a tremendous excitement. *I'm feeling what she's feeling. I'm that close to her! We'll be even closer as parents.*

By the sixth month, however, Wayne's euphoria turned into nervousness. Both he and Patricia worried that the baby might be born with some defect, especially since Patricia didn't get very big. *Why isn't the baby growing normally?* he worried. But the doctor assured them everything was okay.

Then Wayne began to worry that Patricia would have the baby at home, and he would have to deliver it. Again, the doctor assured him all would be fine. Only after the doctor told them what to expect and how much time they would probably have to make it to the hospital, did Wayne feel any better.

Late one evening several days later, Patricia called desperately from the bathroom. The panic of another incident like the miscarriage almost froze him on the spot. But he forced himself to run to her.

"Look," she gasped. "Look at what I did."

He saw a wet mess all over the floor.

"I think it's the water around the baby," she whispered nervously.

Wayne raced to the phone. When he got the doctor on the line, he began blubbering, "This is Wayne—Patricia's wife."

The doctor laughed. "Calm down and go over this again."

"I mean, this is Wayne Andre, Patricia's husband. I think her water burst, and she's fixing to go into labor. She's having some cramps right now."

Patricia took the phone from him and explained what had happened. She listened to the reply, then shook her head. "We'll go crazy if you don't let us go to the hospital."

The suspense over what the doctor was saying was killing Wayne. Finally Patricia hung up. "The doctor said to go ahead to the hospital and check in. The nurses will call him and let him know what's going on."

Wayne rushed her to the hospital and began pacing in the father's waiting room. As the hours dragged by, husband after husband joined him, then got called in to see a new baby. But no one came for him.

Just when he despaired of ever seeing Patricia again, a nurse allowed him into the delivery room. "How do you feel?" he asked, grasping Patricia's sweaty hand.

"The pain is tremendous," she told him. A contraction gripped her, and she squeezed his hand.

"Are you going to have the baby right now?" he wondered.

The nurse who was standing nearby smiled, "No, she hasn't dilated enough yet."

He held Patricia's hand through several more contractions before the nurse ushered him out.

He was allowed to visit several more times after that, but with each visit, his anxiety grew. In the morning, his parents and a few friends dropped by to see if he had any news. But the day dragged on, and Patricia looked more and more worn.

Late that evening, the nurse walked into the waiting room with a broad smile. "It's a seven-pound baby girl."

Wayne's anxiety left with a rush, replaced with joy and pride. He embraced his mother and trotted off to see the new mother.

"Let's call her Natalie," Patricia crooned. "I think it's a pretty name, don't you?" Wayne patted her hand in approval.

He took several days off to help Patricia bring the baby home and get adjusted. She sat on the couch and cuddled the little bundle while Wayne imprinted the picture of them on his mind. He wondered how anything else could be as wonderful as bringing home a new baby.

But being a new father wasn't as easy as he expected. Natalie seemed to cry all the time. Patricia rocked her, breast-fed her continuously and tried to soothe her. But nothing seemed to help. At night, she took the baby to bed with her. By the time Wayne went back to work, he was relieved to get away from them both for a few hours.

Finally the doctor discovered that Patricia didn't have enough milk for Natalie. He suggested several different formulas, but Natalie was allergic to them all. Then he prescribed Canana Banana Flakes and tea. Patricia tried to supplement Natalie's hunger with bottles of tea and smashed, dried toast.

To his alarm, Wayne began noticing that Patricia seldom put the baby down. The minute she did, Natalie screamed.

He decided to put his foot down. "Patricia, you can't keep coddling that baby."

"Why not?" she demanded.

"'Cause you're spoiling her. I just don't believe in letting children have everything they want. It's not good for them."

Patricia's face took on its stubborn set. "If my child cries, I can't just turn my head."

Despite a full-blown argument, Patricia wouldn't budge. Complicating the situation, she insisted the baby sleep with them.

"But we *can't* sleep with the baby in bed with us."

"Sure we can," Patricia countered. "It won't be a problem. She can sleep on this side of me and you can sleep on that side. You won't have to worry about rolling over on her or anything."

"You know that's not the point," Wayne snapped. "Natalie will get used to sleeping with us and won't stay in her crib. We'll never be alone."

As the arguments continued night after night, Wayne felt a tightness forming inside his chest. Bad enough that the apartment was so small that Natalie's crib had to be in their bedroom. But he suspected Patricia was using the baby to avoid him at night. And why did she have to spend every moment with her? Didn't he deserve some time alone with his wife to get his needs met?

Wayne tried subtle methods to seduce Patricia. Some evenings, he would start early. "How are you feeling?" he would ask, anticipating her excuses. "If you have a headache, I'll get you some aspirin. Would you like a relaxing soak in the bathtub?"

Then he would kiss her a few times and pull her into the bedroom.

Sometimes his efforts turned into verbal battles.

"With you, it's just like 'bim bam, thank you, ma'am.' You just satisfy yourself. What about me?"

"Having sex with you is like making love to a log," he'd shout back. "You're just there and nothing happens." Then he'd egg her on some more. If she got angry enough, they would eventually make up and she'd give in to his advances.

Something else about Patricia bothered Wayne. When he had courted Patricia, he had admired her spunk. Now the trait seemed domineering and offensive. He believed a wife should submit to her husband's decisions and not talk back. But Patricia stubbornly held to her own views. She just did not fit the mold.

Wayne began to look for ways to relieve his tension. If only he could get a position in Baton Rouge, he'd be happier at work. The beauty shop in Livonia just wasn't panning out. If only he could make more money, he and Patricia could move into a bigger apartment—a place where they could feel good about entertaining their friends, an apartment with two bedrooms so they could move Natalie's crib out of their room. Furthermore, a bigger paycheck could buy more things and allow them to go places.

Wayne began searching for his next move upward.

9

Like a Hot Desert Whirlwind

Wayne threw open the streaked glass door of Stephano's barbershop and announced, "I'm through. I can't work here anymore."

Stephano's mouth dropped. His hand holding a comb paused in midair. "But, Wayne, I thought we had an agreement?"

Wayne shrugged, turned and walked away before Stephano could plead his case.

Wayne knew that with the right break he could achieve success in the salon business. His talents, he reasoned, were being wasted in a small city like Livonia. When the opportunity came to work at one of the top salons in Baton Rouge, he jumped at the chance.

The owner, Lance Justin, offered him a position in the Paris Set. Although he would start as an assistant to Carol Nathan, one of the hairdressers, he would bide his time and eventually make his move up.

Although Stephano Nicholas would lose his substantial investment in the building and equipment, Wayne was determined to leave.

To ease his conscience, Wayne returned most of the salon equipment to the original seller. But nothing could make up for the money and time Stephano had spent on the building and in arranging for Wayne and Chad to get started. In the end, Wayne still owed Stephano $250, but he told himself he would pay back the debt when the money started rolling in.

Wayne fit in easily at the Paris Set. It was a different world. Everything was neat and in its place; the decor was airy and the stylists professional. They could finish hair, cut exquisite styles and do the latest fashions without even trying. And Carol was one of the best in the city. Wayne learned her technique as he assisted her with clients.

Four months later, one of the hairdressers became sick. A few days later, Lance approached Wayne. "Eva Manning won't be able to work for quite a while," Lance said. "She has a full clientele. Would you be willing to take her appointments until she returns?"

"Of course. I'd be happy to," Wayne agreed. He threw himself into his work, watching the other stylists for tips on how to develop his abilities. Little by little, he realized that his way with customers and his natural talent made him an extremely desirable hairdresser. When the owner learned Eva wouldn't be back, he turned her clients over to Wayne.

Now that he was making more money, he began to feel dissatisfied with the cramped garage apartment. Not only did he want a larger place, but one that would match his new position as well.

He suggested the move to Patricia one evening at dinner. "Honey, I found a beautiful rental house with a half acre of land," he began. "No more concrete, but a real lawn. And a bedroom for Natalie."

Patricia toyed with her pasta. "How much a month?"

He evaded her question. "The rent's affordable. I'm making good money now. And I'll be doing even better in a couple of months."

Patricia had that tight, scared look on her face. "But we've just begun to get on our feet financially. And we still have that car payment. What if you get sick?"

Wayne poured himself another big glass of iced tea and gulped a long drink. "I've got insurance."

Patricia wasn't satisfied. "What if you lose your job?"

Wayne's answer was edged with irritation. "Well, if worse came to worst, we could give up the house and move into a cheaper place. There's no lease."

Patricia slid her plate away. "What if you don't make enough money to live in this house?"

"Listen, Patricia," he snapped. "I'm doing well at the salon, and I'm bringing home bigger paychecks all the time."

Tears filled Patricia's eyes. "If we get too far in debt, I'll have to go back to work. I can't leave Natalie. Not when she's so little."

Wayne's anger surged. "I never suggested such an idea. You won't have to get a job!" He tossed his napkin onto the table. "No woman in my family has ever had to work outside the home. I'll make enough, even if I have to take a second job. Your place is here with the baby."

At last Patricia seemed relieved. Wayne paid the first month's rent on the house, and they began packing.

Moving into the new house brought new conflict. Wayne was content to let Patricia arrange the kitchen as she pleased, but he couldn't stand the way she decorated the living room. To him she just didn't have a good eye for where things should go.

When she set one of the knickknacks on an end table already cluttered with figurines, he exploded. "Patricia, you can't put that there!"

That stubborn look came into her eyes. "Why not?"

"It looks terrible."

"Tough!"

He snatched the glass ballerina from its perch and placed it on the other table. "There. That looks much better."

Only Natalie's crying stopped the yelling and arguing that followed.

Hanging wallpaper in the kitchen created another confrontation. As Patricia handed Wayne a dripping wet sheet, she accidently ripped a corner. "Now look what you did!" he spat. "Watch what you're doing, will ya?"

"I *am* watching," she shot back. "And quit yelling at me. You can't even match the pattern right." It took hours of snapping and shouting at each other to finish the job. And neither of them were satisfied with the results.

One consolation kept Wayne going. Natalie had her own room, and he would have Patricia to himself at night. No more battling to keep the baby out of their bed. One of the first things he assembled was Natalie's crib.

The next night Wayne came home with high expectations. The house looked good, and so did Patricia. She had her hair curled and wore a light blue blouse that highlighted her blonde hair. He settled down in front of the television and waited for her to put Natalie to bed. Surprisingly, after being rocked for half an hour, the baby drifted off. A peaceful, proud feeling engulfed Wayne as he watched his wife and daughter sweetly rocking together in the muted lamplight.

Patricia put Natalie into the crib, then joined Wayne in front of the TV. They finished watching a program, and Wayne began flipping channels.

"I'm tired," Patricia yawned. "Think I'll turn in early."

"Yeah, let's." Wayne switched off the TV.

Half an hour later, they lay side by side. Wayne inched close to Patricia and put his arm around her warm waist. Natalie whimpered in the next room.

Patricia's head shot up. "I've got to see what's wrong."

"There's nothing the matter with her." But Patricia flew into Natalie's room to comfort her.

Wayne waited patiently. Soon everything quieted down, and Patricia returned. Once again, Wayne slid his body next to hers. He felt her back stiffen slightly as he put his hand on her shoulder.

Natalie rattled the crib. Patricia sat up. "I hear Natalie. She's awake again."

Wayne's patience evaporated. "You are not getting up and going into that room this time!" he snapped.

He could see her eyes narrow in the semi-darkness. "Yes, I am." She flung off the blankets and hurried out.

This routine went on night after night. Somehow, Natalie never slept long enough to let Wayne have his time with Patricia. He felt cheated, and gradually his emotions built like steam in a pressure cooker.

Finally one night he exploded. Patricia had already gotten up three times to attend to Natalie. When the baby began whimpering a fourth time, Wayne ordered in an ominous tone, "You are not getting up again."

Patricia answered firmly, "Yes, I am."

Infuriated, Wayne growled, "No, you're not! This is *my* child and this is *my* time. You will *not* get up every time she cries or moves around in bed!"

Natalie's whimpering turned into tremulous sobs. Patricia glared at Wayne and began to slide out of bed. Enraged, Wayne grabbed her arm and jerked her back under the blankets.

She started screaming, "The baby's dying. Let me go!"

Wayne shoved her into her pillow and bellowed, "She's <u>not</u> dying. She just needs to realize you're not coming every time she yells."

Patricia heaved herself up, and Wayne pushed her back down. He could see her eyes flashing, her face twisted into a hateful look. "You have no feeling for your own child," she hissed. "You'd let her die in that bed before you'd let me check on her." Her voice rose to a scream. "Let me go! Let me go!" Unable to get up, she lay back sobbing and cursing.

Wayne continued to hold her down and forced her to listen to Natalie's cries. The baby wailed for at least half an hour before she finally sobbed herself to sleep. Then he and Patricia lay side by side, breathing loudly. Wayne could only imagine the dark thoughts Patricia was thinking toward him. He suspected they were no match for his own toward her.

Wayne found no satisfaction that night, nor several others that followed. An awareness that he was leading two lives began to gnaw at him. At work, he was successful and competent. At home, he felt inadequate and frustrated. Most nights, a dull ache gripped him as he drove up to the trim, little house. As much as he loved seeing Patricia and Natalie, the fights and tension drained much of his joy.

One afternoon, he arrived early because one of his appointments had canceled. As he walked into the front yard, he saw Patricia working in her flower garden. As she stooped down, her little red jumpsuit crept up, exposing her buttocks.

Wayne glanced around. Harvey Jennings was out in his yard eyeing her. Wayne hissed, "Patricia, you shouldn't be out here in that outfit. It looks indecent."

She stood slowly. "You're *not* going to tell me what to wear," she scowled.

Wayne tried to remain calm. "It's not that I want to tell you what to wear. I just want you to look decent when you're out in the yard."

She wiped her face and huffed, "I'll wear *what* I want, *when* I want." Then she stooped and started digging again.

Wayne marched up and grabbed her arm. "Patricia, come inside and change. Right now!"

She straightened, dropped her trowel, and glared into his eyes. "I will not."

"You won't, will you?" Wayne picked her up and staggered to the back door while she kicked and screamed, calling him every horrible name she could think of. He felt sharp pains shoot through his legs where her shoes bruised his flesh.

Opening the screen door, he pushed her into the kitchen and threw her onto the tile floor. Her hands slapped loudly as she landed. Immediately, she jumped up and raced for the door. Wayne grabbed her again and pulled her down the hall to the bedroom. By now, her screams had turned into exasperated sobs, and her face was flushed dark red.

He threw her onto the bed and straddled her so she couldn't get up. "You are *not* going to go out there that way. I said it, and I meant it!"

Roused by the ruckus, Natalie began screaming from her crib in the next room. That seemed to fire Patricia's determination. "You better let me up! You better let me up!" She tried to slip from under his arms, but he held her firmly.

Finding herself helpless, she broke into sobs again. "I can't stand you anymore. I don't want to be around you." Her arms flailed wildly. "You're not going to tell me what to do."

"You are *not* going out like that," Wayne shouted with steel in his voice. She began shrieking uncontrollably. He slapped her face hard, then let her go.

Patricia jumped off the bed, then flew at him, wrapping her legs around his. Grabbing his face, she clawed at his cheeks with her fingernails.

With a great heave, Wayne threw her off and stomped out the door, slamming it behind him. The baby's wails filled the hall as he tramped into the living room.

Minutes later, Patricia appeared holding the still-sobbing Natalie and carrying a bulging suitcase. "I'm taking the baby and leaving you," she threatened.

"Oh, no, you're not!" Wayne blasted. He snatched Natalie from Patricia's arms and threw the suitcase at her feet. "You can go, but my child's not leaving."

Patricia's face turned almost purple; her neck swelled and her eyes bulged in rage. "I want a divorce," she demanded and her words were punctuated with profanity.

Wayne clenched his fists; his nostrils flared. "Fine. I can't live with you either. All you do is yell and argue and fuss at me. You never let us have a peaceful evening."

Wayne's eyes suddenly caught the bright red blotch on Patricia's face where he had hit her. The memory of his father's ferocious temper raced across his mind. *What have I come to? I'm just like my father.* Tears of remorse smarted his eyes. "Patricia, I'm so sorry," he murmured. "I can't believe I got so violent. Can you forgive me?"

Silently she fingered the place on her cheek, then lowered her eyes and stiffened her chin. Natalie began crying loudly.

Wayne gripped his daughter tighter and desperately tried to explain his actions over the noise. "I just wanted to protect you from Mr. Jennings' stares. He had such a leering look."

Patricia turned her head, and the curve of her cheek made her look soft and defenseless. A strong desire to touch her, to soothe her, clutched at Wayne's heart. But he didn't know how. His arms suddenly felt sapped of strength.

She whirled on him with an arrogant look, the lines around her mouth still hard. A strange light came into her eyes. "I'm not going to leave you," she sneered. "When you make all that money at that shop, I'm going to be there to collect it. And I'm going to make your life miserable."

Sudden despair extinguished his desire to be near her. He and Patricia brought out the worst in each other. Their marriage swirled and eddied with turmoil like a hot, desert whirlwind. As a Catholic, he could never think of leaving her. Marriage, he believed, was forever. But how could they ever be happy again?

10

The Spanish Room

Wayne settled into the aisle seat beside Patricia and buckled his seat belt. She slid her navy carry-on bag under the seat in front of her and pulled out a *Vogue* magazine.

"New York, here we come!" Wayne grinned.

She smiled back, but Wayne could see tense lines around her mouth. Tears trembled under her eyelids.

"C'mon, the kids will be fine," he assured as he closed his eyes and relaxed. He heard the airplane door slam shut.

After a few moments, a smooth voice purred over the intercom. "We have a delay in take off. Please be patient and keep your seat belts fastened."

Wayne shrugged. This trip was going to be glamorous and eventful no matter how long it took to get to New York. He could pick up a lot of new ideas at the International Beauty Show, and he planned to enjoy himself at night as well. Now he owned his own shop, The Spanish Room. And it seemed like ages since he had worked at the Paris Set.

As they waited in their seats, his mind roamed over the events that had brought them to this plane ride.

Wayne was successful at the Paris Set. Not only did most of Eva Manning's clients remain with him, he began attracting new business as well.

About that time, it became fashionable to go to male hairdressers. When the fad swept through Baton Rouge, his phone rang constantly, and he began acquiring a reputation around the city. The shop manager was delighted. Within a short time, he raised Wayne's commission to the highest level in the shop.

At Christmas time, Julie, the wife of the owner and one of the hairdressers, invited the stylists and their spouses to a party. He and Patricia were thrilled—until they arrived. Instead of the usual bar and dancing and people having a crazy, good time, this woman served an elaborate dinner, then herded everyone around the piano to sing Christmas carols.

"She's really religious," someone whispered to Wayne.

"I knew that, but not this bad," he frowned.

"Yeah, she's always talking about Jesus."

Wayne laughed. "Remind me to never let her convert *me*. I'd probably die of boredom."

His physical relationship with Patricia improved right along with his career. He and Patricia agreed to have a second child, so she was eager to have sex. He got almost as much as he wanted for a change.

When the manager of the Paris Set opened a second salon in an expensive area of town called Oakwood, he asked Wayne to move out there. Wayne jumped at the chance.

That's where he met Dominick Day, an excellent stylist who could do things with hair that amazed Wayne. And his rapport with the customers was exquisite. From the first, Dominick was especially cordial to Wayne. Sometimes it seemed he hovered around Wayne's station almost as much as his own. Wayne felt flattered.

Before long, both his and Dominick's calendars were completely filled. The manager often mentioned how valuable they were to his business. Between them, they could get just about anything they wanted in the salon and not be scolded.

After a while, Wayne and Dominick decided they should be getting a bigger part of the profit pie. They were, after all, the reason the salon was doing such a brisk business. They attracted a rich clientele—doctors' wives, millionaires, elite professionals. So he and Dominick planned a power play.

They went to the manager's swank home and confronted him in his office. Wayne felt terribly nervous, but Dominick appeared cold and calculating. After explaining their demands, Dominick put on the squeeze. "We have other offers all over the city," he informed.

The manager shuffled papers on his desk. "I'm sure you do," he said coolly.

Dominick leaned forward in his chair. "We're not asking anything unreasonable. Just a bigger share of the profits."

The manager took his time answering. "Well, you could raise your prices."

Wayne shook his head. "No. Our customers are paying top dollar now. We'll lose clients if we charge more."

The man smiled grimly and touched his fingertips together. "Sorry. I'm not going to raise your percentage. You already get enough from this company."

Dominick rose abruptly. "Fine. But don't expect our loyalty."

For weeks after that encounter, Wayne and Dominick discussed their plight with the customers. The clients all agreed that Wayne and Dominick were worth more than the manager was willing to give.

One morning, Dominick rushed up to Wayne. "I've got great news," he whispered.

"What?" Wayne set down a bottle of hair spray.

"My future father-in-law has offered to finance a shop of our own. Betty Lou talked him into it. He wants to set me up in business as a wedding present."

Wayne's heart began to pound. Yesterday, one of his customers had suggested an ideal place to rent in a little shopping mall behind the Dairy Queen on Georgia Avenue. It was only a half mile from the Paris Set. The timing was perfect.

That's how The Spanish Room began. Soon after Dominick married Betty Lou, Wayne and Dominick hired a designer to paint, hang drapes and put in all the fixtures. Betty Lou came up with the name—The Spanish Room. The interior had a Spanish design with a rusty-brown tiled floor; the five stations were set into a gazebo and all decorative surfaces were done at an angle. It was a unique, classy design.

Two weeks before the salon was ready, the Paris Set owner heard about their plans and fired them on the spot. But Dominick could land on his feet in a tough spot. He asked one of the local shop owners if they could rent two stations until the salon was ready. So neither of them lost any of their best customers.

After opening their new shop, Wayne and Dominick had no trouble attracting the best stylists and customers from the Paris Set and were soon well-known in the city.

The owner of the Paris Set tried in vain to sue them for stealing his hairdressers, but Wayne and Dominick were on a roll. Nothing could stop them.

Within a year, they drew up plans to expand into a second room that included five more stations and a full manicurist. Dominick laughed at the dour accountant when he advised them to wait before adding on. "Why should we?" Dominick asked curtly.

"It makes good business sense to stay where you are after a growth period until you discover the level of your business," the accountant cautioned. "You could be getting in over your heads."

Dominick grinned. "And we could stagnate, too. We need to grow and develop. Not stay the same. That's the kind of reputation we've built." He wrapped his arm around the man's shoulders. "Anyway, our customers expect a salon that's going somewhere."

To Wayne, Dominick's assessment of their situation sounded logical. Wayne needed the extra income. He and Dominick were making a lot of trips to New Orleans in high style. Many weekends, they hired baby-sitters and took their wives to the hottest shows, stayed in the most elegant hotels and ate at the most reputable restaurants.

Patricia felt uncomfortable about all the money Wayne was spending. "Why do you and Dominick always want to go to the best places and spend so much money when we could have just as much fun doing things a little cheaper?"

Wayne shrugged her off. He wanted to be seen in the best places, wear the most stylish clothes and dress his wife like a fashion model—all with the thought of gaining an even more-exclusive clientele.

As they hoped, Patricia became pregnant again. Over her usual objections, he moved them into a fashionable apartment with a swimming pool. The complex had a French motif, and the interior was airy and comfortable. Although he got a good deal on the rent, the apartment cost quite a bit more than their house. To pay for their expensive life-styles, Wayne and Dominick ignored the accountant's advice, expanded the salon, and hired five more stylists.

Wayne felt confident. He knew he was one of the best hairdressers in Baton Rouge. He didn't see any end to his advancement.

Snapping out of his reverie as they sat waiting on the runway, Wayne flicked a piece of lint off his tailored gray suit and glanced at Patricia. She looked great in the leopard coat with the fur collar that he had bought her. She had slicked back her high-fashion, white-blonde hair into a bun at the nape of her neck. When she walked, the coat draped around her legs and flared as she turned. Wayne was proud of the way she looked on his arm. He prayed she would forget about Natalie and enjoy the trip.

Finally, after a twenty-minute wait, the plane began to move. Wayne's anticipation heightened. But as they taxied down the runway, his throat tightened. The old feeling of being trapped in a closed space gripped him. He tried to shake it off, but it hung onto him like a cold, wet sheet.

The plane lifted off and flew through the scudding March clouds. Patricia sniffled beside him, still moaning about leaving Natalie at home. Wayne watched the efficient flight attendant serve drinks and ordered a stiff martini. He downed it quickly when she handed it to him.

The flight was uneventful until they neared New York. Abruptly, the wind began tossing the plane around like a child's boat on a rapid creek. The conversation in the cabin hushed. Wayne's stomach began to churn. The air seemed to get hotter by the minute.

As the plane lurched, his claustrophobia tightened and he had an irrational desire to jump out of the plane. Patricia began sobbing loudly.

The intercom buzzed. "This is your captain. Because of the turbulence, we will have to circle for a while. Please fasten your seat belts and relax. We'll be out of this in just a few moments."

Patricia gasped as the plane dropped and then held. "We're going to die! I left my little girl at home. I'm pregnant and I'm going to die!" She turned to Wayne

113

and glared at him. "You caused this. You know I didn't want to go so far from home."

Wayne glanced around at the other passengers. Many were staring at Patricia. Embarrassed, he leaned toward her and hissed, "Quiet, Patricia." Wayne rested his head on the back of his seat to pull himself together. Once composed, he tried again to calm his hysterical wife. "Patricia, you know Natalie is all right," he soothed. "And we're *not* going to die. It's just the wind tossing the plane around."

Patricia pulled her purse into her lap and began fumbling with the clasp. "We are too going to die! You always have to bring us to places where we don't belong." Her voice rose. "We're not jet-setters. We never were and we never will be!" She burst into sobs.

Wayne could barely conceal his disgust. "We're just coming here for a show, Patricia. Don't blow it out of proportion." He glanced at Dominick and Betty Lou across the aisle and noticed how calm they looked. His face flushed.

The plane continued to circle for almost an hour. By the time it landed, Wayne had turned away from Patricia and tried to ignore the scene she was making.

In the airport terminal, Patricia's attitude miraculously changed. "New York!" she said breathlessly. "I can't believe we're really here."

They checked into the hotel and then left for a tour of Rockefeller Plaza. After spending some time sightseeing, Betty Lou spied the restrooms.

"I don't know about the rest of you, but I have to take a break." She disappeared through the shiny, double doors.

Wayne followed Dominick into the men's room while Patricia waited outside, standing delicately on her spike heels, her coat soft and chic.

Minutes later, Wayne came out of the men's room. "Where's Patricia?" he asked Betty Lou who was waiting impatiently.

"I have no idea," she said. "Maybe she went in the restroom after I did."

Betty Lou checked the ladies' room while Wayne and Dominick looked around the plaza. Wayne noticed a security guard standing near the main entrance. "Have you seen a woman in a leopard coat, six months pregnant?"

"Yes, I did," he answered. "She fainted and they carried her to the doctor's office."

The guard pointed Wayne in the right direction, and he ran to find her. The receptionist in the doctor's office led him to Patricia. He found her lying in a bed, her face ashen.

"Patricia! What happened?"

"I want to go home," she cried.

He took her hand. "Are you okay?"

"No, I want to go home. We don't belong here." Her lips stiffened and her voice became sharp.

"What more can she do to ruin this trip?" he muttered to himself. Aloud, he said, "Patricia, we're here. We're going to stay. We can't change the reservations, and we've got tickets to a show—"

Tears gushed from her eyes. "I don't care. I just want to see Natalie."

It took him half an hour to calm her down before he and Dominick could help her out of the office. By the time they reached the hotel, she had recovered quite well.

The next evening, the four of them went to the Copa Cabana. Wayne had looked forward to this evening for months. The host checked their reservations, then led them to a crowded room with a stage at one end.

He threaded the congested aisles between tables and sat them among two other couples at a table that looked hardly more than four feet long and about a foot wide near the center of the room.

The waiter pulled out Patricia's chair, and she reluctantly sat. Wayne held his breath as he saw her face tighten. *She'd better not ruin this evening.*

Dominick and Betty Lou began talking to the couple beside them. Patricia sat quietly for a moment, obviously assessing the situation. Suddenly, she stood up and pointed her manicured finger at the waiter. "Do you think I'm going to pay all this money to be crushed into this little seat?" Her eyes flashed.

Wayne watched the horrified expressions on the faces of the others at the table. It seemed everyone in the room turned to watch the commotion.

"Please, Patricia, sit down," he whispered loudly.

She ignored him. "This is ridiculous! I expect more for my money."

The waiter's eyes narrowed. "Ma'am, if you don't sit down, I'll have to ask you to leave."

With that, she shoved her chair back and sat heavily. Her face steamed. When her meal was put in front of her, she wouldn't touch it. No matter how much

Wayne tried to pacify her, she wouldn't give up. *Maybe she's right*, Wayne mused. *She doesn't belong in the jet set.* He turned away and began talking to Dominick.

Despite the trouble with Patricia, Wayne learned many new ideas at the beauty show. When he and Dominick returned to Baton Rouge, they ordered the equipment they needed to implement the new ideas and increase their image at the salon.

"How are we going to pay for it?" Wayne worried. "Our account is a little short because we spent so much on the trip."

"I don't know," Dominick pondered. "How about the federal withholding taxes? If we dipped into that fund for right now, we could cover our expenses."

"Good idea," Wayne agreed enthusiastically. "And next month, we can make up for the deficit." It wasn't the first time they had dipped into the fund to cover expenses.

Wayne also decided that with another child on the way, he needed more room for his family. They moved to a three-bedroom duplex with a front and back yard. When Natalie ran out to roll in the grass, Wayne's heart swelled with her joy.

Natalie was old enough to start nursery school, and he thought she needed a pet. All the hairdressers had poodles, so he bought her one. Oddly enough, both he and Patricia hated dogs. Right from the first, the dog began to cause problems. Every time they left the house, it would whine and beg to come along. Patricia made it clear she didn't like the dog, and the poodle often left "presents" on her side of the bed just to let her know the feeling was mutual. The animosity between her and the dog became so strong, Wayne gave the dog away.

A few weeks later, Patricia gave birth to a son. He was smaller than Natalie, not even six pounds. Wayne could almost hold him in one hand. The nurse laughed and joked that they could use a shoe box for a crib.

When baby Todd came home from the hospital, Wayne renewed his commitment to be a good father. As a child, he had longed for his parents to hug him and touch him. So he played on the floor with Natalie and cradled Todd. But he could never bring himself to actually say, "I love you." Somehow, the words froze in his throat.

Some months after Todd was born, he and Patricia began fighting over how to raise the children. Wayne expected Natalie to obey after one command. Patricia would repeat her orders five or six times, until she was screaming at the child. Wayne expected the children to be in bed at 8:00, no matter what. Even when they had company, he didn't vary the bedtime. He wanted time alone with Patricia, without the children. But Patricia liked to keep the children near her as long as possible.

She fought him at every point. When she got really angry, she'd shout, "You're just like your father!"

That, of course, infuriated Wayne because he considered himself affectionate and loving, nothing like his father.

As Todd began to grow, Wayne realized more and more how much responsibility he had with his little family. Todd had a strong constitution and cried often. That got on Wayne's nerves. The medical bills, food, and clothing expenses began to pile up. Wayne sometimes felt trapped as the sole breadwinner.

To prevent another pregnancy, he insisted that Patricia take birth-control pills. "It's not right," Patricia argued. "The Church teaches against it."

"Well, I don't care. I want two children, no more. We can't afford another."

After many heated battles, Patricia finally deferred to his wishes, and he felt relieved.

Meanwhile, problems at the salon had begun to surface. Patricia and Betty Lou each took turns working at the desk. But they couldn't get along. Patricia arranged everything her way, and Betty Lou put it back the way she liked it. Sometimes, they had verbal battles right in front of the customers. Neither Wayne nor Dominick could stop them.

Because of the bickering, a couple of the stylists quit. With the high overhead, The Spanish Room could not afford empty stations. Or the loss of clients.

Then the withholding taxes came due. The accountant called Wayne at home. "Do you realize that you owe the government almost $30,000?"

Wayne's mouth dropped. "$30,000? Does Dominick know?"

"Yes, I talked to him some time ago. He says you don't have the funds available to pay."

Wayne's head spun. Where could they come up with that kind of money?

Their financial crisis caused tension between the two men. Although both had been responsible for overspending, neither wanted to acknowledge the source of the problem. Gradually, the customers began noticing the strained atmosphere in the salon, and business fell off even more. Wayne found himself with time on his hands, something he was totally unaccustomed to. He began to panic.

He and Dominick agreed that the only solution was to move to a smaller salon and scale down their expenses. They found a building to lease across the street in the new shopping center that had less than half the square footage of The Spanish Room. For weeks afterwards, as Wayne drove to work, his heart ached to see the old shop in other hands.

Then, just when they thought their financial problems might clear up, the bank called him at work. "Wayne Andre? There's a problem with your business account," the bank officer said solemnly.

Wayne could hardly breathe. "There is?"

"We have received a $6,000 check written against your account and your balance is almost zero."

"That can't be!" Wayne exclaimed. "Our balance shows enough to cover it. Let me check it out."

He quickly called his accountant and explained the situation. The next day, the accountant called to say that a large error had been made in the books a year ago. Their balance was actually close to zero.

It took them several months to clear the mess. And even then, their finances were in terrible shape. It seemed the more they tried to curtail their expenses, the more they spent.

Wayne's head ached. He couldn't stand the tension. He needed to get away.

He decided to take a trip to Florida. Surprisingly, Patricia was eager to go. She took an interest in all the planning and had her suitcases packed early. She gave numerous instructions to the maid about caring for the children and got teary-eyed at the mention of leaving them behind.

That vacation was one of the best Wayne could remember. He and Patricia had fewer arguments than usual, and she seemed especially responsive to him. The weather was balmy, as only a Florida beach can be in the right season. Wayne got a new perspective on his career and his optimism returned. He and Dominick could come out of their financial problems and, for the first time in a long time, he thought maybe his relationship with Patricia was improving.

By the time they got back home, he felt refreshed and eager to go back to work.

11

The Den Again

Nothing happened that morning to give Wayne any warning that his life was to change traumatically within twenty-four hours. He got up as usual and prepared for work in a strangely quiet house. The night before, his third child, Lane, had been born, so Patricia was still in the hospital, and his mother-in-law had taken the other children home with her. He welcomed the peacefulness and vaguely wondered that he didn't miss his family more.

Driving to work that morning he was conscious of a quiet anger in him, like a fire stoked for the night. His thoughts moved sullenly over the past few weeks. He felt no rush of joy at the birth of this latest son, probably because he thought Patricia had tricked him. All along she had said she was taking her birth-control pills, but suddenly right after their return from the vacation in Florida she had made her announcement.

The memory of that evening still angered him. They had been watching TV. He moved gingerly in his chair because of his sunburned back. Patricia's face glowed— he had thought from sunburn—but later he decided she was fired by some personal satisfaction. "Wayne, I've got something to tell you. I'm pregnant."

Wayne nearly dropped his Coke. The movement caused spears of pain to run up his back. "You're what?"

"I'm pregnant."

"How can that be? You told me you were taking the pill. When did you stop? Why didn't you tell me?"

Patricia stirred the ice in her glass with the tip of her finger. "These things happen." She teased, "What do you want me to do about it? Certainly not get an abortion."

Wayne knew that abortion was not an option. Nominal Catholic he might be, but he didn't feel comfortable with terminating a pregnancy. He picked up the empty glass and went to the kitchen. Patricia followed him.

"Everything will work out," she said brightly. "We've got insurance for the hospital bills and everything."

"Hospital bills!" Wayne exploded. "I was thinking of things like rent and utilities and Natalie starting school in the fall. We don't need another kid. Besides, you know the business has been falling off."

"It'll turn out okay. You'll see." Patricia's voice faded as she left the room.

Wayne had kept his anger locked inside for the next few months. He even cooperated when Patricia asked him to take pictures of her one day. "I just saw Donna this morning. Remember my friend from high school?

She told me I looked real good." Patricia was admiring herself in the mirror and pulling her hair back. "I'm looking great, don't you think? I want you to take some pictures of me. You know, like you used to." Patricia placed a chair at the right angle to the window. "There. I'll sit here. Take some now. I may never look this good again."

So Wayne had complied. Patricia had been pleased with the pictures, but inwardly he grew increasingly angry.

One morning around the seventh month of the pregnancy he had announced that he was going to get a vasectomy. "You're not going to get me again, Patricia. This will be the last baby in this house."

Patricia was combing Natalie's hair before the schoolbus came, so she said nothing. The child ran to her father for a quick hug before running out the door. "Bye, daddy. See you tonight."

Patricia peered at him strangely. "This vasectomy deal. It's an operation, isn't it? It means you can't have any more kids, doesn't it?" She began gathering the breakfast dishes, taking them to the sink.

Wayne stopped at the door, his hand on the latch. "Yes, that's exactly what it is. So?"

"Well, shouldn't you talk to the priest, or something?" Patricia seemed worried as she looked up from rinsing the dishes.

"As far as I'm concerned, it's none of his business." And Wayne went out, shutting the door hard behind him.

Wayne parked in his usual place by the beauty shop and went in. He'd had the vasectomy, and the baby had come just last night. *Wonder how Patricia and I will get along now*, he worried.

Dominick and Ryan, his business partners of five years, were already busy doing last-minute preparations before the first clients would come. "Morning, Wayne. How's the new daddy today?"

"Great," Wayne lied. "Baby was born last night. A boy. Everything's fine, I guess."

Ryan stuck his head out from the supply room in the back. "Congratulations," he called. "Heard the news. So I suppose you're all alone for a while."

Wayne nodded and mumbled something about "nice for a change." The first customer came in, then another and business began in a flurry.

Later, while Wayne was giving a permanent, he went to the back room for a fresh supply of neutralizer. Dominick came by. "Any plans for tonight?" he asked. "If not, why don't you join Ryan and me for dinner at Dini's? You know, to celebrate the new arrival?"

Wayne looked up, surprised. "Why, sure. Why not? Better than eating alone, I guess."

After work, at 5:30, the three men set out for Dini's, a seafood restaurant not far away. They all ordered drinks first, then enjoyed their dinner over cursory conversation—mostly shop talk. It was not until they started on a second round of drinks that the conversation changed dramatically.

Ryan toyed with the salt shaker. With a tentative glance at Dominick, he turned to Wayne. "Ever been to a gay bar?"

Wayne looked up, startled. "A gay bar? Like, what's a gay bar?"

Dominick and Ryan exchanged amused glances. "It's where gay people go. Guys dance with guys, and girls dance with girls."

Wayne set down his glass. "You can't be serious. You mean they have a place like that in this city?"

"Oh, yes," Ryan nodded. He paused a minute. "In fact, I've been to it. So has Dominick."

Wayne was wide-eyed. "You mean you're both gay?"

"Yes."

The single word hung in the air a moment before falling like a lead weight into Wayne's consciousness. He picked up his glass, realized he couldn't drink anything and set it back down again. Finally he found his voice. "Do your wives know? What do they think?"

"No, they don't know. Why should we tell them?"

Wayne was still grappling with the shock. "And your children. What about them?"

Dominick patted Wayne's arm with a fatherly air. "You know, Wayne, you've got a lot to learn yet. I bet you'd like this gay bar. You don't know what you're missing."

Wayne was still sputtering. "Hypocrites! You're deceiving your wives."

None of his protests seemed to affect Dominick or Ryan in the least. "We know you'd like it," Ryan insisted.

"You're missing a lot," Dominick agreed. "More than once at the shop, I made a pass at you, but it went right past you. Wake up, man."

Wayne's head swam. The lights in the room blurred, and he wasn't sure where he was. He passed his handkerchief over his damp forehead and blinked. "Gay," he said again, "and I never guessed it. What do you guys—you know?"

Ryan glanced at Dominick. "Well, mostly I guess we have anal sex." He said it without embarrassment the way someone might say, "We have a brass mailbox."

Wayne remembered having once heard of that kind of sex. "But why do you do that?" He found the idea disgusting, but he didn't tell them that.

"Because it feels good," Dominick shrugged.

Wayne felt his face flushing and wiped his brow again to cover his confusion. He felt naive, green, and countrified, to say the least. "Is that all you do?"

"Oh, no," Ryan went on. "There's oral sex, too."

"Oral sex?" Wayne picked up his drink and sipped. "I can't believe you'd put your mouth—." He choked on his gin and tonic. When his spasm of coughing ended he said, "I can't believe you do that."

The smile on Ryan's face seemed a mixture of amusement and triumph. "I think you'd like it. You should try it sometime."

Wayne gulped. "Never in a million years would I ever do that."

"That's all right, Wayne," Dominick's voice soothed. "You don't have to start with oral sex. Anal sex is great. I enjoy it."

"You mean you allow somebody to put their—gosh, what kind of feeling would that be?"

"It's a good feeling." Dominick's eyes glowed with something close to missionary zeal.

"I don't understand. How could you get a good feeling? You're not built for that."

"Look," Ryan insisted. "Explaining is not good. You need to see for yourself. No one's going to hurt you. Come with us to the bar." With that he rose from the table followed closely by Dominick. Wayne trailed behind, trembling as they walked toward the door.

"Don't tell anybody," he pleaded. "And remember I'm just going to—ah—ah—observe." He felt he was going to a sideshow.

The drive was a short one and when they parked by The Den Again, Wayne thought it looked quite dingy and unprepossessing. Inside it was very dark. *These people don't want to be recognized,* he decided. The three sat up to the bar and ordered drinks. The place reminded Wayne of a disco with cheaply painted pink walls and a strobe light that flashed dully. Dimly he could see people in the corners talking or embracing.

"Well, not so bad, huh?" Ryan baited.

Wayne nodded. He had expected things to be more shocking. He began to notice the music; some of the tunes were his favorites. Lots of men were dancing together, and Wayne had always loved dancing.

Suddenly Dominick appeared beside him, a man in tow. "This is my friend, Wayne Andre," he said. "He's never been to a place like this before."

The friend was welcoming and warm, and the other men that his partners introduced him to were just as friendly and accepting. Wayne began to feel more re-laxed. *It's really not so bad*, he thought.

By this time both his friends were dancing with part-ners—sometimes they jitterbugged; sometimes they waltzed. *I can't believe this*, he thought. Yet, at the same time, he began to feel almost at home.

Suddenly, a man was standing beside him. He was tall and his voice was warm, but it was hard to see his face in the darkness. "My name is Gary," he said. "I'd like to dance with you."

Wayne gulped and drew back on his bar stool a lit-tle. "But I've never danced with a man before. I don't think I can do this."

"Come on. Nothing's going to hurt you." The voice was soothing. "I'll just hold you and we'll dance. You can be the man and I'll be the woman."

Wayne turned back to his drink. "I don't think I'd better."

As the strobe light flashed across the bar, he saw Do-minick and Ryan along with Gary taking stools farther down the bar for another drink.

They bent close to each other, obviously talking over something. Then Gary stepped up to Wayne again. The strobe light sparkled across the wine glasses and lit up Gary's face. His eyes were very blue. "Come on," he encouraged. "I know you can do it."

Almost before he knew what he was doing, Wayne got up and went to dance with the man. They faced each other and Gary put an arm around him. "How do you feel?" Gary asked kindly.

"I feel weird." Then he put his arm around Gary's back, they clasped hands and the waltz began. Wayne could feel Gary's muscles rippling. *He's strong*, he mused.

Suddenly Wayne felt electrified with an indefinable sense of belonging. *This is what I have been looking for*, he realized with a rush. Other thoughts came thick and fast, almost burning in their intensity. *The touch of this man holding me. This is where I belong. I don't belong in the heterosexual life-style. Oh, God! I'm gay. These are my people.*

The dance ended, and Wayne went back to the bar more shaken than he cared to admit. He had another drink and thought about Patricia in the hospital. A wave of guilt overwhelmed him. He drank some more, and it subsided. Then Gary asked him to dance again.

Erotic feelings began to tremble in him. *This is a man,* he thought. *I'm actually being turned on by another male. Oh, God, why does this feel so good? I must have been born gay.*

Wayne danced and then stumbled back to the bar again. Whenever he was alone a few minutes, he thought of Patricia and his two little children. Oh, yes, and there was Lane—the little red-faced, squalling, new one. *He doesn't even know me yet, and already I've let him down.*

Dominick and Ryan strode up to him grinning. "So how was it?"

Wayne gulped and steadied himself. "It was all right, I guess. Not as bad as I thought it would be." He swallowed the last of his drink and stood up. "I want to go home. I don't want to be here anymore. I'm feeling scared. I want to go home."

After leaving the bar, Wayne drove his two partners back to the salon to get their cars. He wanted to go straight home, but Dominick and Ryan begged him to come into the shop. "We forgot something," Dominick lied.

Once inside Dominick took hold of Wayne's belt and began to unbuckle it. "We want to see you," he enticed. "Pull your pants down."

Wayne protested weakly while Ryan unbuttoned his clothes. Wayne's mind was in an alcoholic daze, his brain still burned with the good feeling of Gary's embrace.

So Wayne learned about oral sex.

When he finally got home that night, trembling, dazed, and exhausted, he couldn't shut out the thoughts of his wife suffering in the hospital, nor of his tiny dependent son, nor his other two children. Their trust reached out to him until he cried out, *O God, I'm a very wicked man, but it isn't fair because you made me this way.*

Gary's blue eyes shimmered in his mind. Once again the feeling of belonging came over him. To be accepted by the men at the bar, to be held as he danced, these were good feelings. He felt as if he had come home.

The telephone jarred him from his thoughts. It was Gary. "I just *had* to talk to you again," he said sensuously. "You're so good-looking. You really turn me on—"

Wayne had never been able to believe that he was handsome. The alluring voice went on. "I've got to see you again. I'm coming over right now."

Wayne shook his head and tried to sober up. "No, not tonight. My wife's in the hospital, and I don't think I can do this."

"Well, tomorrow then," the voice persisted.

Wayne hung up.

All the next day at the salon, Wayne's partners talked of the gay bar and their plans for the evening.

Right after work Wayne paid a visit to the hospital. As he hurried down the corridor, he could hardly believe that his last visit had been only the day before. With a great force of will, he put a smile on his face and entered Patricia's room. "Hi, honey." He planted a dutiful peck on her cheek. "Had a good day?"

He supported her as they walked down the corridor to the nursery to see the new baby. Wayne listened carefully to all Patricia's chirping mother sounds. "Isn't he beautiful, dear? I do think he looks a little like you. He has your hands."

Wayne didn't say much, and finally after a quick hug and another dutiful kiss, he was free to meet his friends.

All through the hospital visit, he had kept his guilt well buried, and he hoped to keep it submerged until he got to the bar and could fortify himself with a few stiff drinks.

That night the bar was much the same. They all had several drinks. Wayne danced again with Gary, and this time Gary persuaded him to go with him.

Once at the house, Gary seduced him—

When Patricia and the baby came home after only three days in the hospital, Wayne was exhausted from all the unaccustomed sex, the late nights, and the weight of guilt he carried.

"Why are you so tired?" Patricia probed. She had just settled the baby in his crib and was sitting in a big chair fanning herself.

"Oh, I don't know," Wayne lied. "Something going around, I guess. I just don't feel good."

A loud knock at the door startled Wayne. Patricia jumped up, then sat down again. "That hurt. Guess I'm not ready to jump around. Will you get that?" He headed for the front door. "It's probably mom and the kids and Aunt Jane and the rest of the gang," Patricia called after him.

Somehow Wayne made it through the next few minutes, the hugs and congratulations, the ooh's and the aah's over the new baby. Then he quietly excused himself and went to his room weary, ashamed, and full of remorse.

Faintly he heard the phone ring. Someone from the living room called. "Wayne, somebody named Gary wants to talk to you." When he emerged from the bedroom, Patricia was holding out the receiver to him. "Who's Gary?"

Still in a daze, Wayne tried manfully to be calm and casual. "How should I know?" He picked up the phone, and Patricia returned to the chattering guests.

"Hi, how are you feeling?" came the sensual voice.

Wayne was annoyed. "I can't believe you're calling me here. My whole family is here. My wife answered the phone. She wants to know who you are, and I don't have an answer to give her." Wayne hung up the phone without waiting for a reply.

Back in his room, his mind began to turn madly. *I've ruined a woman's life. I'm a homosexual—exactly what her family always told her I was. What all those guys in school said I was. They knew it and I didn't. But now I know. Oh, God, I was born to be gay.*

12

Breakup

Wayne's mind was made up. If he had been born gay, he reasoned, it was foolish to fight it. *What choice do I have*, he thought, *but to be part of the gay culture?* Yet, despite his decision, he had to be cautious. Homosexuality and deviant sex in general were against the law in Alabama.

At work the next day, Wayne told his partners of his decision. The last client had left, and the three of them were closing up shop. Dominick and Ryan warned, "You can't let people know you're a homosexual. Not in this state. It'll ruin your life!"

Wayne stood on a stepstool to put away bottles of conditioner, unsure of many things about his life. "How do you stay with your wives and still do all these things?" He tightened the cap on a bottle and reached up to set it on the shelf. "I mean, how do you get away with this double life?"

"It was different when I was first married," Dominick confided as he sorted hair rollers and set them in their tray. "At first I never did anything like I do now, but finally I realized my homosexual urges were too strong. I had to get away and satisfy my needs."

"How do you get away?" Wayne probed.

"We've got an arrangement," Ryan put in. "We take turns with our wives. One night it's their turn to have a night out while we stay home and watch the kids. The next night it's our turn to be free." Ryan looked up from his sweeping. "It's easy," he went on. "My wife is glad for time off and so am I." He dumped his dustpan full of gray and brown hair into the trash bin. "You could do the same. You can't just walk out and cause a scandal."

Wayne shook his head. "I don't think I could live like you two," he mused. He seemed almost to be talking to himself. "I've never been a very good liar, I guess." He picked up a box of trash and started for the door. "I've always been up-front about everything. Yet, I can't go on the way I am at home, that's for sure. I can't live without—" He could feel the warm blood flooding his face; his new life still seemed strange.

"Not now that I know I'm gay—" he added. It embarrassed him to make such an admission aloud.

Dominick chuckled, "Yeah, we knew you weren't straight, Ryan and me. We could just look at you and tell."

But scandal notwithstanding, Wayne knew he would have to be honest with Patricia. He had never been clever at deceiving people, and as far as he was concerned a double life was out of the question.

Yet, for the first few weeks after the baby's birth, Wayne lived at home. That is, he slept at home. Every night he would meet Gary at the salon, go out for dinner, then stay out till midnight or later. When he got home, he'd go straight to the shower, and then to bed, making sure he always slept with his back to Patricia.

She would usually wake up and demand an explanation. "Where have you been? What are you up to, Wayne Andre? Are you seeing another woman?"

He would mumble something like, "Just didn't feel like coming home. Had a couple of drinks, and I was just fooling around town."

After a few nights the excuses ran out, and he refused to answer at all except to say, "Shut up, Patricia. Can't you see I'm dead tired?"

The truth was that he didn't dare talk civilly to Patricia. Above all he avoided touching her. He was terribly afraid that if he held her and she started crying, he might, even now, melt into tears himself and be persuaded to return to his family. Despite the stunning discovery of his gayness, he didn't want to admit even to himself that he still had feelings for his family.

Nevertheless, his mind was made up. He would join the gay culture. God had made him gay, he reasoned, so he wouldn't pretend to be otherwise. All his life he had longed for male acceptance, for a man to love him, to hold him, and now everything had come together. He could touch another man, and the man would touch him back without blame or rejection. He could hardly believe it, and he wasn't about to give it up.

Finally one night Wayne came home around midnight and found Patricia sitting in the living room waiting for him. The children were all asleep and everything was quiet. Under the lamplight he could see that her eyes were rimmed with red, and he remembered with a pang of guilt that she had been crying a great deal lately. But now she had dried her tears and was looking at him with calm desperation.

"Wayne, I've got to talk to you. Are you going to leave me?" Her question chilled him.

His voice seemed biting when he answered. "Yes."

"I just can't believe you're going to leave me, just like that," Patricia whined. She blew her nose fiercely, then put the tissue in her pocket. "We can't get a divorce. Not us." She trembled a little and drew her worn, blue robe more closely around her. "Sit down and tell me what's wrong."

Her words tugged at him, but he was determined to keep his resolve. "*You* is what's wrong," he shot back. "I can't stand to live with you anymore. I don't like the way you yell and scream." His voice had risen in anger. He hadn't planned such a speech, but since telling the truth was out of the question, blaming was the easiest way. "You bring out the worst in me," he shouted. "You always have." He was still standing with his hand on the doorknob. Now he dropped into a chair.

"But what about the children?" Patricia coughed. "How can you leave us here like this?" She leaned back in her chair, exhausted, her face pale.

Wayne fought back the wave of pity that threatened to choke him. He lifted his chin. "I want a divorce. That's all I have to say."

Patricia glared at him as though the full impact of his decision had only then hit her. She swallowed hard and her eyes glittered. "All right, you creep, if you don't want me, I don't want you! I'll make it. I've been down before. I'll survive. I always have!" Her voice quavered a little; then as if to cover her weakness, she screamed, "You can just get your ever-lovin'——out of here!"

Guilt rose in Wayne as he clenched and unclenched his fingers. Despite her harsh words, she suddenly seemed very vulnerable to him. "You can have everything," he said quietly. "You can live in this house. I'll make the payments and provide for the children. I don't want anything except my clothes."

The baby started crying, and Patricia got up to tend to him. Wayne, finding himself alone, put out the light and went to bed.

The next day he found an apartment, then went back to the house to get his clothes. As he was leaving, he dropped a cup in the yard that carried the name "The Den Again." He wanted to make sure that Patricia would find out the truth.

When Wayne's friends and relatives learned that he had left his family, he began to meet opposition at every turn. An old high school friend met him in the street one day. Without even a greeting, he came right to the point. "I can't believe you're doing this, man. People are going to think so badly of you for abandoning your three children. It doesn't matter what a crank Patricia is. You just can't do this."

But Wayne found he could, and the interference of his friends only drove him farther from his family and closer to the gay society he had chosen.

When Patricia found the cup he had dropped, she asked Wayne about it, but he denied having seen it. Then she asked her brother-in-law to check on it. With the help of one of his police friends, he had traced the cup to its source. But even when she knew The Den Again was a gay bar, Patricia would not believe that Wayne had actually chosen such a life-style.

Still she confronted him. "I can't believe you went to a place like that," she exploded. "What were you doing there?"

Wayne looked at her coldly. "I was there because I wanted to be there."

Patricia's father said nothing to Wayne about the separation, but her mother came up to him after Mass one Sunday. Her voice was unsteady and she was dabbing her eyes. "Please, Wayne, don't do this. Please, you don't know what you're doing." She blew her nose, then with a quick little sob she turned to pat his arm, her gray eyes red and misty. "Patricia will calm down. Please give your family a chance."

Wayne said nothing as he turned away in disgust. Although he felt guilty and distraught, his resolve was unshaken.

Another day at lunchtime when he was just leaving his usual restaurant, another brother-in-law, Allen Williams, stepped up to him. Wayne knew that this man had a lucrative business working on oil rigs and that he was generally known to be wealthy. "Listen, Wayne," he offered, "I know what your financial situation is. Why don't I take all the bills you've accumulated and pay everything off? Would that keep you from leaving Patricia?"

Wayne tried to suppress his rising irritation as his old feelings of inadequacy came back. "No, that wouldn't help," he snapped. "I can't live with her anymore."

Allen walked away silently, then suddenly turned back and said, "I'd be willing to give you more than what your bills are—something to put into your business maybe—"

"I just have to go!" Wayne shot back. "You don't understand." He walked on, his feelings in turmoil.

He was touched that Allen cared enough to make such an offer, but at the same time he felt a great emptiness at not being able to confide in people—not even kind people. He was beginning to realize that he had chosen a lonely road.

Wayne knew he couldn't keep his new life a secret for long. He dreaded the moment he would have to tell his parents. His mother had invited him to Sunday dinner, and he decided to break the news then.

His father, Wayne knew, had surmised he was into drugs and had hired a detective to follow him. Wayne determined to set his father straight. He would tell Albert that he was not a drug addict, but that he was gay. And that would be that!

He knew this would not be easy. He and his father had never been able to communicate beyond the "How are you doing?" level. The conversation would always be one-sided, usually about Albert's deer hunting. Wayne would avoid any type of conversation with his father because it usually ended in an argument. This time, he determined to take the upper hand. As he headed back to work, he tried not to imagine his father's response.

13

Into the Fast Lane

Albert Andre stiffened in his recliner and narrowed his eyes. " And don't think I don't know what you're doing! You're dealing drugs." His arrogant tone was all too familiar to Wayne. "I can't believe a son of mine is a drug addict," he hissed.

They had just finished Sunday dinner and taken their places in the living room, Albert in his recliner and Wayne on the ranch-styled sofa across from him. In the kitchen, Grace Andre slowly washed the dishes. The conversation between the Andre men had been tense at the table, but their tones in the living room had quickly degenerated into open hostility. Taking a deep breath, Wayne tried to stay cool.

"Well, Dad, I don't know why you spent all that money having the detective follow me around." Wayne bit hard on his lower lip, his voice edging closer to his feelings. "You could have just asked me in a humane way, and I would have told you everything."

Andre's recliner snapped forward as he jumped out of the chair, eyes flashing and mouth expelling curses. For a moment it looked like he wanted to hit Wayne. Instead, he stormed to the back of the house, grabbed his car keys, and bolted out the front door. Wayne heard the squeals of his father's car as it backed out of the driveway and roared down the highway.

Wayne sat stunned as his mother rushed into the living room crying. It seemed the only thing she could do was weep and stare at him, her hands covered with dish suds. Although overweight, she looked nice in her Sunday dress and wore a print apron to keep from getting the dress dirty while doing her kitchen chores. She appeared in sheer contrast to Albert who preferred to wear blue jeans and T-shirts. Her rimless round glasses magnified her pleading brown eyes. Grace sat in a chair, dabbing at her face and eyes with the apron and shaking her head from side to side. Her hair, still black and curled slightly at the ends, didn't reveal her age.

Wayne felt panicky. He had never seen his mother this way before. She just was not the emotional type. He had to make her understand.

He leaned closer to her from the sofa. His voice quavered. "Mom, I'm not like the rest of your children. I'm different." A lump forming in his throat, he chose his next words carefully. "I am in love with a man. I know you can't understand, but—"

Grace broke into uncontrollable sobbing. "I can't believe it—I just can't believe it. This isn't happening; it can't be true."

"It's true, mom. Believe it. You're just going to have to accept the fact that you have a homosexual son."

Suddenly Wayne could no longer hold back his own tears, and for a few moments both of them sat crying.

"Mom," he finally choked, "please understand. I'm a homosexual. God designed me differently." Wayne stood. "I'm not supposed to be married to Patricia. I made a mistake. I can't stay with her."

He bent down to hug his mother's bowed form, then picked up his keys from the coffee table. He bit his lip once more. "Thanks for the lunch, mom. I'll talk to you later."

Wayne felt numb as he slammed the door on his battered Camaro convertible and sped off. He had never seen his father so upset. Ever since his accident, Albert had to take morphine to deaden the severe pain he suffered. At one point, he had become so desperate that he tried to take his own life. What would he do when he learned the real reason for his son's separation?

When Gary learned what had happened, he hurried over to Wayne's apartment to console him. The son of a Church of God preacher, Gary was a handsome, muscular, nineteen-year-old who loved gospel music. He brought several albums with him and played them softly as Wayne poured out his troubles with the family. Wayne found Gary's compassionate tones and touches soothing.

Over the next few days, Wayne's conversations with Gary portrayed Patricia as a mean woman and highlighted the hatred he felt for his father. Eventually, Gary moved in with him to escape his own family problems.

Gary, Ryan and Dominick lost no time in pulling Wayne into the fast lane of alcohol, drugs and gay living. Partying, drinking, smoking pot, and ending up in bed with his new lover filled Wayne with excitement.

Gary also introduced Wayne to the occult. During a vacation trip, they visited friends of Gary in Charlotte, North Carolina. One evening a woman named Carlotta who dabbled in witchcraft held a meeting in the home where they were staying. Discovering Wayne's fascination with the supernatural, she tried to hypnotize him. At first he fought it, then pretended to go along with her.

But Carlotta carefully seduced her subject. "You have powers you don't realize you have," she baited in soothing tones. "We need to check on them." She placed a small lamp table between them, then grasped Wayne's hands and lifted them onto it. Her touch seemed cold. "Now concentrate," she instructed, positioning her hands opposite his. "We're going to make this table move."

Wayne smiled to himself. *This table will never move.* But he decided to humor her. For several minutes, with her gentle coaching, he focused his mind on moving the table. Suddenly, it began to rise, stopping about three inches off the floor. *This can't be real*, he mused. The table tilted slightly, and Wayne became suspicious. He peered under and all around it for a reasonable explanation but found none. Jerking his hands off the table, he scooted back in his chair. "I can't believe this!"

Carlotta stiffened. "Why did you pull back?"

"I was frightened."

"There's nothing wrong," she chuckled. "It's just that we got in touch with that part of our minds that can do things like that."

Wayne wasn't so sure, though the idea intrigued him.

Several weeks into his new life, Wayne remembered some things at the house that he still wanted: a small chest, a chair, a couple of pictures that had more sentimental value for him than for Patricia. He was in the back of the salon making coffee when Ryan came in.

"I don't know what to do, Ryan," he fretted. "There are a few things at the house that I forgot to pick up when I walked out, but I have to go after them." He carefully poured water into the coffee machine and turned on the warmer switch. "Patricia will scream at me. You know what she's like. Maybe I could phone and—"

Ryan laughed. "Sure, I can get them for you. No problem. I've never liked her anyway."

Wayne couldn't give his real reason—that he was afraid his guilt and compassion would overwhelm him if he had to see Patricia again.

For months after that, Wayne never met Patricia face to face. He still feared that she might attract him back to his family again. They had numerous conversations, but always on the telephone.

One night Patricia called to say that she was concerned about the future. "I know you won't be able to support us this way forever," she went on. "I'll probably have to go to work. Something will have to be done about the children. You'll probably have to watch them."

Patricia's voice trailed off. Wayne said nothing, waiting out a long pause for her to continue. "Wayne, are you really a homosexual?"

"Yes. But we've been over this before. Don't you believe me?"

"It's just that I can't understand." Another pause. "If I had lost you to another woman, I'd be able to see it, but to lose you to another *man*...." Her voice broke with a sob. "I don't know how to handle it." Then she hung up.

Wayne endured several repetitions of this conversation over the months before he finally told her what had happened to him while she was in the hospital. The long silence on the line after he told the story reflected her dismay. Finally, without saying another word, she hung up.

A few nights later Patricia called to say that she had some questions for him. "Are you willing to answer them?"

"I'll do my best," Wayne promised.

"When we were married, were you looking at men and thinking about going to bed with them?"

"Yes," Wayne answered honestly. "I noticed men's bodies, but I didn't realize at the time that I wanted to go to bed with them."

"Were you thinking about men when you had sex with me?"

Wayne was silent for a moment. "Well, I remember how I used to watch Tarzan films. I would think of Tarzan's body and get stimulated and want to have sex with you."

Wayne could hear a choking sound with sniffles and sobs. Finally in a shaky voice Patricia said, "I can't believe it. I think I'm going crazy. I can't deal with this." A little silence. "I'd know what to do if a woman took you away from me, but you've gone to a *man*." More weeping. "It's so weird. I don't know what to say. I don't know how to react."

When Patricia finally hung up, Wayne thought, *Maybe at last she's realizing that I am a homosexual. Maybe now she'll believe that I'm gone for good and that I won't ever be back.*

In the meantime, Wayne's world was beginning to collapse at the salon. Business had been declining steadily for months. To ease some of his financial pressure, he decided to sell his interest in the shop to his other partner, Dominick, and work as an employee. Soon afterward, however, an IRS agent showed up at the salon demanding immediate payment of delinquent federal withholding taxes on Wayne's wages. Dominick stepped to the back of the salon and told Wayne.

"How much does he want?" Wayne held his breath.

"About a thousand dollars," Dominick shrugged.

Wayne's eyes blazed. "A thousand? He can't do that!" Storming toward the reception area, he threw curses and insults at the agent. "You no good——! You're taking bread right out of my children's mouths— I have to pay alimony outta that money, too!" Customers turned and stared as Wayne continued his tirade. But the agent only became more insistent, and Dominick had no choice but to write the government a check for the full amount.

Wayne's financial troubles quickly deepened until bankruptcy seemed to be his only option. Although he maintained his alimony and child-support payments, he could no longer pay his bills or continue his high rolling life-style at the gay bars.

Things weren't going smoothly between Wayne and Gary either. Almost from the beginning, their sexual relationship sparked conflict. Each preferred the aggressive sexual role, which proved especially disappointing for Wayne. At times when Gary came home drunk, Wayne tried to take advantage of his condition and have intercourse. But drunk as he was, Gary would always manage to stop him.

Wayne also felt frustrated because Gary seemed more interested in having fun and using him for financial security than building a relationship. It had been nothing for Wayne to front seventy-five to a hundred dollars a night on liquor as they visited the bars. Playing the big spender made him feel important. But with his financial problems, much of this activity came to a halt, and they had to rely on Gary's income as a waiter in a local restaurant.

Wayne wanted a monogamous relationship. But Gary was the type who preferred many men, sometimes three or more in the room at a time. This went totally against Wayne's sense of decency. He quickly learned that objecting to his partner's disloyalty only seemed to drive him further away.

One evening in a drunken stupor, Gary brought a "trick" home, leaving the bedroom door slightly ajar as they had sex. For a while, Wayne sat in the living room waiting for them to finish. At one point he passed by the door on his way to the bathroom and caught a glimpse of the stranger doing to Gary what Gary had not allowed him to do.

Infuriated, he bolted for the kitchen, grabbed a butcher knife, and threw the bedroom door wide open. "Okay, this is over!" he swore, breathing heavily. He moved close to the bed, swinging the razor-sharp knife back and forth in front of him. Wayne would have killed the guy had he not jumped out of bed, put on his pants and fled out the front door.

Wayne cried, "I can't believe you're allowing that man to do that to you!"

Gary swayed in the bed and cocked his head. "What's goin' on, man?"

"Why are you doing this to me?" Wayne yelled.

"Doin' what, man?" Gary rolled backward on the bed and fell asleep. Wayne threw the knife on the floor in disgust, then stalked back into the living room and slumped onto the sofa.

He felt drained and limp. The relationship he had longed for all his life had turned into a disaster. He thought of Patricia and the kids. He remembered their fights. The traumas in their relationship didn't seem so bad. Still, he couldn't go back. Here is where he wanted to be. With Gary and no one else. He had to do whatever necessary to make their relationship work.

After that incident, Gary seemed distant. "I think we should separate," he announced one day. "I'll still live here, but I just don't want us to be lovers anymore."

"Why? Why are you doing this to me?" Wayne pleaded. Gary started to walk away. Wayne dropped to his knees and wrapped his arms around Gary's legs. "Don't leave me. Don't leave me," he begged. "Don't tell me I don't have a relationship with you." Gary met his pathetic pleas with coldness.

To keep his hold on Gary, Wayne finally agreed to three-way sex. Everything in him felt it wasn't right, but he couldn't bear the thought of losing him.

Gary's drunkenness complicated matters as well. Coming home from a bar one evening, Gary was so intoxicated he could hardly walk. Disgusted, Wayne managed to help his brawny lover stagger up the stairs to the third floor and down the hall to their apartment. Gary mumbled something which two husky men who were passing thought was meant for them. Shouting "faggots" and "queers," they attacked, kicking Gary several times in the face and genital area. He fell to the floor groaning with pain. Turning on Wayne, they pummeled him in the face. Wayne tried to fight back but couldn't find the strength and fell to the floor bleeding heavily from cuts on his face. Hearing the ruckus, a neighbor threw open her door and shouted, "I'm calling the police!" The attackers fled.

For the first time, Wayne allowed himself to question his future with Gary. His acceptance into the gay lifestyle and his desire for sexual fulfillment with a man had outweighed his doubts about Gary. Wayne tried not to think of his life apart from Gary, but he knew it was just a matter of time before his lover would be gone.

Their breakup finally occurred a short time later when Wayne threw a birthday party for Gary. Many of their acquaintances from the gay community gathered at a neighbor's apartment on the first floor for the event. Wayne found Gary's drunkenness and sexual behavior intolerable and angrily confronted him after the party. In the heat of the argument, Wayne began tossing Gary's belongings into the hallway. "I've had enough of you," Wayne cursed. "Get out. Get out. Get out!" He shoved Gary out the door and slammed it behind him.

A feeling of despair settled over Wayne as his anger wore off. The Christmas season was in full swing, but he felt anything but festive. His love affair with Gary was over and his finances were in disarray. Wayne began to think back on the beginning of his gay life just six months before. What had seemed the path to pleasure had turned into a troublesome, lonely road.

The loneliness hit even harder when he walked onto a sawdust-covered Christmas tree lot a few days later. Instead of the giant tree he usually bought for Patricia and the children, he settled for a tiny one and set it up on a table beside his apartment window. Seated on his sofa near the tree, he shook his head at the thought of his family and wondered, *What did I do?*

His cousin Jessica, who had separated from her husband, visited Wayne occasionally at his apartment. He thought of her as a "nice girl" who as a Baptist never danced, never drank, and never did anything wrong during her upbringing. Both hurting over broken relationships, they took comfort in each other's woes, talking endlessly about their childhood and the events that had led them to this point. He felt closer to her than anyone else. She seemed comfortable with his gayness, even agreeing that he must have been born that way since as a child he had often worn a dress and played dolls with her.

When Jessica wasn't with him, Wayne found himself in a cruise bar after work trying to drown his loneliness in booze and socializing. Sitting at the bar one evening, he noticed a handsome youth glide through the door and approach a group of friends. Wayne took a quick drink and set his glass down. *Real cute little guy*, he mused, taking note of his stocky build and protruding buttocks.

Wayne nudged the guy seated next to him. "Good Lord, isn't that something!"

"Who?"

"There," he pointed to a crowd across the room. "The guy with the tomato buns. The one with the wad of money."

"Oh, him. That's Luke Adams. Wanta meet him?"

"Well, I don't know," Wayne hesitated. But deep inside he had no doubt that they would meet. He turned and motioned for the bartender. "Give me another. Make it a double!"

14

Climbing to the Top

Meeting Luke Adams turned out to be easier than Wayne thought. Across the room, Luke was impressing his friends by flashing hundred-dollar bills and keeping the waiter busy supplying them with drinks. Finally, catching Wayne's eye, he swaggered toward the bar and slid onto the empty barstool beside him.

"Wouldja like a drink?" he grinned.

"Yes, I would."

"Hey, bartender! Drink for my buddy here—on me!" Turning to Wayne, he spoke suggestively. "You look like you need a friend. What's your name?"

Wayne picked up the glass and nodded a thank you. "It's Wayne."

Suddenly his pent-up emotions spilled into a stream of conversation. Luke listened attentively as Wayne related his problems and breakup with Gary. "I was with him once," Luke confided. "Didn't like him at all!"

As they talked, Wayne's eyes searched Luke thoroughly. His physique seemed to possess all the qualities Wayne lacked—a muscular, stocky build with well-developed buttocks; a handsome young face with blue-green eyes and strong chin; fair skin with dark hair. *Luke looks a little younger than Gary, about eighteen,* Wayne decided.

He gulped the last of his drink and slid off the stool. "Gotta go. I'm bushed. Thanks for the—"

"I'd like to see you again," Luke invited. "Meet me here Saturday night?"

"Sure."

Wayne could hardly wait for Saturday to come. He danced and partied with Luke at The Den Again until late in the evening, building each other's passions. Finally, holding Wayne tightly as they danced, Luke breathed, "Come home with me."

Since Luke was still living at home with his parents, he asked a friend for the key to his apartment. By now Wayne knew the game well. First you had sex, then you became friends. After that, you fell in love—if the sex was good. Tonight would be the test.

Luke became the pursuer in their developing relationship. After their first encounter, they frequently went to dinner together or sat beside a lake, talking for hours. Their intimate moments set the atmosphere for their nightly sexual encounters.

Luke, Wayne learned, was the son of a Baptist deacon who set high standards of behavior for his children. And since Luke was the oldest, it was his role to set the example for his brothers. Luke loved his father but could never measure up. In the gay community, he received the acceptance he could not find at home.

Soon after Luke's relationship with Wayne began, the senior Adams learned of his son's secret life. Luke was with Wayne in his apartment one Sunday afternoon when the telephone interrupted their conversation.

Wayne handed the phone to Luke. "It's your mother. She sounds upset."

"What's going on?" Luke's voice was calm.

Mrs. Adams's panicky voice was loud enough for even Wayne to hear. "You're daddy has just lost his mind. He's found out what's going on, and he's coming over there to kill you—both of you."

"What should we do, Mom?"

"I think you both should leave the apartment where he can't find you!"

Luke dropped the receiver into its cradle and they dashed out the door.

After that they saw each other only on the weekends at the bar. Luke and his father fought constantly over Luke's homosexual relationship until finally Luke left home and moved in with Wayne. Even then the arguments didn't stop. It got so that when the phone would ring, Luke wouldn't answer it because he knew it was his father.

Wayne did everything he could to keep his life-style a secret from his children as they grew older. He and Luke moved into a two-bedroom apartment with a pool and garden-like surroundings in a nicer section of town. Whenever the children came to visit, he would put them down in "Luke's bed" and explain that Luke would have to sleep with him. Moreover he wouldn't allow Luke to touch him when they were present. He had scolded Patricia for having a man over with the children at home, and the idea of him having sex with Luke while they slept in the other room offended his sense of morality as well. Neither did he allow any of his other gay friends to visit while his family was around. Drinking wasn't allowed either.

Luke's apparent love for the children amazed Wayne. To deal with the guilt he felt over his life-style, Wayne had learned to block out any feelings that would bring him close to his children. But they seemed to bring out the father instincts in Luke. Whatever they needed he was there to provide, right down to changing the baby's diapers.

"Luke, I can't believe you want to do this!" Wayne shook his head incredulously.

Luke folded a soiled diaper and set it aside while he wiped little Lane with a damp cloth. "Well, they're your kids. You have to have a relationship with your family."

Wayne stared blankly at Luke. *Here's a man I'm in love with, and he's telling me I've got to have a relationship with my children?* Wayne's feelings for Luke warmed even more. *Here's a guy who not only cares for me, but my children, too.*

The senior Adams died from a massive heart attack a few months after Luke moved in with Wayne. After that, Luke began to form a relationship with Wayne's father. Luke liked to hunt, and this gave him a common ground with Albert Andre. During their visits to the

Andres, Wayne would sit in the kitchen with his mother listening to Luke and Albert banter about their hunting experiences. Wayne felt jealous that Luke now seemed to be daddy's son. If Albert's illness sent him to the hospital, Luke was the first one there. And it was Luke who bought the Andres their first color TV.

Albert refused to accept the homosexual relationship between his son and Luke. Every time they came for a visit, Albert would manage to interject, "When are you guys going to get married? Where are the girls?" Wayne would feel irritated at his father's not-so-subtle attempts to edge him and Luke into heterosexuality.

Early in their relationship, Wayne and Luke had decided to climb to the top of the gay society. Eventually Wayne left the salon where he had been working with Dominick and Ryan and opened another shop in Baton Rouge where he continued to attract an affluent clientele. Among them were prominent doctors' wives and a millionairess who owned a women's department store. The richer women of the city seemed attracted to gay hairdressers, possibly because they were more artistic in their work than their heterosexual counterparts. Wayne took advantage of this preference and eventually built his salon into one of the top shops in the city.

One of his most faithful customers, Viveca Stone, a prominent physician's wife, eventually invited Wayne to the governor's mansion for a birthday party in honor of her husband. Wayne asked another of his clients, a pretty young woman who seemed quite adept at social functions, to accompany him. He found himself the hit of the party as he mingled with the high-society guests.

Many of them gathered around him asking questions about their hair and wondering, "What can you do with mine?"

Climbing the Baton Rouge social ladder not only brought Wayne the success and the respect he longed for, it gave him seemingly unlimited funds to do anything he wanted. At the crest of their social life-style, Wayne and Luke spent $250,000 in just one year buying things for each other and keeping up with their social calendar. They lavished money on an elegant car, expensive rings, gold and other costly items, and on travel, entertainment and girls. Rarely eating at home, they made sure they were seen in all the important social settings. Whenever they wanted to look heterosexual to the straight community, Wayne and Luke made sure they had attractive girls with them. Wayne didn't care how he used the girls; they were just objects to him. *Besides*, he rationalized, *they're having a good time. Anyway, they're using us to get a free ride, and they don't have to worry about Luke and me hitting on them.*

Wayne liked flashy clothes and spared no expense buying them at specialty shops in New Orleans. He felt macho when dressed in a loud shirt and purple bell-bottom jeans laced up the sides with leather. His hand-tooled boots completed the outfit.

Wayne believed he had achieved the ultimate in life when he and Luke flew to Denver one New Year's weekend for a skiing adventure. On New Year's Eve, friends picked them up from an apartment they had rented. As they were leaving, Alvin, one of the friends, handed them a tiny blue capsule.

"What's this?" Wayne asked.

"Oh, just a little something to give you the most wonderful time of your life!" Alvin grinned.

"Well, what can a little dot of plastic do to you?" Wayne shrugged.

"Put it on your tongue and let it melt," Alvin instructed.

Wayne did, and Luke followed suit. That was Wayne's first experience with a new form of acid called "pyramid." It didn't take long for the acid to work on their empty stomachs. A light snow had begun to fall when Wayne and Luke followed their friends down the stairs and into a new Lincoln. Wayne felt on top of the world as Alvin chauffeured them around Denver. With his lover beside him, friends around him, and the outside shining with falling glitter, what could be better? They spent New Year's Eve dancing virtually non-stop in a bar, caught up into some higher plane.

Wayne and Luke made frequent skiing trips to Colorado, always making sure they were around celebrities. On occasions they visited The Lodge, a resort in Vail where the President of the United States often stayed. Once Luke snapped pictures of Wayne waving to President Ford as he left in the company of the Secret Service for their turn at the slopes.

Wayne felt a strange sense of accomplishment. *Here I am, a common faggot from Louisiana, in the presence of the President of the United States!*

In all of his extravagance, Wayne had neglected to keep up with his $400-a-month child-support payments. Patricia would call him periodically asking for the money, but he always had an excuse for not giving her any. He had taxes to pay. It cost a lot to run his business. He didn't make much money. He managed to deceive her about his trips, saying Luke was paying for them. Except for the one to Europe. For that he invented another lie. He had won the trip, he told her, and it didn't cost him anything.

In truth, Luke's mother worked for a lumber company and had won a trip for two because of her high sales. She asked Luke to go with her, and Wayne decided—at his own expense—to meet them in London. During the day, they'd tour with Luke's mother, but at night after she went to bed they'd take in the gay life. To Wayne the highlight of their trip was a three-way sexual encounter with a man from South Africa. He could hardly wait to get back home and tell his friends.

Living in apartments didn't seem to fit their affluent life-style, so Wayne and Luke rented a large, restored historical home in downtown Baton Rouge. For the gay society, the area was a nice place to live. An L-shaped porch wrapped itself around the white frame house. Inside, the ceilings were twenty feet high, and French doors led from the living room into a spacious dining room. A huge kitchen off to the side provided ample room to prepare meals for large groups. A beautifully landscaped garden accented the large fenced-in patio in the back.

In that setting, Wayne and Luke threw lavish parties and entertained their pick of other gays in the bedrooms. Homosexuals from around the country, London, and other parts of Europe networked at the parties, increasing Wayne's sense of prestige. Among those who attended was a wealthy contractor who built highways for the state and restored old, historical plantation homes. Some of his homes were used as sets for movies like *Hush, Hush, Sweet Charlotte*. He and Luke once had been lovers. Occasionally Wayne and Luke would visit one of his restoration sites where they would have four-way sex. The man would find somebody in a gay or model magazine who looked good and rent him for the occasion.

Most of his gay life, Wayne was the one who tried to impress others by flaunting his money. But now that they had climbed their way to the top, things were different for them. Their new friends had more money. Because Wayne and Luke were an attractive couple, others wanted to be seen with them and thought nothing of picking up the tab.

Even so, all was not well in Wayne's world. His life seemed a paradigm of success. But in riding the crest of prosperity, he ignored the inexorable undertow of failure. His rising wave of glory would soon crash into a turbulent foam of churning emotional pain and violent lust.

15

The Dark Side

Parties, prestige, and sex were not the only attractions at the top of Wayne's social ladder. The world of the occult held increasing fascination for him as well.

At first he and Luke didn't take much stock in the stories that their house was haunted. According to legend, long ago someone living in their now-restored historical mansion had been killed suddenly, and his spirit was trapped there until it could find its way into the next life. Other tenants through the years had experienced strange phenomena in the house and had spoken of conversations with the ghost. But when Wayne's piano began playing by itself while no one was in the room, he and Luke began to believe the tales were more than rumor.

The clincher came one night while they were having sex. In a standing position, Wayne suddenly felt dizzy and began to rise off the floor and hover in the air. Luke screamed. Wayne floated backward then fell to the floor.

"What was that?" Wayne gasped.

Luke shook his ashen face. "I—I don'tknow."

Afterward, tales surfaced of a little boy who many years before would levitate and move about the house, three or four inches off the floor.

The idea that one could travel in the spirit world especially intrigued Wayne. Lee, a friend studying peermantology at Louisiana State University, introduced him to the phenomenon.

"It's called astral projection," he commented.

"That can't be real," Wayne laughed. "You can't leave your body!"

"Sure you can," Lee insisted. "I'll show you how."

Wayne agreed to participate in an experiment.

"We'll need to lie down," Lee said. "Can we use your bed?"

"Yeah, sure." Wayne got up from his chair and Lee followed him into the bedroom. Setting the scene with soft music, he invited Wayne to lie down and quietly hold his hand. Lee's voice was smooth. "Now, I want you to completely relax. Thaaat's it, compleeetely relax. Now begin to feel your spirit moving up out of your body."

Wayne followed Lee's soothing instructions until suddenly, for a short moment, he could look down at himself from outside his body. Fascinated, Wayne began attending the peermantology classes at the university with Lee. Students—some of them witches and warlocks—would sit under pyramids and meditate.

During one session, he and several others projected to what they believed was the lost continent of Atlantis. Still able to communicate with the real world, however, each student would describe the scene and the people he saw to other members of the class. Suddenly the teacher said, "Now let's pull ourselves away from this scene and back from planet earth and look at the Appalachian Mountains."

As Wayne attempted to pull away from the earth, he accelerated rapidly. "There's light flashes going by me like I'm in space!" he gasped. "Stars are flying past me."

"Stop!" the instructor commanded. "You're accelerating away from this existence. You'll break your silver cord."

A "silver cord," Wayne had been taught, connected one's spirit to his body. If you went too far and broke the cord, you would cease to exist.

Wayne managed to stop his flight and returned to his body. Frightened by the experience, he stopped attending classes.

Meanwhile, two of his clients at the hair salon were into astrology, and he asked them to chart his life. According to their predictions, Wayne would never be rich, but he would live a comfortable life into old age.

Lulled by such a promise and blinded by the bright lights of his social success, Wayne could not see the dark side of his life. The possibility that anything could go wrong seldom entered his mind. Yet as the years of his life with Luke passed, the dazzle of Easy Street began to dim.

Luke preferred to remain in the closet with his homosexuality, making sure he was seen in public only in the company of beautiful girls. This frustrated Wayne because he longed to walk the streets with his lover in hand. The promise of freedom and acceptance in the San Francisco gay community often tempted him to openly declare himself. But participating once in "gay pride" week in Houston, Texas, was as far as he dared to venture out of the closet.

The night he met Luke, Wayne was looking for a lover who would be the ideal partner. At first, Luke seemed to fulfill that dream. Now, however, the dark side of their lives fed on jealousy, boredom, drinking, violence and infidelity. Nothing Wayne could do seemed to stem the undertow.

Wayne's desire for a monogamous relationship drove him to feel jealous of Luke from the beginning. Frequently while they were drinking and doing drugs at a bar, Wayne would catch Luke looking at another guy.

"What are you looking at him for?" Wayne would demand. "You know you have what you want in me."

"I *wasn't* looking at him!"

"Don't lie to me! I saw that look in your eyes." Luke's denials always infuriated Wayne, and they would spend the rest of the evening arguing.

Wayne felt drained by Luke's flirtations and sought refuge from the conflict in hard drugs and alcohol. Finally, to keep himself and Luke together and put new excitement into their relationship, he agreed to "three-way" and "four-way" sexual orgies.

But even these encounters seemed to lose their appeal. Ever searching for something new, Wayne and Luke would visit the gay section of Bourbon Street in New Orleans. Their most erotic times came during Mardi Gras when people openly had sex on the street and in the back corners of the gay bars.

Wayne was not prepared, however, for one of their encounters. On the guise that he wanted to go to the bathroom, Luke led Wayne into a dimly lighted bar. Men dressed only in leather jockstraps hung by their hands from construction scaffolds positioned around the crowded room. Facing different directions with their feet resting on platforms, they appeared like statues luring nude customers to perform illicit acts on them as they passed by.

Wayne turned to leave, but Luke stopped him and pointed to the restroom. "Not yet. You've gotta see what's goin' on in there."

Luke described an antique bathtub which served as a urinal. "There's a naked guy lying in the tub, and everyone's urinating all over him."

"I don't believe you."

"It's true."

Reluctant but still curious, Wayne trailed Luke into the crowded restroom. "This is disgusting—and satanic," he gasped. "We've gotta get outta here." He turned and marched out of the bar onto the street. Outside, men clad only in jockstraps milled about the street, while others dressed in elaborate Mardi Gras guises participated in a costume contest outside Laffite's, a bar named after the infamous pirate.

Their sexual escapades on Bourbon Street only led to more jealousy and restlessness between them. Luke even talked about getting married and having children.

"What do you mean?" Wayne demanded hotly. "I'm doing all this and you want to go get *married*?"

"Yes!" Luke's tone left no doubt about his resolve. "I don't want to live like this the rest of my life."

Wayne faced Luke squarely and narrowed his eyes. "Are you telling me right now, Luke Adams, that you are thinking about leaving me and getting married and having *children*? How could you do that to me! Who is she?"

In high school Luke had dated the daughter of a famous Cajun cook. They had been seeing each other recently.

"Does she know you're gay?" Wayne challenged.

"No. She just thinks we're roommates."

Wayne argued to no avail about the value of fidelity and how women were manipulative, emotional, and only married men for what they could get out of them. He saw himself as a loving, giving person and couldn't understand why Luke would give him up for some woman who would only spend his money and complain because he couldn't give her more. "Besides," Wayne concluded, "we're in this relationship for keeps. You know—'till death us do part'!"

"Not me! I'm going to get married!" Luke huffed and continued his dates with the girl.

Wayne's fear of abandonment and the thought of living alone drove him to tighten his grip on Luke, and their fights escalated. Complicating matters, Luke seemed to lose interest in work. He had been helping Wayne at the salon, but business had increased and when more hairdressers were hired, Luke decided to leave the shop and pursue his own career. He went to work for the Lincoln dealer, grew tired of that, and began selling vacuum cleaners. Soon, he quit work entirely and stayed at home, always with the excuse, "I can't find a job." Wayne found this intolerable, and often he and Luke would load up on gin and do battle. Sometimes Wayne would throw him to the floor and they would pound each other mercilessly, cursing and shouting obscenities.

His dream of a better life shattered, Wayne pictured himself with his family and fantasized about the happy life they could have lived had he not left them. But he couldn't go back.

Conflicts between him and Patricia had been frequent ever since their divorce. The courts had awarded him visiting rights to the children, and whenever he came to pick them up, he and Patricia would get into heated arguments—usually about money. He stopped seeing her and the children after a particularly violent fight.

Patricia had found a job and moved to a poor neighborhood. One day she needed a ride to work, and Wayne went to pick her up in his convertible. Todd rode in the back seat. Fighting as usual over money, Patricia screamed uncontrollably in Wayne's face. "You fag! You've taken my life and everything I've ever had and destroyed it."

"Would you please be quiet, Patricia?" Wayne spoke calmly. "I'm letting you use this car. We don't need this discussion today."

But Patricia only grew more furious. Veins standing out in her neck, she turned red and screamed more obscenities.

Wayne faced her and shouted, "Shut up, Patricia!"

"I will not shut up!"

Wayne backhanded her in the mouth, but Patricia raged on.

"If you don't quit it, I'm going to beat the——out of you!" Wayne shouted. Patricia persisted and he slammed on the brakes, spun the car around, and raced back to her apartment. Rushing around to her side of the car, he jerked the door open and threw her onto the ground. Grasping the now-crying Todd by his arm, he spoke resolutely. "Todd, come with daddy. Don't go with Mama."

Patricia jumped to her feet and grabbed Todd's other arm. "Give me my child," she screeched.

"You *can't* have him. He's *mine!*" Wayne stormed.

Back and forth they shouted and pulled and tugged the crying child caught between them.

It was two years after that incident before Wayne allowed himself to call or see his family again. Perhaps he would have made his marriage work had Gary Ross not touched his deep inner need for male affection and acceptance. All the time Wayne was looking at men, he had thought something was wrong with him. But his attraction to Gary and later to Luke convinced him that God had made him homosexual. Contemplating his failed marriage and struggling to make his homosexual relationships work, Wayne began to realize just how much homosexuality was draining his life. He felt trapped and began to resent God for making him homosexual.

The final blow to Wayne came when he caught Luke having sex with his cousin. Enraged, Wayne raced out of his cousin's house and, for spite, jumped into Luke's new Lincoln, and roared down the street. Luke followed in close pursuit, driving Wayne's car.

Close to home, Wayne jumped the railroad track on North Street, flew into the air, and barreled the wrong way down the street toward their house. Steel posts protected the porch beside the driveway, and Wayne aimed for them, deliberately ripping the right side of the car. Crunching to a stop and shouting obscenities at Luke, he ran into the house and locked the door behind him.

Infuriated by the damage to his car, Luke bashed in the front door and attacked Wayne. Wayne struck back. Luke grabbed a knife from the kitchen and tried to stab Wayne. Wayne managed to disarm him and throw the knife to the floor before pushing him out the front door and shoving him down the front steps into the street.

When Luke returned to pick up his belongings, the atmosphere was tense. Separating their possessions like a couple getting a divorce, Luke claimed a fur rug which they had purchased together. "Hey! Wait a minute. Where do ya think you're goin' with that?" Wayne demanded, grabbing one end of the rug.

"It's mine, and I'm goin' to take it!" Luke jerked on his end of the rug, his voice edged with ice.

Wayne tugged harder, whipping Luke around until he nearly lost his balance. "Well, you can't have it. I want it!"

Tempers flared and fists flew until Wayne bolted out the door in disgust, leaving Luke to continue sorting out his things. After that, Wayne had the door locks changed.

Even after their separation, Wayne tried to patch things up with Luke. Several times they had sex, but feelings of jealousy and anger within them ran too deep for the relationship to work.

As the dark side swirled around him, Wayne clung even tighter to the top rung of his social ladder. His popularity with clients continued, and friends rallied to his side in sympathy over his breakup with Luke. But what kept Wayne alive was his hope of finding another man.

16

Close to Hell

For several months after his breakup with Luke, Wayne partied evenings at The Den Again hoping to find a new relationship. Scanning the crowd he would single out men younger than himself who had strong jaws, a beefy chest or well-shaped buttocks—features which Wayne believed he lacked in himself. But when the "right one" came along, he was far from Wayne's ideal for a lover.

Wayne was perched on a barstool facing the room when he locked eyes with a skinny youth prancing toward him. The stranger wore tight Levis and a white pullover shirt cut off at the sleeves. Something in his face attracted Wayne, and his heart raced with excitement.

"Hi! I'm Stuart—Stuart Duncan. And you're—?"

Wayne stretched out his hand. "Wayne Andre. Join me for a drink." Wayne surveyed Stuart with a lusty gaze as they shook hands and Stuart straddled the stool next to him. "What'll ya have?"

Stuart was eighteen and still living at home when Wayne and he began dating, much to the ridicule of Wayne's friends.

"Hey, Wayne, whataya see in that guy anyway? He's ugly! A real tramp," they taunted.

"No, he's not. He's handsome. Just wait and see," Wayne defended. Excited over his new young lover, Wayne invited him to move into the old mansion, bought him new clothes, and found him a job.

Stuart came from a Christian home, though he didn't attend church. Like Wayne, Stuart couldn't get along with his father on anything. His mother seemed to accept his homosexuality and appeared glad to have him in a place where she didn't have to worry about him.

His sexual preferences intoxicated Wayne. A masochist, Stuart liked to be tied up and tortured. He coached Wayne in S & M (sadomasochistic) techniques until Wayne could inflict pain without harm. Wayne soon began to enjoy his sadist role.

Stuart had a knack for setting romantic scenes. Wayne never knew what to expect when he walked through the front door at night. Frequently he would come home from work to find a room in the house decorated like a garden or forest interspersed with dozens of lighted candles and Stuart dressed in a seductive outfit. One night Stuart chose to set his scene in the bathroom, then gagged and tied himself with ropes in the bedroom to await Wayne's homecoming.

"Stuart?" Wayne called when he saw the light in the bathroom. No answer. "All right. Where are you?"

A muffled "Mmmmmm" from the bedroom answered.

A lusty smile twisted Wayne's lips as he glided toward the sound. The smell of pot lingered strong in the room. Wayne lit a joint and inhaled as he undressed. The pot put him in the right mood. It would be wild tonight. Wayne lunged at Stuart, grappling with him in violent lust. Afterward they staggered into the soothing bathroom to relax in the flickering light and a hot tub of water.

The more hard-core their encounters became, the more abandon Wayne felt. Matt, a friend who worked as a deejay in a huge disco bar in San Francisco, invited Wayne and Stuart to the Bay Area for a visit. He took them to a club where guests needed passes and had to dress in army uniforms to get in. Decorated like an army barracks, the club offered S & M entertainment and beds for sex.

When they arrived, the benches lined in rigid rows in front of a stage were nearly full. Wayne, Stuart and Matt found places among the crowd and watched a performer dressed in a military police uniform strip the clothes off a "private," hang him by his arms and beat him.

In another room, bunk beds equipped with canisters of Crisco and undulating bodies were arranged in long rows, barracks style. A Mack truck and trailer was parked at the rear entrance of the club where other customers engaged in orgies. Stuart wanted to check out the action in the trailer. Wayne's eyes wandered curiously about the dimly lighted trailer. A man hung from a rack and was being beaten while someone thrust a policeman's baton up his rectum. Wayne could barely see what was going on in the back and would have left had Stuart not begun his seductive foreplay.

Wayne's first visit to a bathhouse came the following night. Following Stuart through the front door, Wayne felt strange, like a compelling force was pulling at him.

"I feel like I'm in the pit of hell," he muttered.

"Don't be silly," Stuart laughed. "C'mon."

Wayne and Stuart paid the cashier for their towels and headed for the showers. A low buzz seemed to charge the air. Finishing their showers, Wayne and Stuart draped their towels about their waists and surveyed the scene.

In the center of the building, a round room built as though carved out of a rocky cave provided ample space for group orgies. The primitive atmosphere encouraged participants to pursue their most basic carnal desires.

Around the cave were weight-lifting areas, showers, a steam bath and rooms equipped with televisions and snack bars where customers could arouse themselves and lure partners. Other rooms were available with beds for private encounters.

Wayne followed Stuart to the cave, past a rugged, low-arching doorway, to one of the tiny viewing windows where they could see the action. In the center of the room, swarming naked bodies with legs and heads intertwined and protruding at odd angles seemed lost in erotic ecstasy upon a large bed-like platform. Wayne estimated the number in his mind. *There's gotta be at least twenty or thirty of them!*

He shook his head in disbelief and groaned. "This is evil. Like Sodom and Gomorrah. I think Satan is right over there." Wayne pointed to the center of the moving mass. "This is how close we are to hell." He turned to leave.

"Where ya goin'?" Stuart called, obviously irritated.

"I've gotta get outta here. You comin' or not?"

Stuart refused, and Wayne marched away to pick up his clothes, dress, and wait for him at the entrance.

Wayne felt frightened and used. Not only did he find the bathhouse repulsive, he was jealous over Stuart's attraction to others. Furthermore, he suspected Stuart of using him to escape from his parents and their near-poverty level of living in order to get ahead in the gay society.

The first year of their relationship, Stuart had worked very little and Wayne put him through beauty school. After getting his license, however, Stuart found a job as a hairdresser. Meanwhile, Wayne had left his beauty salon in Baton Rouge to work as a style director for the salon at Gardener's. The shop was operated by Simms & Logan, a company which managed beauty salons in department stores worldwide. His new job gave him the additional prestige he craved, and he made sure he and Stuart were invited to all the necessary parties to maintain his status.

When the opportunity came for him to manage the Simms & Logan salon at the newly opened Sak's Fifth

Avenue department store in San Francisco, Wayne had jumped at the chance. He wanted to get away from Baton Rouge, his family and out of the low-income neighborhood he and Stuart had been forced to live in when they could no longer afford the rent at the old mansion. The store would boost his social life, and moving to the Bay Area would allow him to be more open with his homosexuality. But at the last minute the company decided to transfer Wayne to the Phillips Department Store in Birmingham instead.

Wayne's eyes peered through the doorway of the S & M club's waiting room for any sign of Stuart. None. Wayne shook his head and exhaled loudly. Glancing at his watch, he leaned his head against the wall behind his chair and smiled. "Phillips." The name made him laugh when the company's account executive called him from New York to tell him about the job. His heart set on San Francisco, Birmingham was the furthest thing from his mind.

"It's the pits," he told the executive. "That's where they kill black people. I don't want to go to Birmingham."

The executive insisted he fly to New York to discuss the opportunity further. The job seemed more attractive when Wayne learned he would be supervisor over thirteen salons in the area and make a good deal more money. Wayne and Stuart drove to Birmingham to interview the owner, Simon Phillips, and fell in love with the city. The first place they found was the gay section, and Wayne felt drawn to it immediately. The district, Wayne recalled, looked like a mini-San Francisco. Another drawing card for Wayne was Atlanta. Only two hours away, the city was filled with bathhouses and gay activity that rivaled New Orleans.

They moved to Birmingham where they immediately became known as the city's "hottest new couple." To maintain a high style of living, Wayne made sure Stuart had a good income by appointing him manager of one of the salons he supervised.

They moved into an old, two-bedroom, two-story servants' quarters in one of the historic mansions that circled Birmingham's Fountain Park. Some of the homes in the neighborhood had three and four stories. Wayne and Stuart got a huge bag of pot from a friend and stayed high on it for several months after arriving in the city. The pot seemed to make it easier for them to accept leaving their old friends while they worked their way into a new gay society.

Birmingham is in the Bible belt. Frequently Wayne and Stuart found religious notes at their door when they came home from work, and sometimes clients would ask Wayne if he were a born-again Christian.

"Yes, I'm a Christian," or "Yes, I'm Catholic," he would answer, thinking to himself, *I was born and I consider myself a Christian.* Beyond that, Wayne didn't give much thought to religion. His only desire was to climb the social steps of Birmingham's gay society.

Eventually Wayne and Stuart moved from the two-story servants quarters to a less-expensive apartment overlooking a park frequented by homosexuals. Bob, one of their friends who had the reputation of being the "stud of Birmingham," began making advances toward

183

Stuart and boasting to everyone how he was going to take Stuart away from Wayne. Stuart seemed to enjoy the rivalry. The more jealous Wayne became, the more he flirted with Bob. Eventually Wayne's jealously got the best of him.

One Sunday Wayne and Stuart mixed a jug of vodka and orange juice and downed a quarter of a Quaalude before sunbathing in the hot afternoon sun. Not realizing the sun would intensify the liquor and the drug, they became quite intoxicated. In the late afternoon, they decided to take in the "happy hour" at the Basics, a bar frequented by their friends. The liquor was cheap and they wanted to dance. Wayne eyed Stuart ruefully as he found his way into Joe's arms. Someone slipped more Quaaludes into Wayne's drink and, high on the alcohol and the drugs, his tenuous toleration of Stuart and Bob vanished.

Staggering toward Stuart, Wayne tore him away from Bob, threw him on the floor and began pounding him in the face with his fist. The owner of the bar quickly pulled Wayne and Stuart apart and escorted Wayne to a back room to cool off. A half hour later, Wayne again found Stuart in the arms of Bob. Wayne lunged at Stuart and severely beat him before the two of them could be separated again.

"I want you outta here, both of you!" the owner fumed as he jerked Wayne and Stuart apart. "You're drunk. Get out, and don't come back!"

Wayne grabbed Stuart who was still on the floor and pulled him to their car just outside the front entrance. He yanked open the passenger door, threw Stuart inside, slammed the door, then stormed around to the driver's side and dropped himself behind the wheel.

"I can't believe what we've just done!" Wayne shouted. "We've ruined our life here!"

Wayne started the car and zoomed into the left lane of traffic. As Wayne slowed to stop at a red light less than a block away, Stuart gave him a frightened look and jumped out. Immediately he was struck by a car in the adjacent lane and thrown into the air. Both Wayne and the driver of the other car screeched to a stop. While the other motorist went to Stuart's aid, Wayne leaped out of his car and began pounding his forehead on the top of the door until he bled. Then, rushing to Stuart's side, he cried, "Oh, Jesus; oh, Jesus; oh, God. I can't believe this!"

Stuart lay still on the pavement, bleeding, a bone protruding through the skin on his left leg. A couple of lesbians from the bar rushed to their rescue and someone called an ambulance.

Stuart remained in the hospital until he was able to complete his recovery at home. His mother stayed with him for a while during his convalescence, often begging him to come home. But it wasn't until after she left and Wayne caught him having sex with Bob that Wayne decided to end their two-year relationship.

Gun-shy over yet another failure in his relationships, Wayne doubted he would seek out another. He felt guilty that his actions had nearly crippled a man, but angry that his lovers had brought out the violence in him that he never thought existed. In the straight world, he was known as a kind, sweet, loving and gentle person. The realization that his homosexual lovers were proving him different was hard to take, even though violence was a fairly common thing in the gay community.

Stuart took much of their furniture with him when he moved out, leaving the apartment almost empty. Hoping to bring some cheer into his life, Wayne decided to redecorate. He painted the walls bright-white and covered the hardwood floors with a deep-red carpet. Next he rented furniture to replace the items Stuart had taken.

This fresh start seemed to renew his energy, and he began to party with his friends again. But underlying his facade of happiness, he felt angry. If the good Lord had made him gay, why was there so much tragedy in his life? It would be years before he learned the answer.

17

Gliding on a Wilder Plane

It was several months after the fight with Stuart before Wayne was allowed to return to the Basics Bar—and then only after the manager gave him a good talking to.

Bearded and dressed in a tee-shirt and Levis, Wayne leaned against the bar to watch an obviously intoxicated tall youth who had just come in with an entourage of friends. As the stranger plopped himself on a barstool, his friends crowded around him. Wayne took a sip of beer and stared at the boisterous group. Suddenly the youth caught his gaze. Embarrassed, Wayne nodded a "hello" and turned away to finish his drink.

Moments later the bartender tapped Wayne on the shoulder. "This beer's from the blond guy over there." He motioned to the smiling stranger. "He wanted me to introduce you to him. His name is Thomas Whitney. He says he would like you to have this drink on him."

Wayne took the beer, lifted it up in a toast, then quickly drank it down. At first Wayne took no interest in Thomas. Tall, blond, blue-eyed and white-skinned, he was unlike any of Wayne's former dark-complexioned lovers. But after talking to him a couple of times, Wayne found himself attracted to Thomas and invited him home.

"Wow, this is beautiful!" Thomas slurred as he stumbled through Wayne's freshly decorated apartment. Wayne lit up a joint of marijuana and the two sat intimately on the sofa before heading for the bedroom.

At first Wayne considered this just one of those one-nighters where two people meet, go home and sleep together, then pretend they don't know each other the next day. But he liked having sex with Thomas and detected something different about him. Wayne wanted to know more about this kid.

The son of rich parents, Thomas lived in Hilburn, a northern Alabama town. Every day he drove to Birmingham, nearly 160 miles round trip, to work at his grandfather's lumber company. But Thomas didn't have to work. He could get all the money he needed from his family, sometimes $500 to $1,000 at a time. At Christmas he could easily collect $5,000. The job at the lumber yard was a deal he had made with his grandfather just to keep his big white Cadillac.

At eighteen, Thomas was a full twenty years younger than Wayne. He appeared tender and vulnerable, like a kid who needed a father to raise him and teach him what life is about. As Wayne got to know Thomas better, he sensed a loyalty that awakened his hopes for a monogamous relationship again.

Sometimes Wayne and Thomas drove for hours talking about themselves. Thomas, Wayne learned, had just been jilted by a guy in Decatur. The breakup left him devastated. "At work I'd sit and watch the minutes tick by on my watch, and I'd wonder if he was thinking of me, if he cared for me," Thomas confided. "I'd wonder what he was doing and if he'd ever call me. I swore to God, 'If you ever let me get over this, I will never get myself in this shape again.'"

Thomas needed a man, a father figure, someone to affirm him and give him the identity he needed. "Wayne, what do you have to do to grow up?" Thomas asked. "How do you become a man? Teach me what I need to know. Let me learn from you." Sometimes Thomas would ask Wayne to define words he didn't understand or to help him pronounce them correctly. Wayne would kid Thomas about being the son he never got to raise, and Thomas would laugh that Wayne was the daddy he never had.

Thomas came from a religious family. His grandfather Whitney was a Church of God pastor until he died. He and his mother Kaye attended the church, though she went against its tradition and dolled herself in miniskirts, makeup and earrings. Thomas's father Ben was an alcoholic and, like Wayne, Thomas had grown to hate him. "Dad was never involved in my life," he confided. "I saw him very little. He'd take trips and would be gone for a year sometimes. He was never there for me."

"Same with me," Wayne frowned. The conversation was bringing back painful memories. "My dad and I couldn't get along either. He was always making fun of me. I hated him."

"My mother and dad divorced once when I was in the first or second grade, then they remarried and divorced again when I was eleven." Thomas's voice sounded bitter. "It was just awful. They fought constantly. They would throw things at each other, fight with knives, guns, anything. I would watch murder programs on TV and think how I would kill my father the next time he attacked my mother." He paused for a moment, then added, "Once he shot her."

"Shot her!" Wayne echoed.

"Yeah. Wounded her good. He went to jail, but she wouldn't press charges, and they let him out."

"What happened?"

"They got back together. But it only lasted a few months. That's when they got their last divorce."

After that Kaye would hardly let Thomas out of her sight. "Don't ever show your feelings," she would tell him. "I'm the only one who will ever love you. If you get involved with people, you'll be hurt. Make sure you keep everything secret because if anybody ever finds out stuff about you, they'll use it against you."

At age thirteen, Thomas had his first sexual encounter with a male friend, but it wasn't until he was sixteen that he decided to become a homosexual. He wanted to be a concert pianist and, without finishing high school, enrolled in the Alabama School of Fine Arts. Soon afterward, he was invited to a gay bar.

190

"I was scared at first," Thomas recalled. "But when I walked in, I absolutely loved it. For the first time in my life I felt at home." Several nights later he went with some friends to another gay bar. "I got drunk, I mean major drunk!" Thomas bragged. "And this older guy, he came up and kissed me. I gotta tell you, I never felt anything like that before. I mean, fireworks went off in my head. Nothing ever happened like that when I got kissed by a girl!"

Thomas had several homosexual encounters while attending the school. After he graduated, he enrolled in college, but never attended classes because he was too busy hanging out at gay bars. "I didn't have many sexual relationships," Thomas confessed. "Basically, I'd just get drunk and be happy. I could talk to anybody and do just about anything."

Thomas's family kept themselves isolated from most everyone in their community, trapping him in their sheltered environment. "I hafta get away—be free," he confided. "Maybe I could move in with you and—"

"Thomas, I gotta level with you," Wayne sighed. "I'm having financial problems." Wayne explained some of his difficulties. "I know it doesn't look like it, and that's because I'm acting like nothing's wrong. But all that nice furniture in my apartment? I don't own it. It's rented."

Thomas tried to hide his surprise. "That's okay. Maybe I can help."

Wayne thought it over for a while then decided to let Thomas move in. On New Year's Eve he invited a friend, Ty Andrews, to accompany them to Thomas's apartment in Hilburn. While Thomas picked up his clothes and returned his key to the manager, Wayne and Ty waited in Wayne's old Buick convertible. A woman in a black Lincoln Continental passed slowly by, looking intently at Wayne and Ty. Parking in the driveway, she walked briskly toward Thomas who was just bringing out a load of clothing. To Wayne she looked like a china doll with her hair pulled up on her head.

He could barely hear their conversation. "...And who's that?" she demanded, pointing toward the Buick.

"Aw, nobody," Thomas shrugged with a wave of the hand. He started toward the Buick.

"Must be Thomas's mother," Wayne muttered. "She doesn't look happy!" Wayne and Ty watched the primly dressed woman climb into the Lincoln, back it toward the street and park parallel with the Buick. With a mean look on her face, she lifted a revolver and pointed it squarely at Wayne. Wayne froze and stared back at the enraged woman, afraid she would shoot if he moved. Ty dropped to the floor behind him. Thomas charged around the Lincoln, reached through the open window and grabbed the gun. She held on tightly as the two struggled over the weapon. Finally, she stepped on the gas, and the huge motor roared. Tires screeching and Thomas holding onto the side of the car, the Lincoln weaved a short distance down the highway, then screeched to a stop. After an animated discussion with his mother, Thomas sprinted back to Wayne and Ty.

"Let's go real fast," he panted. "She's crazy. Totally lost her mind."

"No, Thomas!" Wayne refused. "You're staying here. I don't want any part of this. Your mother's a maniac."

"Wayne, *please*. Don't leave me here," he begged, opening the car door. "I can't take her any longer. Don't leave me!"

"Well, get in." Wayne waved him in and started the car. "But I'll never come back here again."

Sliding onto the seat next to Wayne, Thomas spoke breathlessly, his face ashen. "We've gotta get out of the county. They own this county."

"Wait a minute!" Wayne interrupted. "Who's 'they'?"

"My mother. My granddaddy. She'll call the police, and they'll pull us over. She'll make up a story that will put you in jail!" Wayne threw the Buick into gear and roared away while Thomas prattled about his fight with Kaye.

Thomas seemed threatened by the gays who lived in their community and soon wanted to move into an apartment where just he and Wayne could be together. Thomas possessed an extraordinary talent for playing the piano and composing music. He managed to get his piano from Kaye and would often play beautiful tunes for Wayne.

"What's the name of that one?" Wayne would ask.

Thomas would flash a broad grin and shrug. "Oh, I don't know. I just heard it."

Wayne trusted Thomas and was glad he had at last found someone who wanted only him. He put Thomas through beauty school and Thomas proved as talented in hairstyling as he was at music. Eventually Wayne hired him to work in one of the Phillips shops he managed.

Thomas filled the "wife" role in their relationship. He cooked the meals, planned candlelight dinners, cleaned the apartment and generally made things look pretty for Wayne.

Religion was the furthest thing from their minds, except at Christmas and Easter. Wayne preferred the Catholic Church, but one Easter Thomas talked him into attending a service at the Metropolitan Church of God. They walked into church after the service began and sat near the back of the auditorium. Wayne felt claustrophobic, squeezed into the pew so tightly. He focused his attention on women's hairstyles as the congregation sang. He had a stereotyped image of Pentecostal women, many of whom didn't wear makeup when they came into his shop for their big poof hairdos. He was astounded by the women at Metropolitan. They did wear makeup, and some actually looked beautiful.

Taking communion in a Protestant church was a new experience for Wayne. He sat in awe as the ushers passed trays of crackers and tiny cups filled with grape juice up and down the rows of pews. When everyone was served, he joined the congregation as they followed the preacher in partaking of the communion. Wayne's only acquaintance with communion had been in the Catholic Church where participants were expected to go through confession first. He was surprised that churches like Metropolitan even served communion.

Thomas was a heavy drinker when he and Wayne met, and he soon learned to mix alcohol with drugs. It was nothing for him to smoke pot, then drink and take up to fifteen Valiums at one time. To help with the rent, Wayne had taken in another roommate, Kurt Matthews, who eventually introduced him and Thomas to shooting cocaine during a party in Atlanta. Having vowed never to inject drugs, Wayne was reluctant.

"No, I can't do that," he protested.

Mark Davis, Kurt's friend and a medical researcher in a lab at the University of Alabama who had given injections as a nurse, insisted. "C'mon. I'll give it to you. Let's see how it feels. I've never done cocaine either. I'll prepare the coke and give the injections and make sure it's clean. And me, you and Thomas will try it."

"Yeah, try it," Kurt interjected. "It'll help your sex drive. Make it three or four times what it is."

Wayne and Thomas, already high on acid and alcohol, nodded weakly. "Well, okay. We'll try it."

Wayne and Thomas waited in the living room of the apartment while Mark and Kurt went into another room to prepare the cocaine into a liquid state. When it came time for the injection, Wayne volunteered to go first and held out his arm. Mark tightened a rubber tourniquet around Wayne's upper arm. "Give me a fist," he instructed before inserting the needle. Instantly, Wayne felt everything in him accelerate until he was gliding on a higher, wilder plain. Thomas was next. Kurt was right about the sex. Wayne and Thomas seemed to have endless erotic energy for half the night. After the hit wore off, they did more cocaine to repeat the high.

"Man, that's the best high I ever had," Thomas laughed as they drove back from Atlanta.

"Yeah, me too!" Wayne enthused. "We've gotta get more of that stuff."

After searching for three months, they found another batch of cocaine and learned how to mix it. From then on they took hits regularly, trying various mixtures of acid, booze and coke to reach their original high. When they couldn't find cocaine, they would inject morphine. Occasionally they injected Vodka into their bloodstreams to come down off the cocaine. The thought of being coke addicts never crossed their minds. But the drugs and alcohol quickly took their toll.

18

A Face in the Mirror

Wayne and Thomas had left their jobs with Simms & Logan and opened their own salon in prestigious Mountain Brook Village. With financing from Thomas's grandfather, they purchased a salon located in a beautiful two-storied facility leased by a man who was about to go bankrupt. Offering the finest salons and stylists, Mountain Brook was the place to go, and thus they had finally reached the height of Birmingham's hair-dressing society.

They staffed their salon, which they called Essentials, with five of the best stylists from the Phillips group. Simms & Logan retaliated with a lawsuit, charging Wayne with unlawful solicitation of their hairdressers while employed with Phillips. Thomas called his grandfather, and the suit was mysteriously dropped.

Wayne felt apprehensive about their partnership because, with granddaddy Whitney' $150,000 investment,

Thomas was in control. Wayne found himself manipulating Thomas with his experience and knowledge of the business to run the shop.

A couple of months after they opened, Wayne and Thomas hired Jacqueline Kennedy's hairdresser to promote their business during a weekend grand opening. He booked appointments from early morning until late Saturday night and was interviewed on statewide television. This increased the prestige of Essentials and brought in a lot of new business.

But they couldn't maintain this high point of success long. Wayne's and Thomas's drinking and drug addictions eventually became obvious to many of the clientele, and business began to drop off. Adding to this, Wayne and Thomas pillaged up to $4,000 a month from the till to support their habits. This placed severe strain on cash flow. Soon payroll checks began to bounce, Wayne and Thomas defaulted in the shop's group medical insurance payments, and they owed the government $80,000 in back taxes and fell $20,000 behind in other expenses.

Thomas's drinking took its toll on their relationship as well. He and Wayne fought constantly, sometimes violently. One evening Thomas wanted to drive while drunk, but Wayne wouldn't let him. He had already totaled two cars during his drinking sprees, and he was in no condition to get behind the wheel of a car tonight. Chasing Thomas away from his car and around the neighborhood, Wayne finally succeeded in dragging him into their apartment and to the bedroom where he slapped him in the face and sat on him.

Pulling a mirror off the dresser, Wayne held it up to Thomas. "Look at yourself. You're intoxicated. You can kill yourself!" Thomas wrestled free and ran to the telephone.

"Mom, Wayne's beating me! I think he's going to kill me!" he slurred.

Wayne tore the telephone receiver from Thomas's hand and told Kaye what really was happening. "Kaye, this is the end. Something's got to be done about Thomas. I can't take it anymore." Wayne was panting and shouting. "If you don't do something about getting him into an institution where he can get help for this alcoholism, he's going to die!"

"I can't do anything with Thomas." Desperation put a sharp edge on her voice. "I don't know what to do anymore. He's just like his daddy." Wayne hung up in disgust.

Thomas began to want out of the relationship. Often he would cry, "I don't think I'm a homosexual. I think I'm supposed to be married and do other things."

But Wayne, unable to bear the loss of another lover, clung even tighter to him. "No, Thomas, you *are* a homosexual," he would insist.

Wayne considered himself the perfect witness. "Look, Thomas, look at what I did. I ruined a woman's life! And my three kids, I have no relationship with them."

Thomas looked at him as if to say, "That'll never happen to me."

"Look at me!" Wayne growled. "I live in so much guilt, you wouldn't want to live that way. You'll never make it in marriage. Believe me, you are a homosexual!"

But Thomas remained unconvinced. His drunkenness finally landed him in jail. After he and another friend terrorized the Great Sensations salon in the Galleria, they staggered out of the shopping mall toward his car. Thomas had locked the keys in his Lincoln and couldn't remember the push-button code to unlock the door. A patrolman approached to investigate, and Thomas sassed the officer. Later, when Thomas called from the jail, Wayne wasn't sympathetic.

"Wayne, it's me. I've been arrested!"

"You're in jail? Whaja do this time?"

"Tell ya later. I need you to call my mom."

Wayne did, and Kaye tried her best to bail him out. But according to law, Thomas had to stay in jail overnight, and nothing Kaye tried could get him released.

The next day, Wayne drove Thomas home and set him down for a good scolding. "This is real cute, Thomas," he said in his fatherly tone. "Look at you. Look at what we are!" Wayne paced the floor. "Your mother's a basket case over your condition. Our business is in trouble. We're cocained- out and we owe the government thousands of dollars. What are we going to do? I just don't know anymore!"

Thomas stared blankly.

"We have a full salon over there today, and you can't go to work!" Wayne snorted. "I'm going to the shop. If you can come to work later, please call me."

Wayne had to work into the evening. It was late when Thomas finally called. "Wayne," his troubled voice drawled, "I think I've reached the end of myself. I've been talking with my mother and my pastor in Hilburn. I can get into Hillcrest here in the city for twenty-eight days for rehab. What do you think?"

"Thomas, if you're willing to do that, I'll support you and do everything to keep the business going while you're in there." For the first time in many weeks, Wayne thought he saw a ray of hope.

The next day, Wayne drove him to the hospital. On the way, Thomas asked him to stop at a bar. "Why?" Wayne demanded.

"'Cause I'm gonna get drunk before I go," he shot back. "There's a bar. Pull up!"

"Thomas, you're going to the hospital because you wanna stop drinking."

"Please stop!" Thomas spoke angrily.

"No, I don't think so."

"I said *stop!*" Thomas yelled. He looked as if he wanted to hit Wayne.

To avoid another fight, Wayne gave in. "Okay, okay. But just one drink. And no Kamikazes either!"

While Thomas dried himself out in the drug abuse unit of the hospital, Wayne continued to do cocaine. He pocketed enough money from the shop each week to buy three to four grams at a time, at $100 a gram.

Someone caught Wayne shooting coke and called Thomas at the hospital. Thomas flew into a rage and tried to get Wayne thrown out of the salon. Whenever Wayne called him after that, Thomas would get violent. Finally, the hospital wouldn't let Wayne talk to him.

Thomas returned to their apartment after his discharge from the hospital. Their relationship seemed even more strained now that he wasn't drinking or doing drugs. Although Wayne tried to cover up his habit, Thomas was not easily fooled. "You're lyin'," Thomas accused during one of their confrontations. "Let me see your arm!" Thomas pushed back Wayne's sleeve and exposed the fresh needle marks. "I knew it!" He gave Wayne a disgusted look.

Meanwhile, Wayne was suffering from a condition in his hand which was leaving it nearly paralyzed. With Thomas's encouragement, he went to the hospital for surgery. After the operation, the doctor wouldn't let Wayne use his hand.

"You had two tumors, one in your hand and one in your wrist," the doctor explained. "You had extensive damage inside the carpal tunnel. If you continue to do hair, you will lose the use of your hand."

Wayne objected vigorously, but the doctor insisted. "This is it. You can't use this hand on anything but big objects." The doctor looked at Wayne squarely, his voice grim. "As far as your business is concerned, you can't be a hairdresser anymore."

Wayne felt a surge of panic. Thomas had just been through the drug center, the government was after them for back taxes and the shop was on the verge of bankruptcy. Without a source of income, how could he support his insatiable appetite for coke? How would he and Thomas live?

The possibility of losing everything meaningful to him—his lover, his business, his means to buy drugs—

tormented his thoughts continually. He had invested much in his relationship with Thomas. How could he live without him? Wayne considered their business problems. Bankruptcy wouldn't shield them from the government, and to close the salon would make it impossible to generate income. That would mean Thomas's family would have to bail them out. Wayne couldn't bring himself to that, since they had already extended themselves several times to keep the shop afloat.

Wayne and Thomas decided that for the next six months Wayne would manage the salon and collect disability. And the shop would subsidize Wayne's salary until they could determine what else to do.

For the first time, he began to think of his age. Already well into his forties, he recalled Thomas's comment earlier during one of their long talks. "Wayne, I'm not going to love you forever, and it's not fair to let you grow older in a relationship with me. One day I'm going to leave. And you're going to be older, and it's going to be harder for you." At the time, Wayne was willing to take that chance. Now, with his hand virtually out of commission, he felt useless.

Despondent over the turn of events, Wayne tried to overdose on cocaine. He injected the drug into his disabled hand, and dropped unconscious to the ground. But the dose had not been strong enough. After that he had the windows of his truck blackened so he could continue to do his drugs—and possibly take his life—without getting caught.

If Wayne thought he had hit bottom, he was in for a shock at the jazz concert he and Thomas attended some time later. They were invited by Laura, one of the women who worked at the salon. She and her daughter took them one Saturday night to an old barroom in the basement of a building where the concert was scheduled. Wayne didn't know the artists, but since he liked jazz, he had agreed to go. The women talked endlessly through the concert, thoroughly boring Wayne. Sinking deeper into depression, he gazed at the cast on his arm, then at Laura's mouth babbling useless conversation. Finally, Wayne excused himself and headed for the restroom.

Washing his hands, he looked into the mirror. There, staring back at him, appeared a terrifying creature. Its eyes sunken and face gaunt, the entity bore a resemblance to Wayne. *Is that me?* Wayne froze before the image of himself—the drug addict, the old faggot, the queer, the sissy, the *everything* people called him in life. In that brief moment, Wayne saw the reflection of all he had done wrong, acts not worthy of human behavior. Memories of selfishness and greed, his abandonment of Patricia and the children, his unpaid alimony and child support, his life of homosexuality and drug addiction— all of these horrors writhed through his tortured mind.

Wayne threw his hands up in despair. "Lord God. Help me. Save me. Do something. I can't live like this anymore!"

Aghast at the vision he had seen in the mirror, he stumbled back to his friends, more determined than ever to end it all.

19

Breakthrough in Fantasy Land

When Wayne opened his eyes on Sunday morning, he could hear water running in the bathroom. He glanced at his watch. It was 7:30. *Why did Thomas get up so early?*

Thomas sauntered out of the bathroom and began to dress. He didn't say a word, but obviously he had plans. His hair was neatly blown dry and he had already shaved.

Wayne pulled the blankets up to his chin. "What's with you? This is Sunday. We usually sleep late or shop for antiques. Where are you going?"

Thomas buttoned his shirt cuffs. "I've decided to try out one of the steps they taught us at AA. I'm going to turn it all over to God today."

Wayne bolted upright. "You're going to what?"

"I'm going to church."

"To *church*?"

"Yes. Do you want to go?"

Wayne considered the idea. "Well—yes—I want to go. But not back to that Church of God place you took me to at Easter." He twisted the sheet nervously. "Let's go to an Episcopal church. That's something between Pentecostal and Catholic." He wanted a church that would accept gays and wouldn't interfere with his private life.

"If you want to go, get dressed," Thomas ordered with no nonsense in his voice.

Without further argument, Wayne hurriedly put on his black-leather sport coat, black pants, and black lizard-skin cowboy boots.

As they drove off with Thomas at the wheel, Wayne felt uneasy. "Where are you taking me?"

"Why don't you just be quiet and not worry about it?"

Wayne didn't say another word. Disturbing memories began to plague him. He recalled how as a child he had watched Pentecostal tent meetings. The worshipers had prayed while shouting and shaking. Some had even fallen to the ground. He smiled sarcastically to himself. *Holy rollers. The real loony fringe.*

He shuddered as the image of last night filled his mind. He still felt as though he were standing on the edge of a dark abyss. *I'm just going to church for the ride,* he told himself, trying to shrug off the terror lurking in him.

Thomas turned into the parking lot of the Metropolitan Church of God, and they walked toward the small frame building. As they approached, a young man greeted them. Wayne glanced down at his homosexual "uni-form"—black leather sport coat, black pants, black liz-ard-skin cowboy boots. Thomas was dressed in Halston suede. *Oh, God, we must look weird.*

But if the usher thought them queer, he didn't show it. "You guys want to go to a Sunday school class?" he offered. Wayne wondered what a Sunday school class was, but said nothing. Thomas asked what kind of class-es were available.

"Well, there's 'college and career....'" He turned to Wayne. "And what class do you want to attend?"

That reminded Wayne that he probably did seem like the father figure, but in this strange place he wasn't go-ing anywhere alone. He looked the usher in the eye and swallowed, "College and career."

Without a word the young man led them through the entryway of the small building and down a flight of nar-row, wooden stairs. They entered a little basement room where a group of young people were sitting in a circle talking. Wayne and Thomas were seated, and the teach-er smiled a welcome. "We were just talking about our walk with God," he said.

Wayne thought, *Oh —they're walking with God. What have I gotten myself into?*

One of those in the circle, a blonde girl with an inno-cent, eager face, began to speak. "Wednesday night I was in a car accident right at rush hour. It's like a miracle I'm here at all." Her face shone. "Like, it was a real mir-acle! You see, my brakes locked when I stopped at the light, and I did a complete circle in all that traffic. The only thing that happened, somebody dented my fender." She stopped for breath and pushed her hair behind her ear.

"But the best part was when I got home. My sister met me—you know, Annie. She goes, 'Where were you at ten-after-five?' And I go, 'Like in the middle of a car accident.'

"And she goes, 'Now I understand. At that exact moment I had this terrible feeling that you were in danger. I went to the window and knelt and asked God to protect you.'"

Murmurs of "Praise the Lord" came from around the circle. Wayne twisted the corner of his mouth. *This really is fantasy land.*

Then the boy next to the blonde girl described how God had spoken to him that morning reminding him to pray for someone. Another teen confessed that he had been faltering in his walk with God and asked the others to pray for him.

With a shock Wayne realized that each person in the circle was speaking in turn. A few more and it would be his and Thomas's turn to say something. *Well, I'll pass,* Wayne decided. *I'm only an observer.*

Finally it was Thomas's turn. The group fell silent as all eyes turned toward the two visitors. Before Wayne's horrified gaze, Thomas leaned back in his chair and began talking in a quiet voice. "I'm a homosexual. For years now I've been an alcoholic and a drug addict."

Thomas went on but Wayne quit listening. He was paralyzed with fear; his whole body began to shake. He pressed down on his knees trying to keep them still, but he couldn't stop trembling. At any moment, he expected someone to jump up to find an usher and call the police.

On my way to jail ,I stopped by the church, he mused wryly. *What am I going to do now? Thomas, you have made the major screw up of your life.*

But a strange thing happened. As Thomas stopped talking and began to weep, all the young people rose from their chairs and moved toward him.

What are they going to do? Wayne looked wildly about for a door, but his way out was blocked by chairs.

The college students, however, weren't looking at him. They were focused on Thomas. They all knelt around his chair, laid their hands on him and began to pray. "Lord Jesus, have mercy on our brother. Put your arms around him, Jesus. Pour your Spirit into his heart...."

Some began praying in a strange language, but all showed the greatest tenderness and concern.

Although he was still shaking like a man stricken with malaria, Wayne began to realize that the students were sincere. *They care,* he concluded. *They really do care. They didn't leave. They didn't throw us out.* Wayne felt tears spring up in his eyes, and then he wept, too.

When the group finished praying for Thomas, they turned to Wayne. They didn't ask him anything or wait for him to speak. They just gathered around, and under those gentle hands while the tears rained down his cheeks, Wayne confessed his sordid life how he and Thomas were lovers, how they had done drugs and alcohol and how even now he was still sneaking cocaine behind

Thomas's back. The stream of words poured from him as from a dam that had broken.

Through his tears, Wayne noticed the attitude of the students. He was amazed. No one seemed shocked. No one snickered or giggled. He looked for even one contemptuous glance and found none. Instead, they showed a sweet calmness and—there was only one word for it—a cheerfulness almost like exultation. The whole thing puzzled him.

Suddenly a bell rang, signaling the next service. Everyone rose to their feet and started up the stairs to the sanctuary. When Wayne and Thomas arrived at the top, someone greeted them, "We understand you were saved today."

They were escorted to the front of the church and introduced to Pastor Culpepper, who smiled and hugged them both. "Praise God. I hear you were saved today, and the Lord has entered your life."

Wayne was completely nonplused. So this was what people meant by "being saved." Whatever it was, he knew he could not stop it. He felt like a surfer caught in a thundering wave that was sweeping him inexorably to the shore.

An usher came by with two boxes of tissues. He set one on Thomas's lap and one on Wayne's.

"What's this for?" Wayne wondered out loud.

"Pay attention," the usher answered, then moved on.

The organ began to play and the congregation began to sing.

Jesus, Jesus, Jesus
Let all heaven and earth proclaim.
Kings and kingdoms will all pass away,
But there's something about that name.

Once again, the tears poured down Wayne's face. He glanced at Thomas and saw he was crying, too. As they wept in liberation, the congregation sang about Jesus. The place seemed awash with joy.

Pastor Culpepper got up and began to speak. Afterwards, Wayne could never remember any distinct sentence from that sermon. He knew only that God was speaking to him. He became conscious of two opposite feelings: his smallness and helplessness before God's power, and his great intrinsic worth as that power surrounded him, washed him, and filled him.

At the end of the service, his box of tissues was used up as was Thomas's. *That usher certainly knew what he was doing,* Wayne thought as he blew his nose.

Before the closing prayer, the pastor looked at the two strangers and said to the congregation, "Friends, I have someone to introduce to you." He called Wayne and Thomas onto the platform and turned them around. Wayne panicked. *Oh, God, all these people. What in the world will they think?*

The pastor went on, "These two gentlemen, Wayne and Thomas, were saved this morning in the college and career class. For this we praise God."

"Hallelujahs" and "Praise the Lords" broke out all over the auditorium.

The pastor continued, "I want you to love them."

With one accord, the congregation rose and, one-by-one, they came up to shake their hands, to hug them and to say, "We're so glad you're here. God bless you. Please come again."

The welcoming went on for some time so that, despite the smallness of the sanctuary, it took quite a while for Thomas and Wayne to reach the door. Once outside, they walked toward the car.

Wayne was mystified by what he had just experienced. "You know, Thomas, I don't understand this. I mean like—'I'm saved.' What does that mean?"

Thomas didn't try to answer. He only smiled and said, "Don't you feel freer?"

"Yes, I do."

It was true. That dark pressure was gone. He felt different. He felt good. He felt clean.

As they rode down the hill, he noticed the bright sky. Even the bare tree branches seemed to shine with a quiet beauty in the February sun. And the people walking on the street looked interesting. It was as though he had only now begun to see.

They stopped at a favorite restaurant and were soon eating hungrily, for they had had no food since the day before. Suddenly Thomas indicated a table across the room where Pastor Culpepper and his wife were eating with a group of friends. On the way out the pastor stopped to greet them and to say again how good it had been to have them at church. "Be sure to come back," the pastor said. "We'll always be glad to see you."

His public acknowledgment meant a lot to Wayne. Evidently the acceptance and love they had encountered was real. It reached beyond the small sanctuary and operated in the real world outside.

20

Struggle to Freedom

In the end it was the *people* at Metro Church who kept Wayne and Thomas coming back. They simply refused to forget them. The congregation made phone calls, sent thinking-of-you cards and welcomed them warmly whenever they appeared in the little sanctuary.

The phone would ring and Thomas would usually answer it. He'd return to the kitchen chuckling. "It's Deane again. Says she misses us and wants us to be sure to come this Sunday. She wants to sit by me." Thomas ran his hand through his blond hair as he leaned his tall frame against the kitchen counter. "Almost sounds like she wants to get something started."

"Yeah?" Wayne growled. Remembering some of Thomas's casual remarks about someday maybe "getting married," he was conscious of a twinge of jealousy.

Thomas, as though reading his thoughts, countered, "Cool it, Wayne. She sent her love to you, too."

Whatever their doubts, Sunday found the two of them back in church again, soaking up the welcome, the smiles, the hugs, the benedictions.

A few weeks later, however, they made plans to attend the gay Mardi Gras Ball, a posh annual dance held at one of the city's best halls. Some of Thomas's friends had obtained tickets for them at one of the first tables, so it would have seemed ungrateful to refuse them. They dressed in tuxedos, and Thomas wore a lily in his lapel. Setting out in their Lincoln town car, Wayne felt handsome and elegant.

The evening, however, did not turn out as they had expected. For one thing, this was the first bash they had attended with the old crowd when neither of them drank, and they soon found that nothing is quite so depressing as sitting and drinking a Coke while your carousing friends become increasingly more swizzled. By the time the costume show was over and the dancing began, they had decided to go home.

Just as they were getting up to leave, one of the stylists from their salon tottered over, obviously in no condition to drive home. They supported him out to his car, and Thomas took over the wheel. "I'll take him home to our place." Wayne nodded his approval and drove on ahead in the Lincoln.

The apartment looked normal enough as he approached the front door, but once he had opened it, he noticed first that the television set was gone. Then he saw that the desk and dresser drawers had been ransacked. Running to the bedroom, he discovered all the jewelry of any value was gone. Stunned and frightened, he strode to the phone to call the police when Thomas stumbled in, supporting the now-comatose friend.

"We've been robbed," Wayne shouted. "Looks like whoever it was came in right off the freeway and broke in by the back window."

Thomas bedded down his unconscious charge and joined Wayne as they tried to take inventory of their losses.

Wayne felt empty, invaded, and afraid. He thought of his new-found friends at church and felt a comforting glow. He was glad the next day was Sunday. He wanted to feel free and accepted and safe again.

On this particular Sunday the congregation was meeting in a different place. They had moved to a new and larger sanctuary. But the thing Wayne remembered most vividly that day was not the new building, but the altar call that closed the service and what resulted from it.

As the call was made, Thomas went up to kneel at the altar, while Wayne, a little puzzled, held back. In his former church, he had never experienced anything like this. Next he noticed one of the elders walk up and kneel beside Thomas. After a prayer they rose together and began to move across to a side door where some stairs led up to a room above the sanctuary. The elder turned and motioned to Wayne to follow them.

"What's wrong?" Wayne asked as he hurried to join them.

The elder smiled. "Nothing's wrong, Wayne. God simply told me to pray with Thomas and then to lead both of you up to the intercessors' room. They're going to pray for you there."

Feeling a little strange, Wayne climbed the stairs behind Thomas and found a little room where several people were already gathered. In the center on the floor was a small rug—a kind of prayer rug, he decided.

One woman seemed to be the spokesperson. "I'm Wilma Morris," she smiled. The voice was soft but authoritative. "The Lord has instructed us to pray for you guys today in a very intense way." She was a rather plain woman, but her gray eyes shone with sincerity. Her demeanor resembled that of a commando leader urgently giving orders before a battle.

"I want to explain," she went on, "that we will kneel, and we are going to pray. We may pray in a language that won't be English. It's called 'praying in the Spirit' or 'praying in tongues.'"

Wayne felt uncertain, even a little frightened. As he looked around, he glimpsed a flower in Thomas's button hole and realized that he had worn his boutonniere from the night before.

"What's that boutonniere for?" Wilma was looking at Thomas.

"It's just something I wore to a dance last night."

"What dance?"

"The gay Mardi Gras Ball."

"Would you give it to me?"

Thomas handed her the flower, and she dropped it on the floor at her feet. "I'm going to step on this as a symbol of your past life-style," she explained. "God wants to crush this life-style out of you. He wants you to confess homosexuality as a sin. From now on you are to reject that life."

Obediently, Wayne and Thomas knelt, and Wilma began to pray. The other intercessors joined her. They prayed in a strange ecstatic speech, but after the first few seconds, Wayne didn't focus on the words. The Spirit of God became a living presence among them.

Wayne felt as though he were burning up while at the same time chills rolled over him. That day for the first time in his life, he confessed that homosexuality was sin.

When the praying ceased and they all stood up, Wayne felt again that sense of lightness—lightness in every sense of the word—a weightless freedom as his burden lifted and a sense of meticulous clarity of mind as the darkness fled. Once again he had stepped into God's world.

Before the group separated, Wayne and Thomas had agreed to come to the church on Wednesday evening for counseling.

On the way home, Thomas remarked how clean the world looked, and both agreed that they felt liberated. But they weren't much given to conversation. The sense of having passed a significant milestone was too much with them.

In fact, a kind of solemnity stayed with them for the next few days. They went to work at the salon as usual and moved through their essential chores at home, but neither felt much like talking. It was almost as though they'd heard rumors of an approaching death.

Finally as they drove home after work Wednesday evening, Wayne asked, "You going to show up at that meeting with those counselors?"

Thomas was noncommittal. "Why, are you?"

"I'll go if you will."

Thus at the appointed time they were there. Wayne was feeling more than a little uneasy. Despite the deliverance he had felt on Sunday, all week he had been fighting a sharp, rock-hard rebellion. *How can I say my sexual preference is a sin when I was born this way?*

As they stepped into the church office, Tim and Joyce Miller introduced themselves. "The first Sunday you walked into the sanctuary," Joyce smiled, "we noticed you especially."

Her husband Tim nodded in agreement. He was strong, quiet and supportive while Joyce did most of the talking. "The first day we saw you, God impressed on us to pray for you and counsel you."

Joyce's smile lit up her whole face. "Will Wednesdays be all right from now on?"

But despite Tim and Joyce's warmth and sincerity, Wayne felt increasingly apprehensive. He decided it was time for his announcement. "Let's get one thing straight," he snapped, biting off the words like pieces of steel. "I realize you guys think homosexuality is a sin, but I believe I was born this way."

He hesitated. Something seemed to be interfering with his breathing. He swallowed hard and went on. "I believe—I believe that God is love. I love Thomas, and Thomas loves me. We consent to that love and, therefore, we're not out of God's will."

His speech had been thrown down like a challenge, and he sat waiting for the fight to begin, but nothing happened.

For a moment, a shadow clouded Joyce's clear gaze. "Wayne, we're not here to change your mind; we can't do that. We're here to love you and help you right where you are." She began gathering up her books and papers. "If God chooses to change your way of thinking, then He'll do that for you. It's not our place to do it."

The first counseling session ended with an invitation for them to come over to the Millers' for supper the next evening, and Wayne and Thomas willingly accepted.

The following Wednesday night they all met again for another counseling session. "You see," Joyce explained, "if there were no God, none of this would matter. People could do anything they liked with their bodies, and no one would say the word, 'sin.'"

Wayne could detect nothing forced or artificial in her manner. She obviously believed what she was saying.

"But we have to believe in God because there *is* life," she continued. "Life is *His* mystery. He made us and gave us the marvelous sexual machinery that allows us to pass life on."

Joyce leaned forward and spoke in loving, patient tones. "Life is sacred. That's why we can't treat it irresponsibly. That's why we know it would never be God's purpose that this sexual gift be twisted into a mockery. It's all tied up with life and the nurture of life within the family."

"But why does that make homosexuality a sin?" Thomas interrupted.

"Maybe I should explain sin more," Joyce went on. "The word 'sin' puts our backs up because for centuries people have used it to judge one another harshly, to put people down. God doesn't approve of that either."

Tim, who had been sitting quietly by the window, spoke up. "The closer a person gets to God, the clearer he sees sin. In God's eyes, the worst sins are pride, evil speaking, jealousy—the sins of the spirit. They're the respectable sins, but they're deadly."

Joyce smiled in agreement. "That's right. We're not sitting here in judgment on you. We'll always be your friends, no matter what you do."

Joyce reached for one of her Bibles and announced that they would look at some special passages. "It seems that whenever homosexuality is mentioned in the Bible, it's considered wrong—a brokenness, something outside of God's purpose."

By the time that evening was over, Wayne had become much less sure of his old views. Tim and Joyce knew the Bible well. Moreover, they knew God well. But most of all he was convinced they really cared and that the acceptance he was finding there was more genuine than any he had known before.

Soon Wayne looked forward to the weekly counseling sessions. Instead of rebelling, he began to say, "Joyce, I want to change. Pray that God will help me change."

At that point, Tim and Joyce began to suggest separate living arrangements. "If you really want to change your habits," they advised, "you must begin by breaking the old patterns."

Wayne and Thomas agreed with the advice, but inwardly Wayne was frightened. How could he live alone—without Thomas? The very thought chilled him to the bone.

Despite heavy hearts, the two set out soon after to find another place for Thomas to live. Without much trouble they found a nice condo, and Thomas put down a deposit.

"Well, so far so good, I guess." Wayne sounded as if things were anything but good. "We've come this far; we'd better get on with it. What'll you move first, your collection?"

"Yeah, I guess," Thomas shrugged. "Every one of those clocks is delicate. Couldn't trust them to the movers."

They pitched in, covering their heartache with busy activity. In a couple of days, packing after work hours, they had carefully moved Thomas's precious clock collection to the new apartment.

After the last clock had been placed, they stood in the middle of the living room and looked at each other. "Guess I'd better call the movers to get the rest." Thomas tried to sound nonchalant.

"I suppose," Wayne answered. He reached for the phone book, then drew back. They looked at each other, and tears were running down both their faces. At that point they fell into each other's arms and cried. For a long time they clung together. Then Wayne stopped to find his handkerchief and wipe his face. He blew his nose hard and Thomas did the same.

"I'll call the movers now," Thomas offered.

A few days later when they were finally settling the last of Thomas's stuff, Wayne suddenly got the bright idea of moving into the same building. There was another empty unit nearby, and Wayne hurried to put a deposit on it. "We won't be so far apart after all," he cried excitedly. But in the end he couldn't break the lease he already had, so he ended up staying put. "Probably God working again," he grumbled ruefully.

So separate lives began, and Wayne was alone for the first time in nearly twenty years. That first night he sat looking at his familiar, yet strange, apartment and felt quite desolate. How would he manage?

Suddenly the phone rang. It was Thomas. "Hey, Wayne, I've cooked dinner—ribs and Caesar salad—just the way you like it. How about coming over?"

Well, what could he say? "Sure. Be right there."

Dinner was delicious. They cleaned up the kitchen and sat down side by side on the couch to watch TV, and what might be expected happened. It was the same old sexual encounter, as though nothing had changed.

Fortunately, their relationship with Tim and Joyce was such that they felt free to confide in them—the good times and the bad.

"You just have to stop going to Thomas's place," Joyce would say. "You need to understand that we have a spiritual battle going on here. It's very real."

"What do you mean—'spiritual battle'?"

Tim was sitting beside Wayne and he put an arm across his shoulders. "She means there are two supernatural worlds."

"Yes," Joyce continued, "even as God's world is in a different dimension from ours, there's also an evil kingdom with an equally invisible existence. Both powers are continually fighting for our minds."

Joyce talked with great earnestness. Wayne could feel the force of her words. "In our experience with helping people get free," she said, "we've become convinced that Satan's captives are bound by the influence of particular evil spirits—spirits of jealousy or murder or immorality. When you two are alone together the power of your evil spirits is doubled, so your temptation is that much stronger."

"I've never heard of such a thing!" Wayne gasped. But old memories kept him from arguing with her. He well remembered the gay clubs where orgies went on. He would never forget the cold, dark, palpable evil of those places. All those memories kept him from scoffing at her words.

"So what shall we do?" Thomas's face was pale and drawn.

"Pray without ceasing," Tim said from his quiet corner. He always had a Bible verse handy.

Thus the struggle continued week after week. Sometimes Wayne managed to stay home and get through the evening alone. But many times at Thomas's invitation he would drive over to Thomas's place. One night as he sat on the couch watching Thomas cook, Wayne became increasingly more uncomfortable. Finally he stood up. "I think I need to go home. You know what Tim and Joyce said. It'll just be the same old thing and...."

"Calm down, Wayne," Thomas cautioned, flourishing his wooden spoon. "Everything'll be cool."

By this time Wayne had Tim and Joyce on the telephone asking them to pray, and they did. Wayne and Thomas prayed, too, but in the end, despite their prayers, the old sexual habit won out.

Through it all Tim and Joyce never discouraged them or reproached them. "It's a roller-coaster kind of battle," Joyce explained. "But in the end, you'll overcome. I just know it."

And often they did. Many times Wayne would call Joyce to say, "I'm on my way to Thomas's place. I know I shouldn't, but pray for me."

Later he would call again to say that he had turned around and gone back home, and they thanked God together for the victory.

Some nights while on his way to Thomas's, Wayne would cry and pray, "God, why are you doing this to me? Why are you pulling me away from my security?" Sometimes he would pound the steering wheel. "Oh, God, it isn't fair. Why did you make me this way? Why did you give me these feelings?"

Later, looking back on those months of desperate struggle, Wayne could see that even when he and Thomas failed, they were learning how better to resist.

Neither of them will forget one dramatic encounter. Wayne went to Thomas's as usual, having strongly determined beforehand that this time he would be in control and leave after eating. His confidence was high.

They had finished dinner and were sitting in the kitchen when the old urge came on Thomas who began to make a move toward Wayne.

Wayne, remembering his resolve, got up and began moving away. "No, I don't want to do this," he protested.

"No, don't leave," Thomas begged.

Wayne was adamant. "I don't want to have sex. I'm over with it. This has got to be the end of it."

Suddenly Thomas's face twisted into an evil mask.

Wayne was astounded at the change. *This is not my friend Thomas.*

Quickly Thomas darted to the kitchen, snatched up a paring knife and stabbed the counter with it. "I'll get you for this," he snarled. "You think you're so strong and you're going to get away from me. Well, you're not!" With that he grabbed a cup off the counter and threw it. It missed Wayne and shattered against the fireplace.

All this time Wayne had been moving toward the door. "I'm leaving," he yelled and was gone. He heard Thomas shout something but he didn't wait. Jumping into his car, he drove home. He didn't realize how shaken he was until with a trembling hand he tried to fit the key into the front door lock.

Once in the house, he collapsed in a chair and sat shaking while he thought of what had happened. It was as if Thomas had lost who he was. *That was somebody else. Thomas isn't a violent person. Some other power must have had control of him.*

He remembered Joyce's words about spiritual warfare. They now seemed very real indeed.

By mid-summer, Wayne and Thomas were finally realizing they could not trust themselves to be alone together. Gradually, through many falls and victories, they learned they could only be together in a group, and at least one other person had to be around them at all times.

In mid-August, God brought a special blessing to Wayne. By this time he had begun going to the church whenever it was open. On this particular evening Pastor Culpepper spoke from the Book of John. As he described the compassion of Jesus and His great love for people, it seemed to Wayne that it was no longer the pastor speaking, but Jesus himself.

Oh, Jesus, Jesus, if you would only talk to me, he thought. Reverently he bowed his head. *Please, Jesus, I want to be free.*

Suddenly, without warning, a huge, warm light engulfed him. He could see the glow around his body and feel a great weakness. He determined not to fall. People were standing all around him, yet they seemed not to notice him. Somehow he managed to get out to his car and drive home. As his mind went over the experience afterward, he could never remember that ride.

Once at home, he lay on his bed while the warm, life-giving energy still bathed him in peace. He wept softly while God showed him many things. He saw himself a child again being ridiculed, beaten, and rejected by his father. Yet somehow he couldn't find the usual hatred in his heart. Instead he felt the Power was wordlessly sympathizing, while at the same time a message entered his mind:

Now you see why you have felt emptiness and hunger for so long. Years of rejection have made you desperate. You have been searching for male affirmation, male love. As a child you never got enough acceptance to help you develop properly, and you've been searching ever since.

And still the light caressed him as he began to see his father as he had never seen him before. With surprise, he saw that his father had also been neglected and unloved. He was a man of meager education who had known little tenderness in his life.

Wayne saw him laughing and joking as he left for work in the morning. His life had been rough and full of hardship, but always he had been faithful and cheerful. *Poor dad,* he thought. *He just didn't know. He'd never known anybody like me before, and he just couldn't understand.* And little by little the icy hatred began to melt.

Then the light encompassed his current struggle and his relationship with Thomas. *What you seek in Thomas, you'll never find,* the words continued. *You'll find it only in me because I am your Maker, your Lover, your ultimate Peace.*

Even as the light faded and he drifted into sleep, Wayne knew that he would never be the same again.

After that baptism of light, he got rid of all the pornographic videos and magazines in his house. He also found he could stop masturbating. Now that he knew how powerful and how available God really was, he didn't seem to need or want the useless crutches he had depended on for so long.

Then one weekend evening he found himself alone. Everybody he called was gone. Everyone was busy somewhere else. He was forced to sit down and face the situation. The words of Jesus filled his mind, "Lo, I am with you always, even unto the end of the world." He remembered the embracing light. Somehow it still warmed him. *He's here*, he thought. *He's still here. I never have to be alone again.*

Strangely enough he had the same experience the next weekend and the next. For three weekends in a row he had the special chance to enjoy God's presence, and to realize that to a believer, solitude need never be abandonment.

After that he began to do things by himself which he had never been able to do before; gradually his severe co-dependency began to heal.

Other good things came from that baptism. Wayne began to see Thomas as a child, a kind of lover-son. He began to understand how hopeless the relationship was, because the results he had been looking for—permanent, secure love—would always be impossible to find there.

As his vision broadened, Wayne began to notice other people as people. He started watching an attractive girl in the church who had a craft shop not far from his salon. He brought roses to her one day at her shop. He was too scared to ask for a date, but they chatted awhile and visited again a few times after that. Nothing serious came of these meetings, but they were important simply because they showed Wayne that he was beginning to notice women as people instead of objects.

One evening at church, as he bowed his head in prayer and wept, Wayne was vaguely conscious of a young woman sitting beside him. He probably would have forgotten her, except that she reached out her hand in sympathy and stroked his shoulder in a comforting way. Nothing erotic happened in the encounter; one human being was simply comforting another.

Nevertheless, from then on, he noticed her as she sat in the choir. Her thick dark hair was well-cut, and she lifted her face happily as she sang. There was no special lighting in the choir, but somehow she always seemed to glow with a kind of inner light. Wayne began to wonder who she was.

21

Plowed and Harrowed

After church one Sunday, Wayne tried speaking to her. "Hi, you look like somebody I know." He paused awkwardly. "Haven't we met before?"

She looked surprised. "No, I don't think we have." After a moment in which the silence grew very loud, she walked away.

Wayne's mind taunted him, *Dummy, anyone knows that's a cliche.*

He didn't try talking to her again. Although she still shone as much as ever when she sang in the choir, she seemed remote as a painted angel in an old cathedral.

Things went better, however, on the Fourth of July. Thomas and Joyce Miller organized a picnic at Lake Logan Martin, a nearby resort, and invited Wayne and Thomas along with a number of young people. The weather was beautiful, and everyone settled down to enjoy the sunshine and the idyllic setting. Some hiked along the lake, while others played ball. Wayne and Thomas sat on the pier fishing.

Presently a truck drove up hauling a boat. Wayne paid scant attention until he realized that one of the passengers was the girl from the choir.

Thomas ambled over and the girl said, "This is my brother Peter, and I'm Hinano." Thomas introduced himself and began to help unhitch the boat and get it into the water. Peter started the engine and then bobbed up along the pier, the boat's motor thumping. "Anybody for a ride?" he shouted. "How about you, Thomas?"

Thomas climbed in, Peter revved the engine, and they roared out across the lake, causing no little consternation to a mother duck and her ducklings who huddled in the long grass near the shore.

Wayne turned to the girl, who was now standing beside him. She was wearing a smart, white swimsuit. "I like that outfit better than the one you wear in the choir," he grinned.

The girl laughed, a happy sound. "I expect it'll do better in the water than my choir robe."

"What did you say your name was? I'm afraid I didn't quite hear it," Wayne said.

"No one ever does the first time." She tossed her head. "It's Hinano, but my family calls me 'Nano.' It's a Hawaiian name."

"You really from Hawaii?" Wayne was surprised. At the same time he was noticing that in the sun she glowed more than ever—a kind of rosy glow, the color of ripe apricots, he decided. He brought his wandering attention back just in time to hear "California."

"I was born in L.A.," she was saying.

"Is that a fact? I don't think I ever talked to a girl from L.A. before. To us southerners, that's a fascinating foreign country."

"Not really foreign. Just freer, maybe. More laid-back."

By this time they were sitting on the edge of the pier, swinging their bare feet over the water. The clean wind touched their faces, and the sunlight burned and bounced off the waves that Peter and Thomas were making with the boat. Hinano cast him a laughing glance. "I'll bet you had blonde curls when you were a kid," she said suddenly. "Your hair is sort of chestnut now, but it has blonde highlights in the sun."

Wayne flushed a little under her gaze. "You're really perceptive, girl. As a matter of fact, when I was around four, I had the prettiest blonde curls you ever did see. Mom used to dress me as a girl to show me off in town." Then he really blushed, worried he might have revealed too much about his past.

But Hinano was busy tossing a pebble at the mother duck, and the fuzzy brown babies quickly gathered toward it. "What a shame I don't have some bread crusts," she mused. "I think someone said your name is 'Wayne,' but you haven't told me where you're from."

"Me? Oh, I'm a Cajun from Lou'siana."

"Now that's a place I've always been curious about." Hinano was hugging her knees as she gazed at the misty horizon. "Did you speak French, or what?"

"Well, it's Creole they speak among the Cajuns, but my folks spoke French because my father's people were from France."

235

The small waves were slapping the pier, and nearby the mother duck was quacking softly to her babies. "Tell me more about Cajun life in Louisiana," Hinano said.

Wayne explained the Cajun customs he remembered, all the while feeling mystified at her obvious interest in him. Finally, Peter and Thomas roared up beside the pier. "Anybody for water skiing?" Peter shouted, and soon Wayne was skiing behind the boat while Hinano and Peter steered by turns. Thomas had joined a group on the shore.

Soon it was noon, and after lunch the sunny hours fairly melted away. As the shadows grew longer across the lake, people began gathering their beach chairs and baskets, preparing to go home. Wayne felt an unexpected reluctance at the thought of leaving Hinano. He had a lot more he wanted to say to her. He walked over to where she stood by her brother's truck, brushing her hair. "Why don't you let me drive you home?" he suggested, a little surprised at his own boldness.

She smoothed out the folds of her bright-red cover-up. "Sure. Just let me get my sandals on." Gathering her things, she climbed up into his pickup and they drove off.

"Your windows are really tinted dark," she observed. "Can you see okay?"

"Oh, sure. The windshield's clear." Wayne paused to phrase his next words carefully. "The tinted windows are part of my old life, I'm afraid." He glanced at Hinano's serene profile and went on. "I've never been able to stand being sneaky, so I think I ought to tell you about myself." Inwardly he trembled, but he carried on.

"I needed the windows dark when I used to shoot up with cocaine. That way I could get a fix real easy." Again he glanced at her face, felt reassured, then continued. "You see, not many months ago I was totally taken up with the gay life. Thomas and I were lovers. We aren't now. We separated several months ago."

"What work do you do?" Her voice was matter-of-fact.

"Thomas and I are business partners. We own a beauty salon together. Of course, we're both stylists. The salon is called Essentials."

"Oh, yes, I've seen that place."

"You don't sound shocked or disgusted."

"Am I supposed to?" She laughed her happy laugh. "Gay people are nothing new to me. I've had gay friends. In L.A. there were gays at many of the parties I went to." She patted his hand. "It's okay. Go on."

Wayne continued his story, not stopping until he had told her about his old life, his lost family, his seduction into gayness, his troubled journey and finally his arrival at Metro Church with Thomas that Sunday back in February.

"Yes," she nodded. "I remember that day well. I recognized that you both were gay, and I began to weep and pray for you even as I sat in the choir. God laid you on my heart, and I've been praying for you ever since."

The summer dusk provided just enough light so Wayne could see her dark eyes bright with unshed tears. "We don't go far in this story before we run into God, do we?" she said as she smiled.

"That's right." Wayne's voice broke.

"I guess I have a few things to say, too," she offered. "Yesterday was important for me for two reasons. It was my birthday, and my divorce became final. I almost didn't come today. I was so torn up inside, but Peter insisted."

"Well," Wayne grinned, "I'm glad he did because I've found a new friend."

"Me, too," Nano said.

By this time they had reached the outskirts of Birmingham and Wayne dropped Hinano off at her house. As he drove on home, he worried about Thomas. *He'll be upset, I suppose, because I took a woman with me.*

But as he drifted off to sleep that night, his last thoughts were of Hinano's bright, interested face. He remembered especially one remark she had made. "I'm not exactly from a convent, you know. I've got a rocky past myself. The Lord is healing us both."

A few weeks later in mid-August, Wayne's birthday was approaching. He always liked to take a trip out of town on the weekend nearest his birthday. Often he and Thomas had gone to Thomas's mother's condo at Fort Walton Beach in Florida. This time they invited Thomas and Joyce, as well as Hinano and Susan, a girl Thomas liked.

It was a difficult weekend for Wayne. He and Thomas had been there so many times that he found memories everywhere. But now he had a new life and was determined to walk the path God had given him. And then there was Hinano, always very much in his thoughts, and always very disturbing.

He knew his attraction to her nettled Thomas great-ly, not only because of their old memories, but because Thomas was sometimes attracted to Hinano himself.

By Saturday night the interplay between principles and struggling emotions had reached its peak. "I don't know about you guys," Thomas announced, "but on a Saturday night I'm not hangin' around this place. I'm outta here." He was blow-drying his hair while he talked. Disappearing into the bathroom, he soon reap-peared, his hair shaped in a wild, funky style. "Who's coming with me?" he called.

"I'll go," Hinano chimed in. "You coming, Susan?"

"I wouldn't miss it," she laughed.

"Wait a minute. Let's fix you up, Nano." Thomas was still armed with his blow dryer and hair spray. "Here, sit down. I'll do your hair properly—that is to say—improperly," he chuckled. Working quickly and skillfully, he soon had her hair shaped in wild peaks and swirls. "There, that's more like it. Now, do you have any crazy jewelry, wild clothes?"

Thomas and Joyce were enjoying the show but finally decided to turn in for the night. Susan was laughing as she sipped a Coke, but Wayne could only manage a rath-er stiff, uncomfortable smile.

Hinano returned from her room clad in a psychedelic playsuit of hot pink and green with large, round earrings to match.

"Perfect," Thomas cried. "Let's go." He turned to Wayne. "Coming, father?"

Reluctantly, Wayne followed, anything but carefree. All day the old memories had put him on edge. When

Hinano in her warm fashion had tried to pick up their friendship as usual, he had been annoyed. So she had become distant. Now she was obviously cutting up with Thomas, trying to shake Wayne up a little, and Wayne resented it.

The foursome ate at a nearby restaurant, laughing a lot at the impression Thomas and Hinano were making. The startled expressions on some faces were funny. All the craziness proved to be a safety valve so even Wayne began to appreciate by the time they went home.

Early afternoon the next day as everyone prepared to leave for home, Wayne and Thomas suddenly announced they would be staying one more night.

An awkward silence followed. "Do you really think that's a good idea?" Joyce asked.

"Hey, guys," Thomas waved his hand airily. "No problem."

Thomas was looking serious. "You're not ready for this, guys. I don't really—"

"This isn't what you want, is it?" Hinano's voice showed her dismay. She looked pointedly at Wayne.

"We know what we're doing, Nano. We're adults, okay?" He snapped.

Thus dismissed, the friends turned to go and soon drove away.

When Wayne returned the next evening, however, he could hardly wait to call Hinano. As soon as he heard her voice, his reserve broke, and he couldn't hold back the tears. "I'm so sorry, Nano," he sobbed. "I was so sure. I really thought I could go through that weekend and stay in the clear. But I just couldn't."

"I know, Wayne, I know." Hinano's voice was soothing.

"It's so humiliating. I was so arrogant to you and Joyce and—"

"You know, Wayne, I don't think God wants us to stay down too long when we repent. These things happen. A fall teaches us how to trust in God better."

"Yes, I know. Thomas and I absolutely cannot be alone—especially in nostalgic places. From now on—"

"It's okay, Wayne. Buck up. You'll be stronger for this. You really will. Just wait and see."

Hinano's prophecy proved true. As God revealed to them the roots of their homosexuality, Wayne and Thomas never again had a sexual lapse into the old life.

Later that fall, the skin-care specialist at the salon quit. Wayne brought up the problem to Thomas. "What do you think? Should we ask Nano to come in? She's certified in skin-care —licensed and everything."

Thomas agreed, and Hinano started to work at Essentials. Wayne felt comforted to see her every day, to know he had a good friend nearby, someone to sympathize, counsel, and pray with.

About this time Wayne began coming into the salon at 5:00 in the morning to pray, especially for the business. Because of his previous irresponsibility when he had taken money from the shop to buy cocaine, their financial position was precarious. Sometimes he asked Thomas and Hinano to pray with him. Their only salvation would have to be a miracle, and they asked God for this.

With Hinano working at the shop, she and Wayne went out together more often, but nearly always they invited Thomas to go along. For several months, the Wayne-Thomas-Hinano threesome went everywhere together. Sometimes Thomas would bring another girl, or the three would join a larger church group, but for all practical purposes they held to the threesome for security.

Under these circumstances Wayne and Hinano could persuade themselves that they were just friends. The thought of serious commitment was still frightening to Wayne; and Hinano, who was still recovering from her divorce, often confessed she wasn't ready for anything more than friendship either.

Besides, it was apparent to all who knew them that Wayne and Thomas were still very involved emotionally. Almost daily at the shop the stormy interaction between them continued. They hid their worst eruptions from the clients, but often when they reached the room at the back of the salon, they would explode.

"It's like I've told you, Wayne, you've always got to be in control." Thomas would be washing out the coffee pot to make a fresh batch. "You never listen to me. You just *won't* listen."

Wayne would be rinsing his coffee mug while he glared at Thomas. "If you'd just take some responsibility and quit being a child! I get so sick—!"

"Don't talk to *me* about responsibility! Who got us into this mess? You and your cocaine habit!" And setting the coffee to perk, Thomas would slam the door and be gone.

Hinano would sit in the corner, looking sad. Wayne could see the pain in her eyes. "Do you really think this partnership is still working?" she'd ask.

Wayne would give her some coffee, then pour himself a cup. "I don't feel this has to be broken up," he'd say between sips. "We owe too much money for either of us to try going it alone."

And Hinano would rinse out her cup at the sink, sigh, and go to her next client.

On Valentine's Day, 1988, Wayne and Hinano went out to dinner alone for the first time. The date was not planned that way. Thomas had been invited, but for some reason, he hadn't come. The evening was rather uncomfortable and certainly not at all romantic.

On the way to the restaurant Wayne said, "I wonder why Thomas didn't come. Did he say something?"

"No."

Once at the restaurant, Wayne went on in the same vein. With the salad, he wondered what color Thomas would want if they redecorated the salon. Over the steak, he said he had to ask Thomas about how they would manage their next IRS payment. Over dessert, he wondered what Thomas was doing that night. Then he noticed that Hinano hadn't been talking much. He paused a minute.

Finally she set down her coffee and looked at him. "Have you been listening to yourself?" she asked. "You've talked of nothing but Thomas since we left the house."

Wayne stared at his plate and said nothing as Hinano went on. "I really feel that this is dysfunctional. You really need to take a look at this."

Wayne mumbled something about "business partner," picked up the check and started for the cash register. They rode home in silence, both feeling unable to continue talking face to face.

Once he was home, however, Wayne thought of more to say. He phoned Hinano, and the discussion continued with Wayne propped up on his bed and Hinano on hers. "I know it's tiresome for you when I talk about Thomas so much, but he *is* my business partner, and he comes into a lot of my decisions."

Hinano sighed. "Sure, Wayne." She sounded disgusted. "But when you go out in the evening, you should drop your business cares. Cultivate some other interests. This is a sick dependency, Wayne."

He had heard something similar from the Millers, but he couldn't let Hinano think he had no answer. "Well, God is helping me. Little by little He's changing my interests."

Another disgusted sigh came over the line. "Don't use God as a cop-out, Wayne. You have a responsibility, too."

"Well, so does Thomas!"

"Sure, but you can't change Thomas. You can only make decisions for Wayne."

"I'm trying, Nano." A little humility always helped.

The voice on the other end softened immediately. "I know, Wayne. I know it's hard."

"You're very patient, Nano. You do know I care for you very much, don't you?"

"Yes, I feel the same about you, but I'm not ready for anything else right now."

"No, neither am I. Good night, Nano."

Wayne revealed a lot about himself at the shop, often unconsciously, and Hinano, who didn't miss much, sometimes commented on her observations. One day Wayne charged into the back room, furious at one of his women clients. "That old hag," he raved. "Never knows what color she wants. Then after she chooses one, and I apply it, she isn't happy. And she blames me!" He threw the plastic cape he carried across the room, then slammed things around as he gathered supplies for his next permanent. "She has the *nerve* to blame me!"

Hinano watched him thoughtfully. "You should see your face, Wayne. You have an issue here, and it has to do with women. I think you hate them."

"Whataya mean, I hate 'em? I do their hair all day, every day." He sat down and glared at Hinano.

"Maybe that's *why* you hate them," Hinano suggested. "But you'd better get in touch with this because I think there's a real problem here. This is really deep anger."

For several minutes after she left the room, Wayne sat deep in thought. He began to pray silently, then remembered Miles Hamilton, a man at church who was carrying on a deliverance ministry—"prayer counseling" it was called. The counseling helped people get in touch with their hidden problems so they could be brought to the light and dealt with. Usually the process included deliverance from demons. Wayne decided that he would seek out this man at his earliest opportunity.

He told Thomas about his plan, and together they went to Miles. For three months they studied several books and attended individual counseling sessions before the deliverance itself was attempted. At these sessions, they answered probing questions, then joined Miles in prayer.

"I feel as though I'm being plowed and harrowed," Wayne confided in Hinano, "but I know God is there. It's terrible and yet good."

"You and Thomas are the bravest men I've ever met, Wayne," she assured him. "I love you for the way you seek God with such determination. You're going to overcome. In fact, you're winning already."

Finally in early March, Thomas was ready for his deliverance session. It was an all-day process. He took the day off from work and asked his friends to have special prayer for him. When he returned, he was a noticeably different person.

Wayne was interested in Hinano's analysis. "I've never seen such a change in a person," she said. "Didn't you notice? That agitation, that haunted look he gets at times? It's gone now."

Wayne nodded. They agreed that Thomas had become much easier to get along with, more reasonable and mature to talk to.

Wayne was hopeful, yet fearful, of his own coming deliverance. Miles explained how evil spirits actually inhabited the minds of those who put themselves in their power. He even had a special name for the spirit that controlled lust and deviant sex. He called that power, "the spirit of Jezebel," after the wicked queen in the Bible who tried to kill God's prophet Elijah. "This spirit often controls homosexuals, especially if they have dabbled in the occult as you have."

When Wayne went in for that long-looked-for liberation, he was surrounded by an atmosphere of prayer. He, too, had all his friends interceding for him.

After the deliverance, Miles told him what had happened. When Miles called the demon, recognizing it by name, Wayne sank to the ground, his face distorted, tears pouring down his cheeks. Then Miles commanded the spirit to depart in the name of Jesus.

At that moment, Wayne felt a force go out of his body and heard the sound of something that fled.

He too was a changed person after that. He began to realize that when he had lived in the gay life-style, he was not doing his own will. He was under the will of demons. Though he had said his rosary and repeated the old prayers he had learned as a child, he had lived in Satan's will, not God's.

Once the demon left him, he felt released from a great load of hatred that he had never suspected was in him. Wayne also felt freer of his dependency on Thomas, and he and Hinano began to have real dates. One night as they were driving home from a movie, it occurred to Wayne that he ought to give Hinano some proof that he was becoming a normal, heterosexual male. *I do love her*, he thought, *but I certainly haven't done much to demonstrate it.*

When they arrived at Wayne's place, before he got out of the car (they had taken Hinano's Nissan that night), Wayne drew her to him and kissed her. "Don't go, Nano," he breathed. "Come say good night to me properly."

They slipped out of the car and stood a long moment in the moonlight by Wayne's front door, holding each other and talking. Hinano snuggled her head against his shoulder, and he kissed her hair, her forehead, her lips. Soon she was kissing him back, her hands on his neck, pulling his head down to meet her eager mouth.

If he had been concerned about his reaction, he soon knew he need not have worried. His next move would have been to invite her in for the night, when suddenly a familiar voice in his mind stopped him. *Wayne, you've always had relationships that started with sex and went on from there. Why don't you do things My way this time? What you need now is a friend who can relate to you as a person. Just let the sexual part be quiet for a while.*

Still holding her, he said, "Hinano, darling, I need to talk to you. The Holy Spirit has been speaking to me. I don't want to start with sex, then decide we love each other, and finally get married." He sighed, kissed her hair again and stood back, his hands on her shoulders. "I'd like to be your friend first. I'd like the Holy Spirit to lead this relationship, wouldn't you?"

Hinano looked up, her eyes bright in the moonlight. Softly she touched his cheek with the tip of her finger. "Yes, I would," she whispered.

22

In God's Plan

Driving home from a short business trip one evening, Wayne heard something on the radio that set him to thinking. A gay pride parade was being sponsored in a California city and some of the participants were being interviewed. One of the activists argued that homosexuality was unquestionably congenital. "We must fight the bigotry in society," the speaker went on. "People act as though gays have a choice about their life-style, but we don't."

"You mean you were born gay?" the interviewer asked.

"Certainly. And that's what people need to understand. Would you think it right if I was denied a certain job because I was Polish or Korean or black?"

"No, of course not."

"Yet there are people who refuse to hire gays for certain positions, but we can't change our sexual preference any more than we can change our race or the color of our eyes."

Wayne felt the blood rise in his face. He gripped the steering wheel, remembering how he once held those same beliefs. How often through all the dark years of his homosexual life-style he had cried in his heart, *O God, why did you make me gay?*

The past months had shown him that he could be free. He snapped off the radio and began to pray out loud, "Oh, God, you have been so good to me. I praise your name for setting me free. Please help me now to tell the world what you have done for me."

He dried his face with his handkerchief. "I must, Lord. I must tell my gay brothers they can be free, too. That they can live a normal life."

Once at home he quickly showered, changed, and grabbed a bite to eat. Then he was off to the meeting of the Ministries Internship Program at church. Pastor Culpepper was training a small group in ministerial methods, and Wayne had not missed a meeting.

As he sat in class that evening, he decided to tell Milton Thorn, one of the assistant pastors, about his growing vision. Milton was sympathetic, but cautious. He reminded Wayne of a principle often stated by the pastor: "If God wants a ministry started, He will make it known."

Milton stood to leave. "Wayne, before we go, let's pray." Heads bowed, they asked God for a sign indicating whether or not the time had come for Wayne to begin a ministry for gays. God's answer came quickly.

When Wayne arrived at work the next day, an employee handed him a brochure and a letter. "Helen Harmon (one of the volunteers at the church) brought it by," he said casually. The brochure contained an announcement for an Exodus Conference being held at the Loyola-Marymount University in Los Angeles. Scheduled for June, it offered a week-long intensive course in the healing of homosexuality and was geared not only to help homosexuals, but also those who wanted to minister to them.

The letter included a note from Helen encouraging Wayne to attend the conference in preparation for such a ministry. "I feel God is calling you to this work," she concluded.

Wayne's heart raced as he read the note. "Thank you, Lord," he said softly. "This is the sign I've been praying for."

Wayne had three permanents scheduled as well as an appointment with Mrs. Beaufort, the client who was so difficult about her hair color. But not even Mrs. Beaufort could dampen his happy spirit.

On his lunch break Wayne told Hinano about the opportunity and the prospect of starting a ministry to gays. "I've called Milton," he said, "and he's made an appointment for us to talk with Pastor."

Hinano was gathering supplies for her next facial. "It's wonderful, Wayne! I've always known God had something special for you to do. I'll be praying."

As Wayne and Milton walked into the pastor's office that evening, they found him waiting. After they introduced their subject, a knowing smile lit his face. "You know," he nodded, "I've had several people talk to me about starting such a ministry, but I've been holding off. I wanted to give time for the Lord to speak."

Pastor Culpepper leaned forward on his desk as if to talk confidentially. "Yesterday something special happened while I was driving. The Lord began speaking to me. He reminded me that the very property the church is sitting on was once ordained for this type of ministry." The pastor looked directly at Wayne. "I was so stunned with that thought that I began to weep. And I knew then, Wayne, the Lord would put a burden on your heart about bringing forth this ministry."

For a moment Wayne was too overcome to speak. He found it overwhelming that the thing he earnestly desired and prayed for was in the Lord's plan from the beginning.

"Here, pastor." Wayne's voice quavered. "This can help to launch the ministry." Putting a hand to his neck, he drew over his head the gold chains he was wearing. "I want to give these." Then he pulled a large diamond ring off his finger. "This will be one more break with my old life. I don't care to keep these gifts from my old lovers, so I want them to be used for God's work." He sighed with relief as though a burden had been lifted. "It's good stuff—you know, solid gold, real diamonds. It should be worth a couple thousand at least."

Surprised and touched, Pastor Culpepper thanked him. "This is one more indication of your utter sincerity, Wayne." Then the three continued making plans for Wayne and Milton to attend the Exodus Conference in Los Angeles.

252

Wayne was happy as he talked to Hinano on the phone that night about the trip. "I feel good about this, Nano, because there's been one sign after the other opening the way."

"Oh, yes, I agree." Hinano's voice held a suppressed excitement. "You'll meet new people at the conference and hear wonderful things. You'll never be the same again, Wayne. This is an important milestone in your life."

Some nights later, Hinano came over to his place to help him pack. He watched her in the lamplight carefully folding his shirts and placing them in the suitcase. She glanced up, her eyes bright, a rosy flush on her cheeks. "I feel so good about this trip. Even though you're going back to my home country and I'm not, I'm glad for the good things I know will happen. God is obviously leading you."

Wayne looked at her fondly and thought how fortunate he was to have such a friend. Really, more than a friend—he finally admitted to himself—a lot more than a friend. "You're looking really pretty tonight," he ventured.

Hinano flushed, then looked up, surprised at his words. Wayne seldom paid compliments.

"You're smart, too," he mused almost to himself, but she heard him.

"Gosh," she laughed. "Maybe you should go away more often. Just the thought of leaving has improved your conversation something great!"

The next morning she drove him to the airport. He gave her a hard hug and a quick kiss and then he was gone, but not before he had said quickly, "Hinano, I think I may be falling in love with you."

The Exodus Conference was all that he had envisioned. While the more than 500 attendants assembled for the first meeting, Wayne began to gather courage. As people were introduced and the meetings proceeded, he realized that most of the families he saw (many with children) had had to overcome problems with homosexuality. They were all fighting against the same myth that had enslaved him: *God made me gay.*

One of the most outstanding presentations came from Elizabeth Mobley, an English psychiatrist who presented a paper recounting the case study of a man whose experience had been similar to his own. The hope he gained came mostly from the heartening news that he was not alone and the renewed truth that, with trust in God, he could overcome anything.

In class the following afternoon, however, Wayne was reminded that the old habits and powers were still alive. He was suddenly distracted by one of his classmates sitting across the aisle from him. He was the most beautiful male specimen Wayne had ever seen: a young man like a sun god—bronzed skin, burnished hair, steady blue eyes under straight brows and an outstanding physique. *He must be a body-builder,* Wayne decided as his eyes began undressing him and his fertile imagination began its erotic play.

Is this why you came here, Wayne? The familiar voice in his mind brought him up short.

No, Lord, never. Forgive me, Jesus.

When break-time came, he chose a seat far from the glamorous stranger and focused his mind on what he had come to hear. The more he learned about the early deficiencies in his life that fueled those deviant desires, the less power the temptation had on him.

He called home to Hinano several times during the conference and was surprised at how good he felt at hearing her voice. The conference was great, but it would be good to get home to her again.

On the last day of the conference, the conferees were invited to a closing ceremony in the beautiful chapel. At the end of the farewell service, all non-Catholics were asked to leave while the church members took communion.

This angered Wayne, and he let Milton know how he felt. "Here we are, all Christians, children of God, and we aren't considered good enough to share their communion!" Wayne huffed. "Like who do they think they are?"

Suddenly that familiar inner voice spoke to Wayne again. *Don't talk about my Church*, the voice said. *I'll deal with it myself. Just let all that bitterness go, my son. Forget your past in that church. I'll take care of it. You have plenty to deal with in your own life.*

While the gentle voice was speaking, Wayne had turned away from the crowd and found shelter under a tree. There he wept and asked forgiveness and once more allowed the dark hatred to melt away.

The week at the conference taught him how much Hinano's encouragement meant to him. The happy families he'd seen showed him how helpful a family would be as a base from which to operate his ministry. His thoughts of marriage became more serious.

After his return from the conference, he decided to have a talk with Steve and Candy King, an older couple in the church who had taken a special interest in him. He appreciated Steve especially. Some men in the church, having once learned of his background, avoided Wayne. But Steve was different. He had always gone out of his way to show Wayne the fatherly love and acceptance he'd never had.

When Wayne confided his thoughts about marriage, Steve and Candy encouraged him warmly. "I'm glad you're looking in that direction," Steve smiled, "but there's no need to hurry. Continue to pray for God's guidance. We'll be praying, too."

Wayne had not yet dared to bring up marriage when he was face to face with Hinano, but as often happened, they had long talks about it on the phone.

One night in the midst of a long telephone visit, Wayne said suddenly, "you know, if I married again I'd still have a financial burden because of my old family. Remember how I neglected my child support?"

He waited for some indication of disgust, but Hinano merely said, "Yes, I remember."

"Well, I've been thinking that if I want God's blessing in this new ministry, I've got to make restitution to Patricia and my kids, even if they are grown already."

He waited for an explosion or at least a negative groan, but nothing came. "Are you listening, Nano?"

"Yes, of course. I was just putting Rocky out."

"Rocky?"

"You know, Rocky. He's my baby. Oh, Wayne, you are something. Rocky barks at you every time you come over."

Wayne felt annoyed. "Well, I guess you didn't hear anything I said."

"Oh, yes, I did. You said that even though you married again, you'd still feel obligated to pay back what you owe your first family."

"That's right, so—"

"Wayne, I'm pleased that you have such high standards. I think that's great. My first husband was terribly irresponsible. He would never have thought of doing such a thing."

"But, Nano, it will probably be a struggle financially."

"Wayne, if you're doing the right thing, I know God will bless you."

"But, Nano, honey, I've got other huge debts. It's going to be tough."

"We can do it, because God will help us. I'd be willing to marry you now if it would help you out."

"Really, Nano? You're wonderful. I've never known anyone like you."

Wayne was so stunned by Hinano's generosity that he never quite remembered how that phone conversation ended. He only knew that what she had said was encouraging. Maybe he shouldn't wait a lot longer.

He began thinking of an engagement ring, but he didn't know her ring size. He imagined all kinds of scenarios in which he might be able to find out. "Nano, do you have some gloves I could borrow?" But naturally she would ask why, and he found no plausible answer for that.

Then one day he happened to hear Hinano at the salon talking to one of her clients while she was giving a manicure. "It's funny about me," he heard her say. "My ring size is the same as my shoe size—six and a half."

Wayne sneaked away unseen, smiling gleefully to himself as he began to make plans for a very special engagement ring. Next morning found him at the jeweler's up the street gazing at a gorgeous diamond ring. Wayne appreciated beautiful things, especially exquisite jewelry, and this ring was superb with its large marquise diamond flanked by two triangular diamonds. They sparkled royally in their solid-gold setting. He knew he had to get it. He could imagine the sensation at the salon when Hinano appeared with that ring on her hand. "Wow, did you see the ring Wayne gave Nano?"

"How much?" he asked the clerk.

"It's on special this week. Only $7,500. It's a splendid piece. You have very good tastes."

Wayne gulped and hesitated. "It'll have to be layaway, I'm afraid."

"Sure, that's fine. How about $600 down?"

It would take almost the last dollar in his account, but he agreed and left the shop walking on air.

But a few days later an unexpected Steve arrived in the mail from his insurance company. He had borrowed $600 on his policy for a limited term. The time was up. He had to pay it back by the deadline or be penalized.

Wayne had only one recourse. He trudged back to the jeweler and sheepishly retrieved his down payment.

"I'll be back for the ring as soon as I can," he smiled stiff-
ly. He knew it was all bravado. He had no idea where
the $7,500 would come from. His heart felt like stone.
His feet moved like weights as he worried. *O God, does
this mean the wedding's off?*

For a few days that grim thought knocked around
in his mind like a shabby sneaker in a clothes dryer.
Then another thought struck him. *Perhaps God is just trying me. Hinano is the woman for me, but this is not the time.*
He kept pondering, wondering, praying.

As his birthday approached in mid-August, he had
no heart for parties and celebrations. He decided to go
to the condo of a friend, a place at Gulf Shores where he
had often gone before. He would go alone to think and
pray.

During his two days there, he walked the beach and
watched the ceaseless waves, longing very much to be
married—properly, lovingly, under God's blessing. He
wanted what he had never had—a secure and loving
home.

Sure, there would be many problems, but Hinano
was so upbeat and full of faith. And the way she accepted him. Even now more than a year since their first
meeting, he never ceased to be amazed at her wonderful tolerance and—yes—her love. He would never find
anyone else like her. Of that he was sure.

"Well, God," he said at last, "I know you led me to
her, but I'm leaving the timing up to you."

He didn't have long to wait.

As soon as he walked into the salon the following
Monday, Tony Vincent, one of the newer stylists, ap-

proached him with a very serious expression. "I have to see you alone," he said.

Wayne wondered immediately if he might be quitting. He hoped not. Tony was a good stylist and a Christian brother besides.

Facing Wayne at the front of the shop, away from the others, Tony began talking about a ring he had once bought when he'd been planning to marry. The plans had long since fallen through, but just the day before he had chanced upon this ring in his dresser drawer. "And the strange thing is," he went on, "that last night when I was praying, the Holy Spirit told me to give this ring to you for Hinano." Tony gulped, his face red. "For y'all to get married," he finished.

He opened his hand, and there was what seemed to Wayne to be a very ordinary-looking ring. Its tiny clusters of triangular diamond chips seemed quite pathetic compared with the splendid diamond he had just lost.

"Well, thanks, Tony, but I just can't take this. I just can't." And he backed away.

But Tony followed him saying, "This isn't my idea, you know. I'm going to be obedient whether you like it or not." He grabbed Wayne's hand, pressed the ring into it, and turned to go. "The Holy Spirit told me to give it to you, and I have and that's it."

Wayne followed him then. "Well, at least let me pay for it."

"Nothin' doin'. Money wasn't mentioned." And with that Tony went off, leaving Wayne with a piece of jewelry he didn't want. Anger and rebellion welled up within him and, avoiding talking to any of the incoming workers, he fled to the shelter of the back room.

Wayne stared at the ring in his hand, then looked up to heaven. Between clenched teeth he said, "O God, what am I supposed to do? This ring looks so puny!"

You were giving Hinano a ring you couldn't afford, came the familiar voice. *That has been the pattern of your life. You always start with things you can't afford.*

Wayne gave a quick sob, pressed his fists to his mouth and listened. *That ring wasn't really for Hinano. It was for you. You didn't want to give it to her because you love her. You wanted people to be impressed when she showed them her ring.*

By this time, Wayne had melted. Sinking into a chair, he began to weep, *God, I never thought of it that way.*

But God wasn't finished. *The ring you're now holding is worth more than anything you could buy because I gave it to you.*

At those words, Wayne put his head down and sobbed. When he finally left the room, he truly did treasure the simple ring.

He went back to the jeweler's and had the diamonds mounted on a gold band that would match the ring he planned for himself.

"When's the wedding?" the jeweler asked.

"Well, I haven't asked her yet," Wayne smiled a little shyly. Then his face brightened. "But I plan to this Friday night."

23

With This Ring

When Wayne carried his anxieties home that Friday night after he proposed to Hinano, he was no more in touch with his Cajun roots than his parents had been when they'd moved to Valverde, Louisiana, more than forty years before. Had he been thinking of history, however, he might have found a surprising analogy to his own life.

Perhaps back in 1803, France did not realize what she was doing when she sold the vast tract of land, known as the Louisiana Purchase, to the United States. At that time, Wayne's ancestors had for a small price entered upon a bounteous country, wealthy beyond their dreams.

God, of course, had known exactly what He wanted when He gave Wayne the simple engagement ring for Hinano, free of charge. And now, because he had committed his life to God, Wayne longed to enter upon the wondrous territory called matrimony.

Sunday morning Wayne drove to church, his mind still in turmoil. Was it only Friday night that he had asked Hinano to marry him—a scant two days ago? It seemed years since Friday. Saturday morning he'd gone to the shop at daybreak to pray that she would say yes. The long, tortuous workday had followed while he waited in suspense. He had confided in his fellow workers, and they all had watched with him for her answer. Thomas had been especially tense, anxiously questioning Wayne whenever he thought Hinano might have communicated with him.

Wayne was sure the clientele had had no idea of the underlying tension. He was proud of his staff. They'd gone about their work as smoothly and skillfully as ever.

And Hinano—without a hint of his ring on her finger—was quite unconscious of being the center of so much scrutiny. She went about work with her usually bright competence, but Wayne could sense an abstracted air about her whenever she had a moment alone. Thus the long day passed without her saying a word about her decision. That night memories of the events that had brought him to that moment had filled his mind. Sleep had been fitful.

As he sat in church, Wayne tried his best to keep his mind on the service. But mostly he found himself praying, "Lord, let her answer be yes. It was you who brought us together. You can't deny it, Lord."

His glance strayed often to the choir where Hinano sat in her usual place singing with all her heart. She seemed quite oblivious to his prayers. And there was still no ring on her finger. Desperately he wondered what she was thinking.

Somehow he got through the day. Much as he wanted to, he didn't pursue her for an answer. This was no time for overkill. Evening came, and he went to the 7:30 church service as usual. Anxiously he watched for her, keeping an eye on all entrances. Finally she came in with one of her girl friends, smiling and nodding at him as they found places a few seats away.

Still no ring on her finger.

Driving home, he wondered what to do. He couldn't live in this suspense much longer. Dejectedly he sat in his living room, staring at the wall. "God, you'll have to give me patience. Help me to be calm." He forced himself to take a deep breath and to lean back in his chair. "Lord, if she says no now, you'll bring her around later, won't you?"

He heard the front door latch and knew it was his cousin Jessica with her son Rob. For the past few months he had been sharing his apartment with them. A few months earlier Jessica had proved to be an answer to prayer. He and Thomas and Hinano had been praying for someone to help run the financial side of the salon, and God had led them to Jessica. She needed work because her husband had deserted her. She'd had business training and had proved to be a true lifesaver in straightening out the business affairs at the shop. Wayne always thanked God for this rescue.

They came in now, first Rob with his bashful grin, and Jessica with a knowing smile. "Any word from the lady?"

Wayne smiled ruefully. "Not yet. But I'm still praying."

It was just at that moment that the doorbell rang, and Jessica, who was still in the entry hall, opened the door.

Wayne's heart gave a leap as he saw Hinano. She greeted Jessica and Rob with a smile, then turned to face him with shining eyes. "Wayne, we've got a lot to talk about." She held out her hands to him. His ring was on her finger.

Wayne took her hands, kissed the ring finger, held her a minute, then led her to a seat on the sofa beside him. There was no passionate love scene. Wayne, having come from such a cold, undemonstrative family, still had trouble feeling comfortable with spontaneous tenderness. Besides, they had conducted their courtship mainly as a friendship, and they were wary of sexual passion. They wanted to make all decisions coolly, under God's guidance.

Jessica and Rob had disappeared upstairs, and Hinano began at once to make plans. She took a pad and pencil from her purse and began jotting down items. Tapping her pencil against her lips, she gazed reflectively at Wayne. "I've just been thinking. We'll have to help Jessica find another apartment before I move in. I was just talking to Peter. He thinks he may know of a good one. Not too expensive, either."

"That's another thing," Wayne put in. "Your brother will have to find a new roommate, won't he? He'll need help with the rent when you're gone."

Hinano giggled. "Wayne, this is crazy. We haven't even set our date yet." They both laughed as Hinano took out her calendar.

Inwardly, Wayne was contrasting his present light heart with the dejection he had felt only moments before. Was he surprised at Hinano's answer? Not really. Now he felt somehow it had been inevitable, that he'd always known what it would be.

Hinano was chewing her finger and making marks on a tiny calendar. "Let's have a May wedding," she bubbled. "What do you say? It's such a lovely time of year."

Six months. To Wayne it seemed an interminable corridor of days. How many pitfalls there might be in six months. But he agreed for the moment, telling himself he'd work on the date later. He changed the subject to the honeymoon, and they continued planning until well past eleven.

That night, though not torn with his former worries, Wayne still had a hard time falling asleep.

Within the next few days they set up a weekly appointment for marriage counseling with Pastor Culpepper. As they walked into his office that first evening, he smiled on them approvingly. "I can't think of any engagement I've been happier about," he greeted them. "I know God has been leading you."

Once they were seated, the pastor began talking quietly. "In recent years, marriage has been going out of style in our western world. Some have even said it's coming to an end." He grinned at the absurdity of the idea. "But I believe the tide is turning. Even unbelievers have begun to see that without a trustworthy commitment a stable family can't be maintained."

"Children need both a father and a mother," Wayne interjected.

"That's right. You've been realizing what an absent father meant in your own life."

Hinano spoke up. "Some people don't believe in marriage because they're scared to death of commitment."

"It's scary," Wayne blurted fervently, then felt his face redden, afraid he might have admitted too much.

The pastor nodded. "It's an awesome commitment. In times past, the constraints of society kept marriage together, but not anymore." He paused a minute, then spoke slowly, "We might go so far as to say that without God, marriage actually demands the impossible of human beings."

The pastor reached for his Bible. "Jesus said in Matthew 19, 'With men this is impossible; but with God all things are possible.'" He looked at them each in turn. "Already you've both known many miracles in your lives, and God isn't finished with you yet. Not by a long way."

"Pastor always seems to put courage into me," Wayne commented as they drove home.

"I'd say God uses him to increase our faith," Hinano agreed. "If we didn't have God to hang on to, we wouldn't consider this marriage for five minutes."

At their second counseling session, the pastor gave them each a marriage profile form to fill out. They recorded their feelings on several issues, including finances and sex. They also described their habits and gave preferences and details from their personal lives. They handed the papers back to the pastor, and after he had perused them for a moment, he said, "Who's Rocky?"

Hinano glanced at Wayne, then replied, "Why, Rocky's my dog."

The pastor stepped around his desk and sat in a big chair facing them. "Well, this may pose a little problem." He switched on the lamp near his chair. "Yes, Rocky may be a problem."

He said no more about the dog, and they went on to discuss other subjects that grew out of their profiles. But in the months to come they were to remember his warning.

Over the weeks they read several books on marriage that the pastor had given them and watched videos on intimacy. Wayne learned a lot about the deep differences between the sexes, things he'd never realized before.

One evening after they had watched one of the videos, Wayne was thoughtful for a while. "Try not to think of me as some kind of savage, Nano, but a lot of this is new to me—like the idea that a woman has rights where sex is concerned. I feel stupid never to have realized that."

He took her hand as he spoke. "Where I came from a man made love to a woman because she was conquered territory. The idea that she had a right to enjoyment, too—well, it never entered our minds."

"The marriage vow does say 'cherish,'" she reminded him.

"It does, doesn't it? You'll have to be patient with me, Nano. I really do want to learn how to cherish you."

Hinano gave him a grateful look. "I guess patience is the key word for both of us," she agreed.

The pastor talked about patience, too. "Where sex is concerned, don't expect great wonders immediately," he counseled. "See yourselves sexually in the same way you see yourselves spiritually. You're developing. If you're a little awkward and things don't come up to your dreams, well, back off a little. Talk frankly about it. Above all, don't blame each other—or yourself. Be patient."

And these words also, they were to remember to their benefit.

Like many other couples before them, they said at first they would have a small wedding, but they soon realized that would be impossible. Their marriage was no ordinary event. To many people, it would be a milestone of historic proportions. Not only did they belong to an ever-growing church full of friends, but Wayne was well-known in the gay community of the city and under continual, though secret, surveillance. Here was a man who less than two years after turning his back on the homosexual life, was now very publicly taking a wife. This was one wedding celebration which simply could not be small and private.

The date for the wedding changed, too. The pastor's calendar couldn't accommodate them in May, so with some not-too-subtle pushing from Wayne, it was finally set for January 21. By the time the decision was made, they had less than three months to prepare for it.

For their honeymoon, they finally settled on Lake Tahoe, a resort on the California-Nevada border. Hinano had hoped for Hawaii but realized that January would be peak season there and crowded. Thus the days rushed by in a bustle of preparations. Usually they closed each day by reporting to each other, often by phone.

Hinano was especially excited one night. "You'll never believe this, Wayne, but God gave me a real miracle today."

"Really?"

"Mom and I went out shopping for my wedding dress—our first trip, you understand. I expected to spend days looking. But the very first shop we walked into and the very first dress I tried on was perfect. It didn't even have to be altered. It cost twelve hundred dollars."

Wayne gasped. "You mean you got it?"

"Calm yourself," she chuckled. "That was the *original* price. I got it for exactly $605."

"Well, I guess like you said about the ring, that has God all over it!" Wayne laughed.

"It sure does. Isn't He wonderful? It's just little things like that that assure me I've made the right decision."

Wayne gave a lot of thought to his choices for the wedding party. He decided to ask Steve King and Tim Miller to be groomsmen, but he wondered about his third choice—the best man. Traditionally, it would be the bride's brother, but the one he really wanted was Thomas. He thought Thomas should go through this experience with him and feel God's official seal of approval on this—the holy estate of matrimony. But would Hinano approve? It was a delicate situation. He went to ask Joyce Miller.

Joyce looked at him a long moment while he felt increasingly uncertain. "Well, I thought it would be—what I mean is—well, don't you think he should go through the process with me?"

Joyce agreed. "I see nothing wrong with it, though there may be some raised eyebrows when people realize who Thomas is." Then she chuckled. "But what a wonderful witness to God's power to deliver."

With that encouragement, Wayne approached Hinano. They were in the back room of the salon, and because of his nervousness, he wasn't very tactful. "I'd like Thomas to be my best man," he blurted. "Is that okay?"

Hinano gazed at him with large solemn eyes; then her face brightened. "Yes, I think so. In fact, it really would be quite appropriate."

Wayne was too overcome to speak. He had truly expected an objection or even an explosion. With an eloquent look of gratitude he said, "Thank you, Nano," and went out quickly to hide his tears.

That night Wayne called Hinano for their usual reporting session. "You know, Nano, I'm beginning to feel whole for the first time in my life. I think maybe I do belong to the human race. I'm a normal male after all."

The tinkle of Hinano's laughter was good to hear. "You know what?" she observed. "Moses is singing— for the first time in months."

"Moses?" Wayne was quite nonplused. He flicked through a mental card file, trying to think which relative he might have missed.

Hinano was still laughing. "My canary, silly. He hasn't uttered a note in months. I think he's feeling all the happiness around here."

24

The Caress of an Angel

Thomas straightened his tuxedo lapel and turned his black Lincoln into the car wash. "If you and Hinano are going to leave for your honeymoon in my car," he announced, "I want to have it washed."

Wayne looked at him strangely. "In our tuxedos? We've only got an hour before the ceremony."

"Plenty of time," Thomas said firmly. He guided the vehicle to the starting point. The two men got out.

"What about my luggage?" Wayne asked, still concerned about the delay.

"It'll be fine in the trunk." Thomas led Wayne to a bench in the waiting area near the viewing window. Wayne carefully inspected the seat before he let his clothes touch it. Then he gingerly sat, feeling awkward in his formal attire.

After a few moments, another man in formal dress rushed up. Wayne recognized him as one of the ushers for his wedding. "Thomas," the man panted, "you're needed at the church for pictures."

"But my car—" Thomas glanced out the window. The huge hula-skirt wash strips wriggled over a small red Honda. The Lincoln was nowhere in sight.

"Let Wayne drive it back," the usher suggested. "He's not supposed to get to the church before the ceremony anyway."

Thomas rose. "Good idea." He turned to Wayne. "Fine with you?" Wayne nodded weakly, and the two men strode out the door.

As soon as they had disappeared, Wayne felt even more out of place in his tuxedo. Everyone seemed to be staring at him. Then a horrible thought struck him. He patted his back pocket and grimaced. *I didn't bring a cent. How will I pay for the car wash?*

Stepping to the window, he saw Thomas's car slide into the wash cycle. Its black surface gleamed under sprays of water and suds.

Sharp edges of anxiety made his stomach tighten. *Hinano will be frantic if I don't make it to the wedding on time.* He brushed some dust flecks off his pants as his old fears resurfaced. *Twenty years and I haven't touched a woman.* Hinano's sensitive face shimmered through his mind. *Am I ready for this?*

The Lincoln moved down the line, creeping relentlessly toward the rinse cycle.

This is going to be a spiritual wedding, Wayne reassured himself. *All Hinano and I want to do is glorify God. That's what we agreed on.* He pursed his lips. *And the marriage will be spiritual, too, even the physical part of it.*

But uncertainty continued to plague him. Did he really love Hinano the way a man should love a woman? Or did he just want to dress her up, buy her jewelry and display her on his arm like he had done with the other women in his past? Could he really tell the difference between his need to be respectable by having female companionship and the deep commitment of selfless love?

His thoughts were shattered by the sight of the black automobile slipping into the dazzling sunshine. Two attendants began wiping it down with towels.

"I'd better go explain my predicament," Wayne muttered as he headed for the cashier.

"I don't have any money with me," he stammered to the slim lady behind the cash register. "I'm the groom. My wedding's at 6:00." He glanced at his watch. "In less than an hour. My best man left me here, and it's his car."

The woman looked at him distrustfully.

"If you don't let me go without paying, I don't know how I'm going to get to the church on time!"

Several bystanders chuckled at his plight.

A tall, lanky attendant outside held up his hand to signal that the Lincoln was ready.

Wayne pleaded with the cashier. "You see my predicament? My fiancee will be in a panic if I don't show up. Could I come back later to settle my bill?"

The lady's face looked immovable. Wayne's spirit sank.

Suddenly, Thomas strode through the door. "Problems, Wayne?" he chortled as he came up beside his friend.

"You came back!" Relief spilled all over Wayne's face. "Nice of you to show up. I have no cash to pay for your car wash."

Thomas grinned slyly, then paid the bill. "Let's go. You don't want to be late for your own wedding, do you?" They rushed through the exit, jumped into the car, and sped off toward the church.

For the next few minutes, Wayne had little time to think. The church hummed with activity, and everyone seemed to have a question or comment for him.

The organist began to play moments before he and the groomsmen were to step through the door into the sanctuary. Thomas approached and put his hands on Wayne's shoulders, tears glistening on his cheeks.

Wayne looked deep into Thomas's eyes, friend-to-friend.

"I'm so happy for you," Thomas declared. Wayne could hear the sincerity in his voice.

"Thanks. That means a lot coming from you." Wayne's heart filled with hope that they could work out the rough spots in their relationship.

Then the moment came. As Wayne stepped into the sanctuary, he looked down the long, empty aisle to the back of the church. The first bridesmaid began promenading toward the altar. As she reached the front, a groomsman took her arm. The organ music bathed the scene with elaborate notes and elegant chords.

As a second bridesmaid started down the aisle, Wayne's hands began to dampen. Joyce flashed him an encouraging smile from the back of the church as she prompted the remaining bridesmaids. Wayne smiled back weakly. But he couldn't stop the fear aching inside. *How will I feel when Hinano walks through the door? Will I see a wife or something less?*

Suddenly, there she was. Her face shone with a special glow, and her gorgeous gown flowed like a cascade around her. She looked like something out of a dream, like Cinderella coming to meet her prince.

Wayne broke into a huge smile. "O God, thank You—she's mine," he breathed. The organ swelled into the bridal march, and everyone stood. Wayne stepped out proudly to join his bride.

Her touch was as gentle as the caress of an angel. As Wayne took her slender arm, his mind wandered back to the pictures of angels he used to see in the ornate Catholic church he attended many years ago. Back in those days, his friend Joan would sit across the aisle from him during the anointing services. At times, he felt a strong holy presence. That's when the vision would come. Waiting breathlessly, he would see angels hovering over the altar. He would look at Joan and whisper, "Do you see them?" and she'd whisper back, "Yes."

That seemed so long ago. If only he could see those beautiful angels again. How their presence would ease his mind about the big step he was taking! As he escorted Hinano to the altar, he prayed, *Lord, if there is one thing you could do for me, let the angels come to my wedding.*

Pastor Culpepper began the ring ceremony. As Wayne looked into Hinano's luminous eyes, a warm, confidence filled him. He repeated his vows in a strong, firm voice.

Amy Rice's moving soprano voice flowed over the congregation as Wayne and Hinano lit the unity candle. Wayne's fingers lingered over the small hand cradled in his. Gazing at each other, bride and groom secured the candle in place and turned toward the audience.

Now came the part of the ceremony that Wayne and Hinano had prayed about so fervently. Pastor Culpepper stepped forward and began speaking in a solemn tone, "While we want to protect the dignity of this moment, we want the Holy Spirit to touch people who may never have heard a message of love and peace. I think of the difference between the Wayne Andre I met a couple of years ago and the Wayne Andre I know today. It is simply found in two words—'personal relationship.' That is a personal relationship with Jesus Christ."

Amy began to sing "Touched Through Me" softly as Pastor Culpepper went on. "The one beautiful quality that brought Wayne and Hinano together is a miracle of love and wholeness. It's been a miracle of Jesus Christ. They desire to share with you that Jesus Christ means everything to them...."

Wayne scanned the congregation. He saw several friends who were trying to free themselves from the gay life-style. Some of his clients were seated there, too. Many had never invited Christ to be their Savior.

Pastor's voice broke in on his thoughts. "The Bible says that if we confess Jesus Christ with our mouth and believe in our heart that God raised Him from the dead, we will be born again into the family of God...."

Wayne spotted Lydia Cole. He had known her for many years, back to his days in Louisiana. She was an influential business woman in Birmingham now. She seemed to hang on every word.

His eyes lingered over his family at the front and then met his mother's gaze. She had tears of joy on her cheeks. How devastated she had looked the day he told her he was gay! That was the only other time he had seen her cry. God had begun to heal so many relationships in his life since he had found freedom in Christ.

The pastor's voice deepened in intensity. "If you will sincerely pray the prayer we are about to say as a congregation, I promise you according to God's Word that Jesus Christ will wash your sins away. You will walk out of this building born again—a new creation in Christ."

The presence of the Holy Spirit seemed intense at that moment. Wayne squeezed Hinano's hand, and she squeezed back.

"Would you repeat after me?" Pastor Culpepper urged his listeners.

Wayne bowed his head.

"Father God, I come to you now—"

Suddenly, a sublime feeling spread through Wayne's body. A quiet voice whispered inside him, *The angels are here.* He looked up.

Gathered over the congregation were the white-robed angels—the same beautiful beings he had seen so many years ago. They hovered over the congregation like a dome, their arms interlocked, creating a glorious network.

Wayne was stunned by the beauty. "Thank you, Lord," he breathed.

Soon the ceremony ended, and he and Hinano strode down the aisle to the back of the church. His heart overflowed with joy.

After leaving the sanctuary, they waited for the rest of the wedding party to join them. As Joan who had been one of the bridesmaids came up, Wayne asked if she had seen the angels.

Her face lit up. "It was the most marvelous display I've ever seen in my life."

"Wasn't it, though?" Wayne said mostly to himself. And he took his new wife by the hand.

Hours later, Wayne escorted Hinano into the lobby of the Wynfrey Hotel. He had reserved a room on the security level since neither he nor Hinano wanted uninvited guests on their first night together.

When they reached the room, Wayne opened the door wide to let Hinano walk through in her gorgeous gown and train. He grabbed their suitcases and set them down next to the bed.

As he returned to close the door, panic tightened his chest. *It's just her and me. What am I going to do now? I don't want to be self-centered and only think about my needs like I did with Patricia.* He noticed the fifty buttons running down the back of Hinano's wedding dress as she set her small case on the desk. They seemed like a formidable barrier. *Am I going to be able to go through with this? She's so sensitive. I don't want to hurt her. Can I have normal feelings again after all these years?*

"This room is magnificent," Hinano smiled as she arranged her dress and sat delicately on the bed.

Wayne's eye spotted the shell-pink telephone beside the bed. "Are you hungry?"

"Yes, now that you mention it. I'm starving."

"Why don't I order us up some dinner?" Wayne called room service and selected a three-course meal. After he put down the receiver, he felt his tension ease a little. He removed his tuxedo jacket and sat next to Hinano on the bed. His hands trembled as he put his arm around her. "Mrs. Andre," he announced in a solemn voice, "you look gorgeous."

She smiled demurely and a blush spread across her cheeks.

At that moment, Wayne wanted to take her into his arms and kiss her, but he hesitated. Then his fears returned, and his desire drained away.

They sat silently for a long time. To Wayne, they seemed frozen in time, side-by-side yet miles apart. *Should I touch her? What does she want? Is she as nervous as I am?*

A knock at the door made them both jump. Wayne answered it. A waiter brought in a tray of covered dishes and set it on the table.

Hinano laughed. "It's going to be a challenge to eat in this dress."

After the waiter left, Wayne helped her up to the table. The white dress billowed up behind her, reminding him once again of the angels who had come to his wedding. He felt his confidence return.

Pulling a chair up to the table, he served her a crisp, elegant Caesar salad. They chatted lightly throughout the meal.

When Hinano pushed away her chocolate mousse, Wayne's nervousness returned in full force. "Let's pray," he suggested.

Hand-in-hand, they dedicated the rest of the evening and their new marriage to the Lord. Some of the tenseness seemed to lighten, and Wayne led Hinano back to the bed where he began unfastening the long row of buttons. His fingers fumbled over each shiny half-pearl. Hinano began describing how happy she felt as she walked up the aisle. Wayne could hear the strain in her voice. *She's trying to make me feel more comfortable*, he realized.

Finally he reached the last button. He frantically tried to remember what the books Pastor Culpepper had given him during the premarital sessions had recommended about the wedding night. The advice seemed clinical now. So cut and dried. How could he put the suggestions into practice to meet Hinano's needs? How would she react if he messed up the evening?

"Let me get my negligee and I'll dress in the bathroom," Hinano offered sweetly. "I want to look perfect for you."

Again relief rushed over Wayne. Hinano always seemed to understand his fears. "That sounds beautiful," he said quickly.

With a rustle of silk, she knelt beside her suitcase and unzipped it. She began gently searching through her clothes, then gasped. "Look, Wayne." She held up a bulging pair of tube socks.

"What on earth?" Wayne knelt next to her. "The tops are sewn shut!"

Hinano pulled out a navy-blue blouse. Its arms flopped oddly.

Wayne ripped open the stitches at the top of the sock. "Birdseed!" he exclaimed as a trickle of seeds poured onto the carpet.

Hinano giggled. "Your family did this! They said they were going to do something to mess up our honeymoon."

Wayne snapped open his suitcase. He pulled out trousers with bulging pockets, fat round underwear and even an oddly shaped sweater. "They've sewn every opening shut," Wayne chuckled. "It must have taken them hours. They got us all right."

"I've got some little scissors in here somewhere," Hinano offered, rummaging through her suitcase.

"Let's use this wastebasket." Wayne slid over a good-sized one.

They sat on the floor and pulled out their clothes one-by-one. Wayne snipped off the stitches and Hinano poured out the birdseed. When a sock-full of seed accidently emptied into Hinano's lap, Wayne grabbed his camera and took a snapshot.

Feigning irritation, Hinano poured handfuls of birdseed onto Wayne's hair and took a picture of him, too. While he picked the mess off his head and clothes, Hinano disappeared into the bathroom. Moments later she reappeared in a pale-blue, sheer negligee. Wayne's heart almost stopped. For so many years, he had only seen and felt hard, male bodies. Now here was this soft creature. Anxiety pierced his mind.

Gently and patiently, Hinano waited until he undressed, and they slipped into bed together. The birdseed lay forgotten on the floor.

She nestled close. Wayne put his arms around her, then lay still. He knew he wasn't ready yet. He felt petrified.

Hinano began to pray softly. When she finished, Wayne did, too. "O Lord," he pleaded, "I just want to glorify you in this marriage. Please help me be a godly husband to Hinano. I know you have forgiven me. Now help me put my past behind and start over. Give us the strength to go through the hard times ahead."

When he finished, Hinano rolled onto her back and began talking about how beautiful the wedding was. Wayne described the incident at the car wash. They laughed about what the other people must have thought.

Gradually, the tenseness eased from Wayne's muscles. He felt Hinano relax, too.

After some time, Wayne admitted cautiously, "Hinano, I saw the most glorious sight during pastor's prayer."

He could sense her eyes on him in the dimness.

He paused, a little apprehensive. "The entire sanctuary ceiling was filled with angels. It was so beautiful, I could hardly breathe."

She raised her head. "Oh, Wayne? Like the ones you saw years ago?"

He nodded. "The same. And Joan saw them, too."

"It was the Lord's blessing on our marriage," she whispered.

"That's what I thought, too. I wish you had seen them."

"That would have been wonderful. But I'm so glad *you* did." She snuggled next to him again, and he kissed her. Silence filled the room. He could hear the numbers turn on his digital alarm clock. He held her tightly. Moments later, he felt Hinano's body relax in sleep.

Closing his eyes, he whispered a thank-you prayer for such a tender, intuitive wife. Then he, too, drifted off to sleep.

The next morning, Wayne and Hinano rose early. They cleaned up the birdseed the best they could and headed for the airport. Their flight took them to San Francisco before noon where they rented a car. Within the hour, they were on their way to Lake Tahoe for the rest of their honeymoon.

The January sun shone pale through the windows. Wayne found a radio station that played soft, Christian music, and Hinano moved close to him. At her touch, sensation shot through his body. "Hinano," he said softly, "I'd like to take you in my arms right now."

She touched his cheek with a whisper-soft caress, her eyes shining like candles.

Wayne's heart began to pound. With a start, he realized how natural and right his feelings were. He didn't have to force himself to physically desire his wife; he felt so masculine and normal. The Lord had given him the right sensations.

Right then, he knew they would consummate their marriage that evening. He took her hand. "It's right, so right," he said with a tremor in his voice. "I know it will take some time to feel completely comfortable, but I really want you."

She looked deep into his eyes. "Yes, it feels right to me, too. Isn't the Lord gracious?"

He nodded and turned his eyes back to the road. They would have a wonderful time in Tahoe!

25

Voyage of Discovery

The first serious trouble after the honeymoon was just what Pastor Culpepper had warned about. Rocky, Hinano's dog, angered Wayne. It wasn't just his yapping or the way he left his toys and half-chewed Kings around the house. The most irritating thing was Hinano's attachment to him. The way she would pick up that little Shih Tzu, cuddling him, petting him, even kissing him, was truly disgusting.

In the family where Wayne grew up, dogs were meant to stay outside. They were supposed to be useful—helping on the hunt or herding cows or guarding the home—not living inside like people, sitting on chairs, sleeping on the beds, or eating fancy food. A dog being treated like family—well, that was just too much in Wayne's opinion.

One night he and Hinano returned late from a meeting at church. It had been a long day because they had gone straight to church after work, and they were both weary. Rocky met them at the door with his usual frantic welcome. That is, he welcomed Hinano. The dislike between him and Wayne was mutual, so the dog had as little to do with the man of the house as possible.

Hinano scooped up her puppy and began scratching his ears. "Did my baby miss me?" she cooed.

Wayne strode through the house to the kitchen. Bits of dog food were scattered around the pet's dish and a little of the drinking water had spilled. "What a mess!" he huffed, stumbling over a half-chewed King by a kitchen chair. "How long will I have to put up with this filth?"

He spied a tattered tennis ball under the stepstool. "Look at the way his stuff is scattered around here. You'd think we lived in a kennel." He kicked the ball, and it shot across the floor to the stove, then bounced back to hit the door jamb just as Hinano walked in from the living room.

"What's *your* problem?" She set the dog down and met Wayne's angry gaze with a fiery glare of her own. "I can't believe a grown man has to make such a fuss about one poor little dog!"

Wayne shoved the water dish with his foot and more water splashed on the floor. "Well, this 'poor little dog' is making a pigpen of this place."

Hinano gave a mocking laugh. "A pigpen! Really, Wayne. Just listen to yourself."

Rocky, hearing the anger in Hinano's tone, began barking sharply. His yapping, harsh and insistent, was not at all difficult to understand. No one was going to threaten his beloved mistress if he could help it. Especially not this large male intruder who now took so much of her attention.

"Can't you shut him up?" Wayne demanded. "Where I come from, animals are animals and people are people. We don't confuse the two."

Without a word to Wayne, Hinano swept up the dog and shut him in the bathroom. "Come, baby," she soothed, "before you get killed."

"Baby! Baby!" Wayne jeered. "You'd better listen to yourself. He's no baby. He's a full-grown, pampered, spoiled *animal*, and I've had enough!"

Hinano's eyes filled with tears. "Wayne, I do believe you're jealous." She blew her nose on a tissue. "I can't believe a grown man could actually be jealous of a poor little dog." She picked up the gnawed King and the tennis ball and put them out of sight in the broom closet. "I can't stand your pickiness," she sniffed. "Human beings aren't meant to live in a sterile laboratory."

Collapsing on a chair by the table, she sat chin in hand while the tears coursed down her cheeks.

Wayne marched by in stony silence and stomped out the front door, slamming it behind him. A spring haze hung over the valley and the smell of growing things was in the air. He looked down the quiet street where each street light carried a halo of mist, took a deep breath and began to walk.

He strolled a good while, his mind in a daze. He couldn't have told how long it was before he was willing to listen to the quiet voice persisting through the layers of anger. *Wayne, is this how you intend to live with your wife?*

Turning then, he quickened his pace and headed back home. When he opened the front door, all was still except for Rocky scratching and whining at the bathroom door. He stepped through to the kitchen where Hinano sat, her eyes red, staring blankly at the wall. Drawing out a chair, he sat down. "Look, Hinano," he began, "we've got to talk."

"Yes, I suppose we do." She gave a long shuddering sigh. "And I guess there won't be any peace around here unless—" Her voice broke and she dabbed at her eyes with the damp wad in her hand. "Oh, Wayne, why do you have to be so unreasonable?"

"I've never had to put up with animals in the house, that's all!" Wayne got up and began pacing the floor. "Maybe I'd better make some coffee."

They talked while Wayne measured coffee into a pot and filled it with water. Their argument over Rocky continued into the wee hours of the morning, at times becoming a shouting match.

Finally, they reached a shaky truce. Hinano would try to find a home for Rocky, but it would have to be the right place. She would not just dump him. And Wayne agreed this would take time.

Tensions eased between them after that. Knowing the dog was only a temporary inconvenience made it easier for Wayne to tolerate him, and so for the time being, peace prevailed.

The weeks passed and things went more smoothly as they gradually got used to each other's habits. Also, they began to realize their hardest adjustments were not going to be sexual as they and their counselors had once feared. The stickiest problems arose from the same difficult areas encountered by many other couples—misunderstandings because of their different cultures and their previous dysfunctional families.

Wayne, for instance, found it hard to show affection in public because his family never had. One Sunday Hinano's irritation at this spilled over as they drove home from church. "What's with you anyhow, Wayne?" she snapped. "Are you ashamed of me, or what? I try to take your hand in church; you pull back." Her voice trembled a little. "I put my arm around you as we're walking out, and you actually push me away. What's going on?"

Wayne heaved a weary sigh. "Oh, it's my family background, I guess." He reached for her hand, and his voice grew gentle. "I'm sorry, Nano. But I never saw my father kiss my mother. And except when I was small, he never kissed or hugged me either."

Hinano shook her head. "That's hard to imagine."

"Well, honey, that's the way it was. I guess I came from a pretty cold family."

After that Wayne tried to be more affectionate in public, but it was hard to alter old habits, and change came slowly.

Being open to showing tenderness, however, was not the only thing Wayne had to learn. His culture was insensitive in other ways. The men often joked about women. They also derided their children and each other. No one was ever safe from ridicule for long. Mistakes were not suffered kindly and weaknesses were gleefully pointed out. Sensitive feelings found little consideration in such a culture.

One evening the Andres invited the Millers over for dinner. The roast beef, vegetable casserole and the tossed salad were all delicious. But Hinano had some trouble with the pie, and the crust was tough. As Wayne tried to cut it, he laughed, "Sorry about this crust, folks." He made a face as he carried a bit to his mouth. "Reminds me of the old song, 'No matter how tough the steak may be, you can still stick your fork in the gravy.'"

The laughter was strained, and Hinano got up to get more coffee, her lips pursed in a thin line.

Joyce Miller quickly changed the subject, and the rest of the evening continued well. But when the guests had gone, Hinano snipped at Wayne. "You really made me feel great tonight, Wayne. Just great!" Her voice resembled the sharp edge of a knife. "Don't you think I felt bad enough about that pie without you calling attention to it?"

The unshed tears in her eyes annoyed him. "Oh, Nano, don't you know I was only kidding? Can't you take a joke?"

"Joke?" she echoed. "Joke? It's not a joke when you hold me up to ridicule in front of people!" Turning on her heels, she swept out the back door, slamming it behind her.

In a few minutes she walked back into the kitchen with a little more calmness, but the hurt look on her face was still plain to Wayne. "I'm sorry, Nano. It's hard for me to change. In my family we always kidded everybody about almost everything."

"Well, I'm just not used to it." She picked up a dish towel and began to dry the last of the dinner dishes. "I'm not sure I ever will be." She lowered her lashes, then looked up with the melting look that always touched him. "This is my home," she went on, her voice soft. "When you expose me publicly like that, I feel betrayed. If I can't be safe in my own home—" She left the sentence unfinished and put a drinking glass in the cupboard.

Wayne had never thought of home in quite that light. "I guess a girl should be able to feel safe in her own home," he admitted.

"Thanks, Wayne." She threw him a shy glance. "And I know I've got to work on not being quite so sensitive." She made a wry face. "I think it's called 'growing up.'"

Wayne also found it hard to trust Hinano out of his sight, mostly because in the homosexual life he'd known for so long, his relationships had all been filled with suspicion and uncertainty.

One night Hinano came home from choir practice around 10:00 to find him quite upset. "Where were you?" he demanded. "Choir practice started at eight and ended at nine. Where've you been all this time?"

She looked nonplused. "Why, I was just talking to everybody. I always do." She set down her Bible and music. "After all, I go to church as much to see my friends as anything else."

Wayne turned to his book and growled, "Next time, call. All you have to do is pick up the phone. Then I won't worry."

Hinano heaved an exasperated sigh. "I suppose so, Wayne. But I've been independent for a long time, and I'm not used to being on a leash."

Wayne said nothing, but he was fighting an inward battle between the panic forces from the old life and the quiet voice that said, *This is your wife, Wayne. She's an individual.*

Later Hinano came to sit on the hassock by his chair. "I suppose you find it especially hard to trust me, after what you went through in your old life." She put her hand over his. "There wasn't much trust there, was there?"

He looked at her gratefully. "Not much," he shrugged. "I'm trying to trust. Marriage has to have trust, but try to remember how hard it is for me."

Despite the miracles they had known in the past and their continuing dedication to God, they sometimes had evidence that the enemy was not giving up easily. One night Wayne awoke with a start, gasping for air. He was dimly conscious of Hinano holding him and saying desperately, "It's all right. It's all right. You're right here with me."

Frantic for air, he bolted upright. "Something was trying to strangle me," he choked. "There were cold fingers around my throat. A dense shadow hovering over me." He took a deep breath. "It was dreadful."

Hinano still held him, stroking his cheek. "Let's pray," she suggested in a shaky voice.

Together they knelt by the bed and committed themselves to God's care. Gradually Wayne stopped shaking. Then setting his mind on the evidences of God's care in the past, he finally fell asleep.

The nightmares continued from time to time, despite their prayers and the prayers of their friends. Finally Hinano began to detect something unwholesome about the house.

One morning after they had struggled through another nightmare, she announced a decision. "Wayne, we've got to get out of here. There's darkness here. It's not just in your head. There's an evil presence here." She hugged herself as if to keep from shivering. "You lived your other life here. There are memories—too many memories. We've got to get out."

Wayne dropped into his armchair looking at her thoughtfully. "Maybe it *is* the house. I don't know." He chewed his knuckle a minute. "Good places are hard to find, but I guess it wouldn't hurt to look."

Hinano's eyes brightened. "Let's go looking tomorrow. God will help us. I know He will."

Hinano was right. The first day they found a spacious townhouse at a reasonable rent. It was in Inverness on the southern side of the city overlooking the beautiful Kahaba Valley. They immediately began to prepare for the move.

Once the decision was made, Hinano realized she could delay no longer about finding a home for Rocky. A friend at church knew of a girl called Sonya who wanted a Shih Tzu and told Hinano that the girl would call. When the phone rang that Monday morning, Hinano's stricken expression startled Wayne. *Anyone would think she was waiting for news of a loved one's death,* he thought.

But as the conversation continued, Hinano's excitement told him something unusual was happening.

When she hung up the phone, her face was radiant. "Wayne, it's really, really wonderful!" She shook her head. "God is so good."

They walked out to the car and Hinano continued explaining as they drove to work. "Well, I don't have to tell you how determined I've been that Rocky should have a good home."

"No, you don't have to tell me."

"Well, anyway I've been praying. And I had these special conditions in mind, but I didn't tell anyone except the Lord." She paused for breath. "Like I wanted Rocky to be an inside dog. He's never had to live outside. And I wanted him to have companionship, not to be alone all the time—a lot of things." She laughed. "You won't believe it, but this Sonya fulfills every one of my conditions, and she didn't even know. And she wants him right away. Isn't that great?"

Wayne smiled and sighed with relief.

One bright Sunday in October Hinano stopped to gaze at the view from the living room of their new home. The hills were still green, stretching to the horizon under a clear sky. Faint in the distance, she caught the pattern of geese flying south, while here and there a grove of trees glowed in bronze or gold.

She turned to Wayne who'd come to stand beside her. "I feel so thankful this morning."

Wayne put an arm around her. "Yes, I always feel glad on Sunday—no work," he laughed. "My old friends would never believe it, but I really look forward to church."

"But of course. And why not? The church is our family," Hinano joined. "They give us the support we never had growing up."

"We'd never have come this far without our church friends," Wayne mused.

Hinano turned to glance at the calendar. "Know what? It's just about a year ago that you proposed to me with that tricky story about your friend and his ring."

They both laughed.

"Sure did swallow that line, didn't you?" Wayne chuckled, squeezing her affectionately. "It was great."

The next weekend they went on a yearly retreat sponsored by the Ministerial Internship Group that Wayne belonged to at church. The big lodge where they met had a large friendly room with a huge fireplace—a wonderful place for singing and praying together, for exchanging stories and sharing testimonies, and for healing.

Saturday afternoon the group gathered around the fire in praise and worship. The leader was about to close with prayer when suddenly he looked up and said, "There's someone here who thinks the Lord can't heal what's wrong with him. He doesn't have faith to receive the Lord's healing."

Wayne felt his heart thumping. He swallowed hard. *He's talking about me*, he thought. Months before on his honeymoon he had severely sprained his thumb while skiing, and it had never healed properly. For all the intervening months it had been painfully swollen and even now, it hurt him to move it. *Yes, he means me.* But Wayne was too embarrassed to speak.

The group sang another song, and several spoke of how God had blessed them. Then the leader said, "The Lord really wants to heal this person."

But still Wayne hesitated. He was no stranger to God's healing power. He'd had a serious bronchial infection, so severe that he'd had difficulty breathing or even swallowing. No antibiotics helped, and he'd begun to fear that he might have AIDS after all and that this infection was part of it.

Then one Sunday God spoke to him in church telling him to go up and be healed. He had hesitated then, too, he remembered. But when he had left his seat, finally, and climbed the stairs to the prayer room, he'd found the intercessors waiting for him. Then one woman had put her hand on his back and prayed, and immediately he'd felt healing warmth and energy, and instantly he was well.

Wayne remembered this, and still he held back. When the leader spoke the third time, Hinano nudged him and whispered, "Wayne, I think he's talking about you. You know, your thumb."

Wayne raised his hand. "I really think—that is, I think the Lord's speaking about me," he faltered, "but I'm scared to—" He grinned uncertainly. "You see, months ago on my honeymoon I was skiing, and I sprained my thumb really bad. All these months I've been suffering."

Suddenly he was conscious of Steve King coming toward him. "I guess I just don't have the faith," Wayne stopped. By this time Steve was standing beside him, laughing.

Wayne felt annoyed. "Steve, why are you laughing at me?" He felt his face grow hot. "I'm trying to be serious, and you're just laughing at me!"

Steve stopped laughing, but he still had an irrepressible grin on his face. "Wayne," he said, "the Lord already told me in the praise and worship service to take this bottle of oil and pour it over your thumb, and He would heal it."

Wayne's mouth fell open. He looked around the room at the others. "Are you serious?"

"Yes. Do you believe He can heal it?"

Suddenly everything made sense and he couldn't understand his former hesitation. "Yes," he agreed. "I do."

Someone brought newspapers to protect the carpet, and Steve poured the oil on Wayne's thumb. It grew very hot, and he began moving it from side to side and up and down. No matter what he did, he felt no pain. The swelling had disappeared. The thumb was healed.

He felt so relieved he began to laugh, and then Steve began to laugh, and the whole group joined in. Wayne knew the chorus of laughter was a kind of praise, a carefree abandonment of joy. He was conscious of a new dimension of faith that allowed them all to trust God so completely that they could laugh like children in His presence.

As January and the New Year of 1990 approached, Wayne and Hinano made plans to attend the Living

Waters Conference given by Andrew Comiskey in Ana-
heim, California.

"I guess you realize," Wayne remarked to Hinano
during one planning session, "that we'll be at this conference during our first wedding anniversary."

"Why not?" Hinano sounded glad. "I can't think of
a better way to spend it. Away from work and from all
the tensions around here. No telephone. I can hardly
wait."

They were not disappointed at the conference with
its intensive program. Although they attended the classes together, the agenda was so full they found little time
during the day to discuss what they heard. When they
finally returned to their room at night, they were full of
exciting ideas and liberating discoveries, so there was
much to talk about.

Because the room had two single beds, they had to
sleep apart. At first they were disappointed, but in the
end their long talks in the dark as they lay in their beds
created a new bond between them, one of friendship and
mutual understanding.

"I'm learning so much about myself," Hinano's eager voice came to him across the dark, still room. "I'm
beginning to see how much I drew into myself as a
child." She paused, then went on, excitement growing
in her voice. "So all these years I've been projecting a
mask to the world, trying to be what I thought people
wanted me to be. When I found Metro Church, the love
and support there began to heal me, but this conference
is helping me further. This sounds crazy, but I'm excited because—well, it's okay for me to be me."

Wayne could say the same of himself. "It's so liberating to be myself and still to be accepted. All my life I've felt either like an outsider or a loner." He stopped to think a minute. "You know, I think maybe this acceptance is another part of what God means by forgiveness. A sort of extension of it."

"Oh, yes," Hinano chimed in. "What I get from all this is that when we accept God's forgiveness, we accept ourselves." Wayne could picture her face intently pondering.

"Think about that awhile," she went on. "That means if we accept God's forgiveness of others, we accept them. There's no way out of it. We have to."

All was silent for some minutes. "You sleeping, Hinano?"

"No—I was just thinking about Thomas."

"What about him?"

"You know. He's been depressed ever since he and Helen broke off their engagement. But the other day, he told me he was relieved because he realized he wasn't ready for marriage yet."

"Yeah. It's much simpler to separate before marriage," Wayne said wryly. Feelings between him and Thomas had been tense for a while after the wedding, but not anymore. Wayne felt glad that Thomas had gotten over his jealousy.

"His new counselor is really helping him," Hinano commented. "Have you noticed how much more upbeat he is? I've never seen Thomas this way."

Wayne yawned. "I think you're right, Nano." He turned on his side and closed his eyes. As he drifted into sleep, Wayne thanked God for the new friendship he was building with Thomas. "Lord, I never would have dared to expect this. Of all the miracles you've done, this is the greatest."

The day of their anniversary was spent in classes as usual. That evening they met with some of Hinano's California family and celebrated with warmth and thankfulness. That night they dropped into bed very weary, but before sleep came, Hinano spoke suddenly out of the darkness. "Wayne, is it true?" She hesitated. "I mean, do you really enjoy making love to me?"

Wayne laughed. "Well, you saw me trying to figure out how to put these beds together, didn't you?"

Hinano giggled. "I guess it wasn't supposed to work. Not this time. I mean, these beds can only fit one way."

The rising wind clattered the palm fronds outside the window, and a rush of rain rattled against the pane. "I didn't think it ever rained here," Wayne remarked. "Listen to that."

"Oh, it does rain, sometimes. It's always news when it does."

Wayne raised himself off the bed with his elbow and peered at Hinano. "We've been having a different kind of bonding this week," he observed. "There are so many ways to be joined. We really do need a lifetime to build a marriage."

"Yes, oh, yes," Hinano breathed. "This week has been a real voyage of discovery."

"You know," Wayne interjected, "a little more than a year ago, just before our wedding—making love was the big question for me. Would I really spontaneously enjoy normal sex? Would I be able to make you happy?"

Wayne paused to steady his voice. "Well, we went into the unknown trusting God all the way, and God has healed me totally. He gave me back those lost desires, all the normal feelings."

Tears rushed to his eyes then, as he remembered what he'd come from—the darkness and fear, the uncertainty, the endless, feverish search. He slid from his bed and went over to Hinano's. "Nano, Nano, don't you know how dear you are to me?" He held her close. "Give this lonely guy a hug. He's been missing you a lot lately."

26

Miracles at Mountain Brook

Wayne's face beaded with perspiration as he knelt in front of the hard wooden chair. He clenched his eyelids tight.

Wayne could see the black shadow on his horizon, mushrooming, ready to smash his business once again. *It's always the same*, he thought. *Finances. They'll crush us like bugs on a windshield.*

Just a few months ago, it had seemed like God was blessing Mountain Brook Salon. Although Thomas and Wayne had declared bankruptcy under Chapter 11, they had been slowly paying back their creditors. Their clients seemed pleased, and the business was growing.

Then Blake, their chief stylist, had announced that he was opening up his own shop two blocks away. Wayne was shocked. To make matters worse, after he left, Blake offered Mountain Brook stylists ten percent more commission than Wayne and Thomas could afford. Three of the best stylists abandoned Mountain Brook for the new salon.

Wayne couldn't even be angry with Blake. Hadn't Wayne pulled the same trick on his employers? Now he faced the other side of the circle, and it hurt.

Wayne looked around the room that was lighted only by the feeble rays of the little Tiffany lamp on his desk. The May sky had not yet begun to awaken.

Wayne glanced through the open door into the shadowy salon. It took $11,000 a month just to open the doors. Rent, high electric bills, payroll, supplies. The expenses never seemed to end. And they still had a year left on their lease. Had God brought them this far to abandon them now?

"O God," Wayne prayed from deep within his soul. "Please show us what to do. Either close this business or provide some way out of this mess. We gave this business to You. Open my eyes and let me see it as you do."

After a few moments of stillness, he spread his Bible on the chair. Turning to Psalm 28, he read through verse seven. Then he sat in the chair and meditated on the words:

> *The Lord is my strength and my shield;*
> *My heart trusts in him, and I am helped;*
> *Therefore my heart exults,*
> *And with my song I will thank him* (NASB).

Suddenly the past two years began to play before him like a panorama. But it wasn't exactly the way he remembered it. Somehow, the struggles and the trials had been gilded with rays of sunshine. He saw the hills and valleys of his experiences in a new light, like the splendid scenery of a breath-taking drive. In every turn and dip and sharp curve, he could see God's hand, guiding, protecting and loving.

It started when Wayne and Thomas came to know the Lord. At first, friends advised them to split up the partnership. "How can two former homosexual lovers continue in a business relationship? The temptation will be too strong," they reasoned.

The advise seemed logical. Yet every time Wayne and Thomas prayed about their situation, they didn't have peace about selling. Always, it seemed, God was leading them to straighten out the financial mess and make things right.

Finally, he and Thomas decided to keep the business together. In 1988 they dedicated the salon to the Lord and began giving ten percent of its income to the work of the Lord. Although turning the salon around financially was a constant objective, their biggest desire was to introduce their employees to Jesus Christ.

That's when Wayne began arriving at the shop at 5:00 a.m. to pray. Wayne would ask God to change the heart and alter the life-style of each employee who didn't know Christ as Savior.

Altogether, the salon employed fourteen people, including hairstylists, manicurists, a make-up person and a shampoo assistant. All eight stylists were gay. Every employee knew the lives Wayne and Thomas had lived as homosexuals. It would take a miracle for them to see the love of Jesus through Wayne and Thomas.

Those days seemed like a maze of troubles. Defaulting on all kinds of payments and loans, they had to file for Chapter 11 bankruptcy. Both he and Thomas still battled homosexual urges. Sometimes, they slipped back and had to ask for forgiveness. The government began investigating their withholding tax records. The general account was nearly always in deficit.

In those early days of their spiritual walk, Wayne and Thomas faced every obstacle with the faith of children, believing God would give them victory if they only kept their eyes on Him. To show their clients they had changed because of Christ, they worked hard to solve their financial problems and keep checks from bouncing.

Miracle after miracle began to happen. Late one night, one of the stylists knocked on Wayne's and Thomas's apartment door.

"C'mon in, Paul." Wayne closed the door and led him to the couch.

Paul wasted no time. "Wayne, I can't believe I'm here. But I'm at the end of my rope."

Wayne studied the gray, harried look on Paul's face. "The HIV?" Wayne recalled the positive test results Paul had received more than a year ago.

"Yes, I'm scared. But it's more than that. I'm just a little over thirty years old, but my life is in ruins. Tonight I went to the bar and began drinking one glass after another." Paul paused to bite his lower lip. "I saw a friend I hadn't seen for a while. He looked horrible. Eyes sunken and that haunted look on his face. He didn't even recognize me. And I didn't even say hello."

Paul's words came slowly, as if he had to search for them somewhere deep inside. "It all seems so empty. Everything in my life is in turmoil. I'm living with a partner I can't stand." He shook his head, took a deep breath and sighed. "I like everything to look professional and proper. The more things deteriorate, the harder I try to look good. The pressure is incredible."

He dropped his head in his hands and sobbed. "I'm so lonely."

Thomas came in from the kitchen. Sizing up the situation, he sat gently beside Paul.

Paul looked up. "You guys have changed. I used to watch you in the salon. You used to be like me. Now you look happy. I guess it's true what you said—that Jesus made the difference."

Joy flooded Wayne's heart. How many hours had he prayed for Paul? "Why don't we pray about it?" he suggested.

Paul nodded and put his head back into his hands. Wayne poured out his heart to the Lord about Paul and his need of a Savior. Thomas prayed when Wayne finished.

Then, unexpectedly, Paul prayed, "God, I'm lost. I don't know what to say. Help me become one of your children."

With a little help from Wayne and Thomas, Paul asked God to forgive his sins and invited Jesus Christ to live in his life. When he finished, his face shone. "I feel great!" he gushed, thanking God over and over for lifting his heavy burden. That Sunday, Paul attended church with Wayne and Thomas.

That had been almost two years ago. Now, kneeling beside his chair in the dimly lighted room, Wayne prayed for Paul.

Paul was still walking with the Lord. His former lover had moved out, and Paul had begun taking an experimental drug from a plant root out of Russia that keeps the C-cell count high. So far, he had no signs of full-blown AIDS. He was the picture of health. To Wayne that was a miraculous answer to prayer!

As Wayne continued his daily prayer vigils, one-by-one the other employees in the salon accepted Christ as their Savior. The number of Christians increased, and the work atmosphere became sweeter. The clients often remarked about the change. When they did, Wayne described what God had done in his life.

Wayne and Thomas began advertising Mountain Brook on the local Christian radio station. Soon Christians began to patronize the shop, and Mountain Brook became a much more pleasant place to its customers.

One day, a customer confided in Wayne, "I'm planning to divorce my husband." Her face was set and angry.

"Don't do anything you'll regret later," Wayne cautioned. "You can never erase the past." He told her about his homosexuality and how he had ruined his marriage.

As he described how God loved him in spite of his sin, huge tears trembled on the edge of her eyelids. "I don't know," she said as she paid her Paul. She left shaking her head.

310

A few days later, Wayne received a call from her. "I'm so glad you told me to stick it out." Her voice seemed bright. "Now I see my marriage in a completely different light."

Wayne rejoiced. God had used him—the one who had walked out on his own marriage—to influence another to reconsider her decision to leave her husband.

He and Thomas used their witness at the salon to introduce people to Christ. As the other stylists came to know the Lord, they also helped others to receive Him. Sometimes Wayne would laugh in amazement at the change that had come over the salon.

One day, Mrs. Raine, the woman who ran the health food store across the street, pulled Wayne and Thomas into the back room. She had been coming in to get her hair done by Tony and had told him about her homosexual son. All of them had been praying for Chris.

"Come quickly," she stammered. "There's something wrong with my son. He came to the shop with a Bible in hand. He insists Jesus is calling him home. I don't know what to do." She began sobbing uncontrollably.

Suicide, Wayne thought immediately. He and Thomas sprinted across the street, followed by a frantic Mrs. Raine.

Tramping down the basement steps, they found Chris at the bottom huddled in a chair. His face was twisted in despair. Wayne glanced at Thomas. His face clearly said, "What do we do now?"

Wayne and Thomas knelt on either side of Chris. "We know how you feel." Wayne spoke quietly. "We've been there, too."

"I think you know the answer is to live for Jesus," Thomas chimed in.

Chris began to cry. Thomas prayed while Wayne put his hands on Chris's shoulders. The musty smell of the dank basement seemed to thicken ominously.

"Bring him out of this life-style to you, Lord," Thomas pleaded. "Change his heart. Forgive his sin."

Wayne shivered. He could feel the spirit of homosexuality hovering around the chair. Again and again, as Thomas poured his heart out to God, a spirit seemed to come out of Chris and float over them.

"I do want to become a Christian," Chris sobbed. "But I've been so evil. The things I've done—"

"Jesus can forgive them all," Thomas assured.

His voice broken and low, Chris began praying for forgiveness. Wayne helped him as he stumbled for the right words to say. When Chris finished, his face glowed. Somehow the room seemed clear and fresh.

Over the next few months, Chris began to grow in his new life. He helped counsel others, and although he sometimes struggled with his commitment to the Lord, he kept plugging away. Eventually, he decided to go back to school and got a job as a waiter to pay for his education.

A little light was coming in the window now. Wayne shook off his memories and began to pray again. It was the financial worries that plagued him most. But hadn't God shown how much He cared for Wayne and Thomas by performing many miracles in that area, too? They had learned that God could do the impossible.

Wayne recalled the mess he and Thomas had faced right after they accepted Christ: checks were bouncing, they had no money for payroll, creditors were calling, and they had to file for Chapter 11.

One day, Diana, an employee, came with disturbing news. "I've just seen my doctor and he recommends surgery for my back. I called the insurance company for approval and they refused to pay. They say you have defaulted on your insurance payments."

Fear chilled Wayne's heart. It was true. With their extravagant spending habits, dipping into the federal withholding tax hadn't been enough. They had quit paying the insurance.

Several days later, Laura approached him with a similar request. More back surgery! Between the two of them, the estimated costs would be as much as $24,000.

Wayne and Thomas made an appointment to see their lawyer, J.F. Dixon. "Is there anything we can do to get our premium up to date?" Wayne asked. "The insurance company refuses to pay a dime."

Mr. Dixon shook his head. "There's no way an insurance company will bring you up to date and then pay such a large claim. You defaulted and that's it."

That night, Wayne and Thomas brought their problem to the intercessor group at church. For the next few days, they also asked every Christian they knew to pray that God would give them favor with the insurance company. Everyone kept telling them the same thing, "Just work in faith."

When Wayne and Thomas went back to Mr. Dixon's office, he seemed even more glum about their prospects.

Wayne's heart ached for Diana and Laura. It wasn't fair that their lives would be impacted so severely because of his negligence.

"There's no use pursuing it," Mr. Dixon frowned.

But Wayne insisted. "Let's proceed as if we could win. Let's keep going until we get a flat no. The Lord can work a miracle."

Thomas agreed.

The lawyer stared at them in amazement. But feeling that what they were doing was right, Wayne stood firm.

For two weeks, the lawyers negotiated. Thomas and Wayne and everyone at church continued praying.

One afternoon, Mr. Dixon called the salon. "You and Thomas come on over to my office. I have some news for you."

Anxiety clutched Wayne's stomach. Could God melt the hearts of an insurance company? It didn't seem possible.

Sitting across from the attorney's huge, wooden desk a short time later, Wayne could see a tiny glint in the Mr. Dixon's eyes. *It's good news*, Wayne realized with a jolt. *Praise God. But how can it be?*

"I consulted several colleagues about your case," Mr. Dixon began. He tapped his fingertips together as if he were underlining his words. "The only recourse seemed a lawsuit." A smile broke over his face. "The insurance people began checking their records. For some unexplainable reason, you didn't owe them any money." He paused to let the next sentence get its full effect. "In fact, the company owes you $4,500 and is sending a refund check."

Wayne's mind whirled. He looked at Thomas who had a blank expression on his face.

Mr. Dixon went on. "The check has been issued and should arrive in a couple of days."

Wayne and Thomas laughed, deep and hard. Forty-five hundred dollars! Exactly what they needed in their checking account to cover the payroll and other expenses.

Wayne and Thomas called those who had prayed and told them the news. Everyone rejoiced. Diana and Laura went in for their surgery, and claims totalling $30,000 were paid.

On another occasion, Wayne and Thomas owed $30,000 to the IRS. While the lawyer was trying to work out terms with the government, the bank called because of a $5,000 overdraft. Wayne's heart sank. He thought he had the accounts well in hand. As usual, his calculations and spending didn't match. Neither he nor Thomas had a dime to spare. How could they cover such an amount?

He and Thomas asked God to help them clear the overdraft, then Wayne called his mother. "Mom," he said hesitantly, "I'm in kind of a tight situation."

"Is it money again?" She knew Wayne's weakness with finances.

Wayne's face burned. "You know it. I have a $5,000 overdraft. Could you help me out?"

"Well, I have $2,500 of the money your dad left me when he died. I'm not using it."

"I'll pay it back as soon as possible," he assured.

"Yeah, I know, Wayne. Give me your bank account number and I'll transfer the money tomorrow morning."

"Thank you so much, mom."

But his mother's generosity didn't resolve the problem. Where would they get the other $2,500? He called a few people to pray, then took it to the Lord himself. Hinano encouraged him to trust God for the situation.

The next afternoon, Thomas hurried up to Wayne in the back room. "You won't believe this!" he shouted, waving an official-looking letter.

Wayne grabbed it from Thomas's outstretched hand and pulled out a check for $2,500. From the Internal Revenue Service!

"What's this?" Wayne sputtered.

"A refund check," Thomas laughed.

"Refund? But we owe $30,000."

When the euphoria had subsided, Wayne and Thomas discussed what they should do with the money. Maybe it was a computer error. Or better yet, a gift from God.

They insisted that Mr. Dixon investigate. Was the refund legitimate? He called back. "Go ahead and use the money. It's a refund from a prior year. If you send it back now, the paperwork will be a snarl you'll never get untangled."

So they paid the rest of the overdraft with thankful and joyful hearts. To this day, Wayne doesn't understand how they got a refund.

It was true that Wayne and Thomas had no aptitude for finances. Even at the beginning of his walk with God,

Wayne knew he could never manage the business finances right. His heart was sincere, but he just had no business sense.

Before Wayne and Thomas went into bankruptcy, they sought the counsel of other Christians, including Pastor Culpepper. Everyone agreed that the Lord required them to pay back their creditors 100 percent. So Mountain Brook went into Chapter 11 with a commitment to settle all accounts in full.

Wayne knew, however, that something more had to be done. They needed a business manager. But where would they get one who could do the job?

One night, Milton Thorn approached Wayne. "The Lord has given me a special message for you," he said. "You will find exactly the right person to help you manage your financial affairs."

Wayne looked at him curiously. He didn't know such a person. How could it happen?

Not long afterward, his sister called from Louisiana. "Jessica, (their first cousin) is really bad off," she commented. "Her husband is an alcoholic and she's living on the river bank, fishing for her food."

When he hung up, Wayne began to pray. "Lord, I'm so fortunate to have all this room." Thomas had moved out a few weeks ago, and Wayne had the town house to himself.

A thought struck him. *Jessica could stay here for a while. We need a shampoo assistant at the salon. She used to be a hairdresser. I could offer her the job.*

He called Louisiana and left a message for Jessica. Two weeks later she returned his call.

"Pack up what you've got and c'mon out here," Wayne insisted. "I need a shampoo assistant. You could stay here with me until you get on your feet."

When she arrived, all she had was a pair of blue jeans and a T-shirt. Her dark hair looked uncared-for and her dark complexion seemed sallow. Wayne's heart went out to Jessica. They had grown up like brother and sister, and he determined to take care of her.

She plunged right into work. For months, she stayed in the back doing her job. One day, she told Wayne about the business she ran in Louisiana.

Wayne's mouth dropped open. "You know how to do accounting?"

Jessica pushed her glasses further up her nose and smiled. "Sure do."

"Well, let's see what you can do."

Wayne put her up front at the receptionist desk and started letting her keep the books. To Wayne's amazement, it didn't take her long to have the account ledgers in order.

In time, she completely took over the financial management of the salon, and her good sense of business helped Wayne and Thomas get back on track. When Wayne recalled the words of Milton Thorn, "You will find exactly the right person to help you manage your financial affairs," he realized Jessica was the one God sent to help them. Jessica moved into her own apartment when Wayne married Hinano and seemed to be getting along quite well.

Wayne stared at the light from the Tiffany lamp, now dim from the sunlight streaming in the window. In his mind he reviewed part of the Psalm he had read, "My heart trusts in him, and I am helped."

It's true! Wayne thought. *The more I trust God, the more He works miracles in my life. The more I thank Him during difficult situations, the more He shows me how much He loves and cares for me. Why would almighty God stoop to touch the life of a sinner like me?* Wayne again thought of his current crisis. "The problem is yours," he breathed.

Wayne's solitude was broken by Hinano's entrance. "Hello, honey," he greeted, kissing her.

"Worries?" she asked.

"Not now," he beamed. "I just turned them over to the Lord, and I can hardly wait to see what He does with Mountain Brook!" He hugged Hinano gently and led her into the shop.

27

Cahaba Plaza

Wayne and Thomas strode into the hazy room. The smoke drifting up from the landlord's desk stung Wayne's eyes.

The landlord snubbed out his cigarette. "What'cha need?" he asked in his thick-tongued voice.

Wayne and Thomas shifted uncomfortably. Wayne prayed silently while Thomas spoke. "We've lost a few stylists in the salon and are having a few financial difficulties. We thought you might be willing to let us rent one of your smaller places instead of Mountain Brook."

The man narrowed his heavy eyelids. "How much ya got left on your lease?"

"A year," Thomas answered.

"A year?" the man exclaimed. He slowly lit another cigarette. Glancing first at Thomas then at Wayne, he sent puffs of smoke into the air. "Can't break the lease!

If you want out, you'll have to find someone to take it over."

"Well—okay," Wayne said slowly. "We'll see if we can sublet it ourselves."

The landlord shuffled through the papers on his desk. Scribbling a few names and telephone numbers on a note pad, he ripped off the sheet and handed it to Thomas. "Here's a few leads. If you come up with anything, let me know."

Every morning for the next two weeks, Wayne, Hinano and Thomas prayed that God would help them find a tenant. They called every name on the landlord's list with no results. Everyday, Thomas and Hinano scoured the city looking for a smaller place to relocate.

Finally, one afternoon the landlord called Wayne. "I've found someone to rent the building if you can be out by the end of June."

Wayne's mind quickly calculated. "That's just six weeks away. Could you give us a week to make up our minds?"

"Sure," he said and hung up.

Wayne, Hinano, Thomas and Helen, a friend, stepped up their tours of the surrounding business districts. But after a week of exhaustive search, still nothing materialized. The four of them gathered again for prayer in the back room of the shop. Forming a tight circle with their chairs, each began sharing their concerns.

"I feel a little frantic," Helen admitted. "It's been five days and we're no closer to finding a place!

To complicate matters, it would take a few more days just to cement a new lease once a store was located. And time was running out.

"But God has it all under control," Hinano encouraged.

They went around the circle praying. When Hinano's turn came, her prayer received hearty amens from the rest. "Lord, show us a sign that the place we find is the right one. Let us know what Your will is for the salon."

After the prayer, Thomas drove them around to different sections of the city. At one point, within four miles of Mountain Brook, Hinano noticed a small shopping center called Cahaba Plaza. An office space had a "For Rent" sign posted in the window. "Pull in here," she proposed.

Thomas turned his car into the entrance and parked in front of an office supply store next to the vacant space. Entering the attractive store, they heard Christian music playing. Wayne noticed Hinano raise her eyebrows. "Could this be the sign we're looking for?" she whispered.

"Could be," Wayne shrugged.

Thomas asked for the manager, and they were introduced to a middle aged man and his wife who freely acknowledged they were born-again Christians.

"We'd like to know about the office space next door," Wayne began. "Is the rent reasonable?"

"Yes, quite reasonable," the supply store owner assured. "The place has been empty for quite a while. Ever since they built it, in fact. The realtor's really hurting. I'm sure they'll bargain with you about the rent."

Wayne asked to use the store phone to call the realtor. He set up an appointment with a woman named J.P. who agreed to meet them at the site in an hour.

While they waited, the four of them drove around to several other locations, but none of them seemed as attractive as Cahaba Plaza.

When J.P. arrived, she showed them the facility. It was brand new and just the right size for their shop. Wayne and Thomas negotiated with J.P. for about thirty minutes while Hinano and Helen waited outside.

J.P. offered six months free rent as an incentive. Thomas glanced at Wayne, then turned back to J.P. "We'll discuss the matter this evening. Can we meet here at the same time tomorrow? J.P. nodded.

As soon as they piled back into the car and pulled into the traffic, Thomas commented, "The realtor will do a credit check."

The tone in Thomas's voice worried Hinano. "Are you sure?"

"They always do. And with our bankruptcy and bad credit rating, we'll never pass. They'll automatically consider us a bad risk."

Thomas's pessimism dampened everyone's spirit, and they rode the rest of the way back to the salon in silence. Wayne thought Cahaba Plaza was perfect for their new location. In two days, they had to give their present landlord an answer. Where else would they find a place as suitable and have time to sign a lease?

When they reached the salon, the four of them again went to the back room for prayer. One-by-one, they committed tomorrow's meeting to the Lord and then went back to work.

The next day, Thomas and Wayne met J.P. at the plaza. On the way over, Thomas suggested, "Wayne, you always give away too much information. Let me do the talkin'."

Wayne nodded. "Okay, I won't say a word."

J.P. let them into the building. Wayne looked around. The layout looked as good today as it had yesterday. Surely, this is what the Lord had provided for their business.

"Well, what did you decide?" J.P. asked as she set down her attache case.

Thomas looked her straight in the eye. "We'll take the deal as is, right now, if you don't do a credit check. Just let us have the building, and we'll sign a three year lease today."

Wayne stifled a gasp. What was Thomas doing?

"Give me a few minutes," J.P. said and went next door to use the telephone.

"That was pretty strong," Wayne remarked after she left.

Thomas laughed. "You bet. But I thought we might as well get our cards on the table. We haven't got time to beat around the bush."

Wayne and Thomas paced about the empty store without a word after that, each praying silently. Wayne believed they had little hope.

After a few tense moments, J.P. returned. "You've got a deal. Let's sign the papers." She opened her attache case, and Thomas pulled his pen from his pocket. Wayne breathed a silent prayer of thanks.

"Only God could have bulldozed the lease through in one day," Wayne enthused later as he climbed into Thomas's car.

Thomas laughed. "That's for sure. That was our sign."

The next few weeks were hectic. Not wanting to lose any business, they tried to time the move around their appointments. Scheduling when to transfer the equipment was essential. Everyone pitched in and despite minor problems, everything went smoothly. The heavy part of the relocation came on July 3, and the new shop opened on the fifth. How good it felt to be free from the high rent and to be working again with all the stations filled!

God began blessing the new salon. As the stylists who had left to work in Blake's shop returned, Wayne and Thomas added more stations. Within a year, the business again had eight stylists and fourteen employees. Wayne and Thomas were gaining financially, and the IRS deficit was reduced to $10,000. If business continued as it had been, the debt would be paid in another year.

With lesser square footage, the salon seemed bursting at the seams. Wayne and Thomas began talking about expanding into the empty office space next door. This time, they proceeded with caution, seeking God's will before they signed another lease.

But what excited Wayne the most was how he and Thomas were touching lives for Jesus through the salon. Although they had not worked out all the emotional difficulties between them, they were united in using their business to testify to God's love in their lives.

One day Wayne was asked to do a live telephone interview on a radio talk show. A few minutes before the broadcast, Thomas turned the radio up in the salon so everyone could hear the interview. As he waited on the phone, Wayne listened to the familiar introductory music. When his own voice blared over the speaker, it sounded strange.

The employees chuckled and joked as they listened. Wayne noticed a gay couple who had just come in to get their hair cut. They glanced at each other with knowing looks, then both turned to stare at Wayne.

Feeling uncomfortable, he could guess only what they were thinking. He wanted to be sensitive to all his clients and didn't want to give the impression the salon was trying to force religion on them. He cupped his hand over the telephone and motioned to Thomas.

"We may have to turn the interview off," Wayne whispered.

Thomas glanced at the gay couple and nodded. He went to the back, turned down the volume and switched to a music station.

Later when the two gay men went up to the front to pay, Danny rang up their total.

"Did you play that religious program just because we were in here?" one asked.

Wayne overheard and his heart froze. Did the interview offend them?

"No," Danny answered. "Wayne was being interviewed on a talk show on WDJC."

The men seemed surprised. "You mean having that station on was intentional? You all wanted to listen to that stuff?"

A smile burst over Danny's face. "Oh, yes!" The men listened with apparent amazement as Danny began sharing with them how God had changed Wayne's and Thomas's lives.

Wayne listened intently as he worked. God had honored his and Thomas's decision to stay in business and commit every part of their finances to Him. The future seemed to shine before them. Expanding the shop was less important to Wayne than the fact God was using the business to spread His message of love. While important, financial success couldn't measure up to the joy of seeing his employees grow in their walk with the Lord.

Wayne sighed contentedly as he sprayed and lightly patted his client's hair. His ministry didn't end at the door of the church or after the counseling sessions at *Free My Children*, Wayne's outreach to gays wanting out of their life-style. He could serve the Lord anywhere. Who could ask for a greater future than that?

Finished with his last customer, Wayne cleaned up his tools and went to the back room. Hinano was sitting in a chair reading her Bible. He greeted her cheerfully. "Got any problems you can't solve today?"

She grinned. "Plenty."

"Great! Then I know just how to solve them." He patted the cool pages of the Bible and flashed a playful smile.

How far the Lord has brought me since I saw the grotesque image of myself in the mirror and determined to end it all. There's no way I can describe the gratitude I feel toward God who not only forgave my years of homosexual living, but also of abandoning my wife and children and hurting others through my greed. I feel clean, secure, loved and destined to share a glorious future with Christ.

Perhaps you too are struggling with homosexuality. Or want to help a friend or relative caught in this life-style. Maybe you wonder, Is a gay person born that way? Is homosexuality a legitimate life-style? Can a person who wants to come out of the gay world ever learn to live differently?

Through my own experiences and the help of loving Christians, I have discovered the answers to these questions. I am excited about the growing movement in the church to minister to gays and to love them as God does. I have seen God perform many miracles in the lives of gay friends.

Perhaps you are a homosexual and want to get out of that life-style or you may be concerned about a friend or loved one who is trapped in a cycle of despair like I was. I urge you to see homosexuality from God's eyes. I encourage you to understand the origins and causes of this behavior, and to live above the circumstances of your past.

God can overcome any sin, heal any hurt, and transform any life. I have told you my story. Now I want to show you how to deal with homosexuality, whether it be your own or that of someone you care for. I want to help you discover how to minister to your gay friends and their families through the power of God's Holy Spirit.

28

Finding True Love and Acceptance

Over the years since my deliverance from homosexuality, I've learned much about helping gays deal with the consequences of their life-style.

Most homosexuals are filled with fear—the fear of being found out, the fear of venereal disease or AIDS, the fear of violence, and the fear of aging. They dread the shame of their life-style. They wrestle with drug addiction or alcoholism. They struggle with guilt. They see little hope for the future. And in their despair, many commit suicide.

Perhaps you are at that point. Let me encourage you. There is hope. There is a way out, and I want to help you.

When I started our ministry to gays, I had a burning desire to help homosexual men and women who wanted out of their gay life-style to find the deliverance I had received from God. I have fond memories of our small beginning.

I invited the men from my old circle of friends who I thought might come. I explained to them what the meeting was about. Then I ran the name I had picked out for the ministry by Hinano. "What do you think about *Free My Children*?"

She thought a moment, then smiled. "Sounds like it suits the purpose."

Only ten men showed up for our first meeting, but each wanted to be set free from his homosexuality.

We kept the service simple. Hinano and Joan Nall led in singing. Then I related some of the miracles God had worked to free me. I found it hard to get up in front of the group. But as I talked, I could see hope dawn on some of their faces.

When I finished, the others described their lives and how desperate they felt. Many asked questions. I answered honestly but admitted I was still learning about the issues of homosexuality myself. We didn't finish until eleven that night.

Was I discouraged with this small beginning? Not at all. I was satisfied to start small. I had a lot to learn and much growing to do. Over the years since then, however, I have gained a clearer understanding of the dysfunctions that tend to move a person toward homosexuality. And having worked through the process of deliverance, I have discovered some basic steps to take in breaking free from sexual brokenness.

The first step is to *believe change is possible*. For nearly twenty years I bought into the theory that homosexuals were born that way. No matter how tough things got, I used this argument to justify what I was doing. Gay behavior, I believed, was unchangeable, like having big feet. I was born gay, and nothing I could do would alter that. But while this rationalization helped ease the guilt I felt, it kept me in bondage to my addiction and gave me an excuse to blame God for my troubles. My thoughts changed on this, however, when I turned my life over to Jesus Christ.

As I searched the Bible and went through counseling, I learned that God created the sexes—male and female. The Book of Genesis says Adam was alone on earth after God formed him from the dust of the ground. Despite all the animals and other good things God had made, Adam was lonely. He needed human companionship.

When God fulfilled Adam's desire, He did not create another man. He formed a woman out of Adam's side. She was a compliment to him, yet in many ways an opposite. From the first, God intended that sexual relationships should be between men and women through marriage. Homosexuality is Satan's perversion of God's perfect union. Satan distorted the beautiful sexual relationship God created, turning love to lust, self-control to indulgence, and truth to lies.

As I studied other Bible verses on this issue, I couldn't escape the fact that homosexuality is sin in God's eyes:

Homosexuality is absolutely forbidden, for it is an enormous sin (Leviticus 18:22, The Living Bible).

Women turned against God's natural plan for them and indulged in sex sin with each other. And the men, instead of having a normal sex relationship with women, burned with lust for each other, men doing shameful things with other men and, as a result, getting paid within their own souls with the penalty they so richly deserved...Their lives became full of every kind of wickedness and sin, of greed and hate, envy and murder, fighting, lying, bitterness, and gossip. They were backbiters, haters of God, insolent, proud braggarts, always thinking of new ways of sinning...They were fully aware of God's death penalty for these crimes, yet they went right ahead and did them anyway, and encouraged others to do them, too (Romans 1:26-32, The Living Bible).

Don't fool yourselves. Those who live immoral lives, who are idol worshipers, adulterers or homosexuals—will have no share in his kingdom. Neither will thieves or greedy people, drunkards, slanderers, or robbers (1 Corinthians 6:10, The Living Bible).

If we were born gay, God could not honestly consider that life-style sinful. He could not justly condemn the act nor demand penalty. It's hard to change unnatural desires and, until we recognize the sinfulness of the act and deal with the root of the problem, we will remain vulnerable to our brokenness.

The second step is to *understand the root of your homosexuality.* In every case I've encountered, rejection has played a major role in the gay person's life. The most serious rejection comes when a child is small. Harsh words from a father in a moment of intense anger can cause a child to shut down and detach emotionally. That's what happened to me. I felt rejected by my father, and in self-defense I grew to hate him. My entry into homosexuality was an attempt to fulfill my natural, legitimate needs for love, acceptance and identity through unnatural sexual intimacy.

A root cannot grow unless it is fed. Once it receives the right moisture and nutrients, it not only spreads underground, it also breaks out into the open. I have observed seven dysfunctions which provide the right growing conditions for homosexuality. Most gay men and women will recognize more than one of these in their lives.

Modeling and imitation after the same sex. Every child imitates someone. If men are not available, he loses his male role models and begins to learn behavior from women. This often sets up an endless pattern of rejection from men.

The rate of homosexuality dramatically increases in homes where the father is absent, abusive, alcoholic or unavailable. My father worked from 3 p.m. to 11 p.m. When I got up in the morning, he was sleeping. I saw him for two hours a day, usually while he was under the car, fixing mechanical things around the yard, working in the garden or mowing the grass. When we were together, he was frequently abusive and I felt deeply rejected. Consequently, my mother became my early role model.

Modeling plays a leading role in one's sexuality. Much of a child's psyche is formed between ages three and six. Adopting female role models can make young men behave effeminately. As a child, I blocked the male image out of my mind and began to relate to women. I even tried to walk and talk like them.

Satan always plays on our most vulnerable parts. If we have a tendency toward impatience, he will tempt us to be angry. If we lean toward stoicism, he may tempt us to be distant or critical. But modeling is learned behavior. Over time, it can be reversed.

A learned aversion to the opposite sex. I didn't consider a woman's anatomy repulsive when I married Patricia. But after I became a homosexual, my mind turned this way. Eventually, I didn't find women attractive at all.

I've counseled many men who wouldn't consider getting near a woman. They think the female body is missing something important in its genitals. They would never consider heterosexual marriage. Called castration anxiety, this frequently comes from a puritanical upbringing that says the opposite sex is not erotically appealing.

The view of women as angels or symbols of virginal purity. This stems from a perversion of religious symbols or from setting women on a pedestal, making them untouchable and unreachable. This attitude can cause a man to shrink away from sexual contact with them.

Over-attachment to a protective mother. This dysfunction affects many men in our society. Single heads of households are prone to overprotection because of extra demands, responsibilities, and cares hanging on their shoulders. Mothers left at home alone with their children for long stretches of time may develop strong, unnatural attachments to their little ones. My mother was overprotective, which prevented me from developing masculine traits.

Early homosexual experiences. This can happen when an older man, such an uncle, brother or stepfather, begins fondling the child at an early age. Often that leads to molestation, sodomy and oral sex. Sometimes, two adolescent boys may experiment with each other. Masturbation in a group can lead to unplanned ejaculation while in bed with another male.

That happened to me, and it left an indelible impression on my young mind. If a child who has experienced repeated rejection suddenly finds pleasure in an act with a man, the child begins to relate acceptance to sex. The youngster begins to think, "He likes me when I do this." That causes him to repeat the behavior so he will be accepted.

Adolescent alienation. All children desire to be accepted by their peer group, but some parents isolate their kids. They fear their son or daughter will get sick, hurt, or get into a fight. By the time the child is allowed to relate to others his age, he has already become a loner. He doesn't know how to interact.

I've dealt with gay men ranging in age from nineteen to forty years. Although they are accepted by their gay friends, they cannot relate to their peers. They never have close relationships. You see their faces all the time, but they remain isolated in the midst of the crowd.

My heart goes out to these lonely people. They will never find the kind of love and acceptance they desire because they cannot reach out to someone else.

Narcissism or abnormal maternal indulgence. Most homosexuals are caught up in self-love. They begin to internalize everything in their lives, which causes them to become introverts.

Many times, self-love develops because of an indulgent mother. Perhaps this was your experience. She spent her life trying to make you happy, giving you everything you wanted and making it look as if life revolved around your every wish. This made your eyes focus on self.

As a selfish introvert, your main desire is to please yourself. You spend your money on things to maintain an image acceptable to your peers or your social group. You put on a front and use all your resources to keep it intact. The real you is hidden behind all the paraphernalia. Self-love doesn't bring satisfaction. The emptiness causes you to build your front even higher, isolating you even more.

The ultimate goal for homosexuality is satisfaction. Tragically, that can never be found until the root of the deep need is exposed and dealt with. The feeling of rejection continues to wound and hurt, causing behavior to become more bizarre.

I was caught in this cycle. For years I tried to cover the hurts and the rejection I had suffered from my father and my peers when I was an adolescent. The older I got, the more I exercised this option.

Trying to fulfill your needs with someone of your own gender, I discovered, is a futile task. Only one Person—Jesus Christ—can truly satisfy your innermost needs and free you from the tyranny of your lusts.

The third step in breaking free from sexual brokenness is to *see homosexuality for what it is.* Homosexuality creates a downward spiral. Lust attracts more lust. Instead of giving satisfaction, it creates a desire for more. As a person continues to pursue lustful relationships, the demonic influence becomes stronger. That's the way my life was affected, and I've seen similar results in many others.

The aim of homosexuality is to empty the other person. You pull everything out of them you can to fill your own desperate needs. When your partner no longer satisfies you, you discard him.

This was disillusioning to me. I tried to establish monogamous relationships with my partners. But because the gay life-style prevented that, I was torn from one person to another. That plunged me into a deeper sense of insecurity and guilt.

The fourth step is to *realize that God loves you and has a wonderful plan for your life.* God sent His Son, Jesus Christ, to pay the penalty for our brokenness by dying on the cross. Our heavenly Father desires to forgive us and make us whole. When we accept His sacrifice for our sins, we become His children and He imparts great value to us. His unconditional love reverses the pattern of rejection and makes us fully pleasing and acceptable in His sight.

When I realized how much God loved and suffered for me, I opened up the emotional channels I had shut down and I found healing. In the process, I discovered how God's love could help me through my hurts and despairs, gently comforting and instructing me as I looked into myself and saw my brokenness.

Homosexuality is a symptom of one's deep need for affirmation and acceptance. God offers complete forgiveness and unconditional acceptance. He will not only give you eternal life, but put purpose in your living for the here and now. I invite you to accept God's love and forgiveness right now by praying this prayer from your heart:

> *Dear heavenly Father,*
> *You are the God of miracles. Only you have the power to make me whole. I believe that you sent your Son, Jesus, to die on the cross for my sins. I ask you to forgive me of my sins and deliver me from homosexuality. Help me to live for you. I thank you that I am now a member of your family. In Jesus' name. Amen.*

The day I accepted Christ as my Savior I had no idea how that decision would impact my life. Miracles began to happen. At first, Thomas and I lost most of the clientele in our business, since ninety-five percent of our customers and employees were homosexuals. But God was faithful. He eventually replaced everything we lost. Other people began supporting us. We became the only "Christian" salon in the city. Our Christian customers in the salon began to give us references. That brought in a whole new clientele.

When our lives changed, the homosexual community in Birmingham began to watch Thomas and me. Many ridiculed us behind our backs. But we welcomed the homosexuals who continued to use our hairstyling services. This gave us a chance to witness to the gay community.

The Lord also helped me love my former sexual partners in a new, godly way. I called each one and asked forgiveness for all the hurt I had caused them. That released me from a lot of emotional baggage. Having come to grips with the wrongs I had committed, I felt clean and free.

God has also given me spiritual strength. Step-by-step, He has built good qualities in my life which have given me more joy and satisfaction than I could ever describe. He has given me a burden for gays and is helping me to see their deep needs. He has provided me with more than I could ever ask for, especially my precious Nano and the acceptance and love she has brought into my life.

But God's deliverance is no instant cure. While some gays seem to find deliverance easy, most struggle for years before they can live a normal life.

If you have committed yourself to the Lord and to getting out of the gay life-style, be patient. God will begin where you are right now and walk you through the deliverance process. As long as you commit your life to Him daily and admit when you have blown it, God will deliver you, and you will begin to experience the abundant life He has promised.

29

New Life From Ashes

A stranger arrived at a *Free My Children* meeting one Monday night. Since I was in the back room praying and preparing for class, Hinano greeted him.

"Hi, I'm Carlton," the man responded. "Is this the Monday night Sunday school class?"

Hinano hesitated. "This isn't a Sunday school class, but it is the only Monday night group that meets here at Metro church."

Carlton looked puzzled. "When I called the church office, the secretary said a group of homosexuals get together here every Monday night for Sunday school."

Hinano realized Carlton thought he had come to a social club for gays. "Well, that's not exactly right," she smiled. "But you're welcome to stay and see what we're all about."

Reluctantly, Carlton took a seat.

When I entered, I recognized him from the hairdressers network. "Hi, Carlton. Good to see you." We shook hands.

Hinano and I started the meeting with music. After I finished teaching, everyone began breaking into small groups. Carlton looked uncomfortable.

"Why don't you stay for the discussion?" I suggested.

He shrugged. "This isn't what I came here for. I have no intentions of changing my life."

I encouraged him to stay nevertheless, and he stuck it out until the meeting ended. Then he rushed out the door.

Carlton didn't show up at the next meeting or the one after that. Then we began seeing him at Sunday morning services. He attended sporadically at first, then every week. On the third month, he responded when Pastor Culpepper asked those who would like to find forgiveness in Jesus to come forward. That morning, Carlton invited Jesus into his life.

That's how ministry begins. God touches one person's life. We provide the human acceptance and love.

Whether you want to begin an organized ministry to the sexually broken in your church or reach out to a gay friend, I want to share several principles that can help you minister effectively.

FIRST, *examine your attitude toward homosexuality*. Ask yourself, "What keeps me from wholeheartedly accepting those who are trying to recover from sexual brokenness?" I challenge you to search out your true feelings.

According to a recent survey, seventy-five percent of church-goers believe homosexuality is wrong. But many Christians have a hard time separating the behavior from the person. They insist that gays must completely abandon their life-style before they will be accepted into the fellowship of the local church. But people coming out of a gay community need a place to be loved and accepted as they work through their brokenness to wholeness. That place is the church. It provides healthy role models for living, accountability for decisions, and a safe place to grow into Christian maturity.

Traditional myths about gays, however, cause many Christians to make serious mistakes when relating to those who are seeking help. The most common of these myths are:

> •*Homosexuals lead happy lives.* In fact, most gays are filled with despair and hopelessness. Many have attempted suicide and struggle with the fear of disease, aging and being exposed. They constantly battle feelings of guilt. They feel unwanted and unloved.

> •*Homosexuality is an unpardonable sin.* Matt. 12:31,32 defines the unpardonable sin as blasphemy against the Holy Spirit. Nowhere does the passage mention sexual sin.

> •*Homosexuals can't change.* 1 Corinthians 6:11, 1 John 4:4, and Phil. 4:13 all describe Christians who have left their former sins, including homosexu-

ality. God considers them forgiven and washed clean by the blood of Jesus Christ.

We cannot let such misconceptions keep us from ministering to the sexually broken. Instead, our love for Christ compels us to help them experience God's wonderful joy and peace.

In dealing with gays and their problems, many people fear what they don't understand. They frequently withdraw from the sexually dysfunctional because they don't know what to say to them. Christians often find it easier to blame and judge them than to show them compassion and forgiveness. Because the road out of homosexuality can be long, they grow impatient with the process. We tend to stereotype people who desire to be treated as unique individuals. But this only creates barriers to communication and relationships—and that keeps many from seeking wholeness.

You cannot begin to help someone break free from sexual brokenness until you come to grips with your own attitudes. As you consider ministering to gays, ask God to help you see and love them as people. Try to understand their deep need rather than to dwell on their wrongful behavior.

SECOND, *understand the process of change.* I have seen Christ touch and restore those who are deeply broken and full of shame. Although God's love and power can heal all types of compulsive, addictive and oppressive behaviors, change comes through process. The first step toward healing comes through a point of change. For many, that means accepting Christ as Savior and

Lord. This decision becomes the foundation for a lifetime of progress, giving the former homosexual freedom and power to conquer his brokenness.

But another step is also necessary. He must wholeheartedly commit himself to go the full distance to freedom. This includes a desire to deepen his relationship with Christ and allow Him to reveal God's intentions for sexuality. Facing his sinfulness and the painful realities that lead to sexual brokenness is also vital. He must be open and honest about what he is feeling and practicing, as well as admitting areas of identity and emotional immaturity. True freedom will come when he receives the healing ministry of the Holy Spirit and truly desires to walk free from sexual bondage and form loving relationships within the Body of Christ.

Sounds hard, doesn't it? But none of us can accomplish freedom and wholeness on our own. As a ministering Christian you can help the gay person begin the process by encouraging him to fellowship with other Christians and join a support group for encouragement and accountability.

THIRD, *demonstrate Christ's love.* The best way we can minister to the sexually broken is to love them unconditionally. This kind of love requires patience with failure. The important difference in dealing with setbacks is to determine whether the person is committed to change or content to live in his sin. The one who is willing to change needs to be accepted and enfolded into fellowship; the one who is unwilling to forsake his homosexual life-style will not want to be part of the Christian community.

As we work with homosexuals who are committed to changing their lives but fail many times, we treat them with compassion and love, not condemnation. We encourage them and ask, "Have you asked the Lord's forgiveness for last night's sin? Have you asked Him to give you more strength when temptation comes again?" Then we pray together.

Let me give you some simple do's and don'ts when developing relationships with the sexually broken:

<u>Do</u>	<u>Don't</u>
Love unconditionally	Preach to him
Accept the person	Condemn him
Be flexible	Convict—that's the Holy Spirit's role
Offer encouragement	
Hold him accountable	Accept gay behavior

Following these guidelines will enable you to be successful in all facets of your ministry to gays.

FOURTH, *help in the renewal process.* The Bible clearly defines how to change our behavior. Romans 12:1,2 says:

I urge you therefore, brethren, by the mercies of God, to present your bodies a living and holy sacrifice, acceptable to God, which is your spiritual service of worship. And do not be conformed to this world, but be transformed by the renewing of your mind, that you may prove what the will of God is, that which is good and acceptable and perfect (NASB).

Renewing your mind takes a lot of hard work. It means denying yourself the wrong things and concentrating on the good ones. But we've found that eighty percent of those who are committed to breaking free will succeed.

Part of renewal is adopting a new life-style. That brings conflicts for a person deeply entrenched in the gay community. Although your friend has experienced spiritual renewal, he still has to deal with tons of emotional garbage. One of the first problems he will confront is what to do about his partner. No homosexual relationship can thrive if one member of the couple commits his life to the Lord.

Losing a lover is like experiencing a death. Be patient with his sense of loss. Help him find new living arrangements and healthy friendships. And offer him substitute entertainment. His whole life is turning upside down. When he feels lonely and disoriented, he will yearn for things to be the way they were. At these times, encourage him to follow through on his decision to break free from old entanglements. When he obeys God's leading, give him the affirmation he craves.

Another part of renewal is pursuing restitution for wrongs committed in the past. After I received Christ as

Savior, I asked Thomas's mother for forgiveness. I drove to her home in Hilburn. As we sat across from each other in the living room, I felt very awkward. Finally I said, "Kaye, I need to tell you something."

She seemed to be intimidated by me, so I decided to get right to the point. "Remember the day you shoved the gun in my face? If I had been in your place, I might have pulled the trigger!"

Her eyes widened with surprise.

I went on. "I never understood what I did to you until I came to know the Lord. There I was, a bearded wonder taking your nineteen-year-old boy away. You were just trying to protect him. Would you please forgive me?"

Tears filled her eyes. "I forgive you," she choked. "I just can't believe you even thought of this."

What a thrill it was for me to have a chance to tell her about my sorrow. It provided a healing that I can't describe. But most people need the support of other Christians to help them begin restitution. Urge your friend to make restitution where he has hurt others. Then help him go on to the next step.

FIFTH, *develop a small group.* Once you have made initial contact, help your new friend find a small group where he fits in well.

Most gays are passive. They have never learned to communicate below the surface. Instead, they leave at the toss of a hat, especially when they might have to deal with emotional issues.

We use small groups in our program to teach homosexuals how to relate to others. Through the care and encouragement of other Christians, homosexual strugglers can delve into their deep needs and find healing.

Through intimate group sessions, we teach them to confront their feelings and to work through their emotions. If that means beating the floor, acting like a child or crying like a baby, we go through it with them. We allow them to get angry, to grieve.

At first, you may feel uneasy about ministering to people with serious sexual problems. Many times you will need the help of a professional Christian counselor. But as you get to know and love homosexuals as real men and women, you will play a vital role in the healing process.

Being involved in small group ministry has many advantages for you, too. Not only will the Lord help you show others how to deal with their sins, He will also change your views and outlook on many things. You will learn to accept and love others as God does. You will develop lasting friendships. You will help the sexually broken learn to develop relationships of trust—maybe for the first time. When they see how much you care for them, they will know that what you tell them is the truth, even if they don't want to hear it.

SIXTH, *expect setbacks and successes.* Every homosexual struggling to free himself from his addiction has good times and bad. We've seen many miracles performed through our ministry, and we've seen people experience setbacks for years. In such times we have learned to be patient.

Recently, a desperate wife called us. "My husband is fixing to leave me," she sobbed. "He's on drugs and says he hates me. He's filing for divorce and moving in with another man. Can you please help me?"

Hinano and I met with the couple. The man explained that although he was a Christian, he believed he had been born a homosexual. "I thought that getting married and having a baby would make those feelings go away. But they didn't. I've just given up fighting my urges."

His wife was in tears. After hearing my story, he agreed to stick it out with her. But his drug habit grew worse. He began stealing money to support it, and six months ago he was arrested for theft.

We didn't give up on him. Someone from our church got him admitted to a Christian-owned, drug abuse center in Philadelphia. Since he was released, he's been doing great. The process of healing is not finished, but he is making significant progress.

Chris Raine began his breakthrough to freedom in the basement of his mother's health food store. You'll recall how Thomas and I ran to help him when Mrs. Raine came to us in a frantic state. Chris accepted the Lord as Savior that day, and we all cried and hugged each other in joy.

Since then, Chris has had his ups and downs. We had to encourage him in his commitment to the Lord. But we have seen miraculous things happen in his life. As he grew and matured, the Lord began to use him. Pat Robertson's *700 Club* invited him to be a guest on the program, and Chris also spoke in Charles Stanley's First Baptist Church of Atlanta. He gave his testimony at a church in New York and before his home congregation and Sunday school. He's become one of our small group leaders.

When someone new comes into your group, don't condemn him for setbacks. I understand the temptations a person feels who is trying to break a habit. For six months after I became a Christian, I slipped back into sex with Thomas. I had to break many other twenty-year-old habits as well.

It takes time to learn how to fulfill your needs in acceptable ways. Every time a gay person feels lonely or the need for love, he goes to a bar and picks up a "trick." Going to bed with a partner feels good for the moment. But the next morning, your companion is gone and you are lonelier than ever.

I urge you to be patient. Just as He helped you in your exciting steps of spiritual growth and in your discouraging times of failure, He wants you to accept that same process in others.

SEVENTH, *be aware of special issues when helping the sexually broken.* As *Free My Children* has grown, it has developed special ministries. Some of our insights may help you deal with the issues you will face in your own ministry.

Lesbianism. Female homosexuals have different concerns than males. Programs like ours are usually geared to men because most gays are male. Only six or seven of those who have gone through our group have been women.

Both men and women, however, get their primary affirmation from their fathers. So lesbians have the same need for healthy male role models. They crave the same acceptance from peers.

But women are more complex emotionally. The attachments between females are much stronger. Where men are primarily interested in sexual contact, women desire emotional involvement.

When a woman pulls out of a partnership, the separation can get vicious. Both partners are devastated. Rebuilding new relationships takes more time and strength. This is important to remember when helping former lesbians start over.

Singles and AIDS Ministry. Our concern about AIDS led us to Jonathan Hunter, who heads a project called AIDS Research Ministry, a branch of Desert Stream. Lee Savage, who works with the drug-abuse program at Metro, agreed to begin an AIDS outreach. He planned to go to a January seminar in California with our group.

That week he had to attend a drug-abuse convention, so Milton Thorn went in his place. Milton got some information from Jonathan Hunter on how to reach out to AIDS patients.

Milton became so enthused, he decided to spearhead the ministry himself. Since he also heads the church singles group, his new responsibilities fit right in with what he was already doing.

The ministry was named *New Life*. As it developed, we formulated these policies that you could adopt also:

- We would not discriminate against anyone be cause of AIDS.
- We would not ban AIDS patients from church

functions.
- We would not give them responsibilities that would endanger their health or the health of others.
- We would not regard the disease as a curse from God.

Pornography and Masturbation. Most people we counsel at *Free My Children* suffer from these addictions. Both are symptomatic of something deeply wrong in their lives. To cure the symptoms, they must discover the root of their problem.

How do you help addicts stop the cycle of behavior?

We first try to find where the cycle begins—what triggers the behavior. We ask, "What makes you want to buy pornographic materials? What makes you begin masturbating?" We call these triggers red flags.

Then we help the addicted person find an acceptable response to red flag feelings. We suggest they decide on something pleasurable that is not sinful. The substitution, we have discovered, will help them avoid addictive behavior.

While they are practicing the acceptable behavior, we help them focus on the root cause of the problem. Many times feelings of rejection from the past trigger their conduct. As you work with a sexually broken person, try to find out why he tries to abandon his emotions in this way. Understanding will help him deal with the root, rather than just the symptoms.

Handling the Concerns of Family and Friends. Recently, I was a guest on a talk program called *The Morning Show* in which I rebutted a psychologist who claimed homosexuals are born that way.

At the time the program aired, Hope Roberts was working in her kitchen. Normally, she didn't watch TV while she cooked, but for some reason that day she had it on. Just as she went to turn the program off, she heard my name announced and that I was an ex-homosexual.

She turned up the volume and sat down to watch the show. The next day, she contacted me and related her story.

Hope and Tom had been married for ten years. He had just left home to go into the gay life-style. She wanted him to come home. The night before, she and her son had prayed that the Lord would intervene in Tom's life.

Hope scheduled an appointment with me. When she arrived, Chris and I shared our stories with her.

"How can I get him to come and hear this?" she asked.

"Just continue to pray," I suggested. "Describe the meeting, and what we told you, to him. And let the Lord do the rest."

"He'll never come. He's a well-known banker and any leak would destroy his career."

"Well, the only thing we have is prayer. God answered your prayer so far. Won't He finish what He's started?"

She called me once a week for a month. Her husband still wouldn't consider meeting with us.

Two months later, Tom called me himself. He was still hesitant. Finally, after three more calls, he agreed to meet me.

We had five sessions. I told him how Satan had robbed me of precious years with my wife and children. I described the lack of intimacy and fulfillment he would find in a gay relationship, the fear of AIDS, and the emptiness of living in brokenness.

Tom decided to go back to Hope. Eventually, he progressed so well that we discontinued the sessions.

Like Hope, family members and friends are affected deeply by a person's decision to become gay. We have just started ministering to parents of homosexuals. When we started *Free My Children*, two parents, Frank and Martha, came to us. Frank had a full white beard and looked like Kenny Rogers. They wanted to sit in on the group sessions. We said, "Fine."

Martha pointed out our need to deal with the problem from a parent's point of view. I had had a vision for doing exactly that, but the Lord had never opened the door.

Frank and Martha eventually began that facet of the ministry. They help families deal with the dysfunctions that caused the problems and showed them how to turn their lives around.

One question we often face from fathers is: if I have rejected my child, can I correct the damage? We answer: If your child is young, his heart may still be open to you. Begin at once to show your love and acceptance. Affirm your child in his gender and don't ridicule him.

If your child has reached an age where he is actively homosexual, your impact may be minimal. Some kids can be caught in adolescence and the problem addressed, but much will depend on the child at this point.

We ministered to one family whose son was seventeen when the parents realized he was gay. The father couldn't erase the past, but he could change his behavior in the future. The son also had to realize what was wrong and respond differently to his parents.

We try to help friends of the family, too. Ron attended our meetings for two years. His family kept in close contact with us. One day, he brought his new fiance to the salon. She had come in from California. We met her, and before she returned to California, they announced their wedding date.

Not long after, Ron backed out of the plans. His fiance was devastated. She arrived in Birmingham, bag and baggage. Ron didn't know what to do and called me for advice.

This young woman sincerely loves Ron. She knows he is HIV positive, but she still cares for him and about him. She's not putting pressure on Ron to marry her, but she moved to Birmingham to be near him. It's a difficult situation for both parties. Emotional ties take patience and love from those who counsel people trying to recover from deep hurts.

We have two men in the group who have young children. Our concern is that rejection is not passed down to them. Other gays are absorbed with overprotective mothers. One man admitted, "My mother calls me four times a day. I have to tell her everything I'm doing." Another young man goes home after every class and tells his mother everything that went on.

Sometimes family and friends can complicate the healing process. Handling these situations helps the former homosexual more clearly realize his need and how to bring his brokenness to the Lord for restoration.

EIGHTH, *help the sexually broken see their potential as servants of the Lord.* Our goal in every human endeavor is to bring glory to God and to serve our risen Lord. In turn, He gives us the power to live in joy and abundance.

When ministering to the sexually broken, we can assure them that their commitment to wholeness will enable them to give back to God a part of what He has given them. Anyone who struggles with guilt over a wasted past will wonder if the Lord can ever use them. The answer is a resounding yes.

Sexual energy is a powerful force. When it is surrendered to the Lord and used for His glory, it will become a testament to the love of a heavenly Father. What was once a devastating addiction can be transformed into a ministry of healing and grace to others who are struggling with the same cycle of brokenness.

The secular world has no answers for homosexuality. Many today criticize and ostracize gays. Others advocate legislation accepting homosexuality as another life-style instead of trying to help people break free from their addictions. Society would have us whitewash the problem, but that will never change the hurt and pain that causes the behavior.

But because of Christ, we have the answer. Forgiveness, acceptance, and unconditional love heals hearts. Christ offers us the power and freedom to live above our circumstances. He changes our brokenness into a glorious testimony to His love and grace. He creates new life from the ashes of the old. All He needs is a willing heart.

What a privilege He gives us to witness the transformation in sexually broken lives as we reach out to those in need, in His name! I encourage you to experience the joy of seeing Him help people grow through the process of change. Your impact in the lives of others will have eternal results.

Free My Children
A Division of
The Turning Point Foundation
P.O. Box 380005
Birmingham, AL 35238-0005